MW01381200

Leisure Studies in a Global Era

Series Editors
Karl Spracklen
Leeds Beckett University
Leeds, UK

Karen Fox
University of Alberta
Edmonton, Alberta, Canada

In this book series, we defend leisure as a meaningful, theoretical, framing concept; and critical studies of leisure as a worthwhile intellectual and pedagogical activity. This is what makes this book series distinctive: we want to enhance the discipline of leisure studies and open it up to a richer range of ideas; and, conversely, we want sociology, cultural geographies and other social sciences and humanities to open up to engaging with critical and rigorous arguments from leisure studies. Getting beyond concerns about the grand project of leisure, we will use the series to demonstrate that leisure theory is central to understanding wider debates about identity, postmodernity and globalisation in contemporary societies across the world. The series combines the search for local, qualitatively rich accounts of everyday leisure with the international reach of debates in politics, leisure and social and cultural theory. In doing this, we will show that critical studies of leisure can and should continue to play a central role in understanding society. The scope will be global, striving to be truly international and truly diverse in the range of authors and topics. Editorial Board: John Connell, Professor of Geography, University of Sydney, USA; Yoshitaka Mori, Associate Professor, Tokyo University of the Arts, Japan; Smitha Radhakrishnan, Assistant Professor, Wellesley College, USA; Diane M. Samdahl, Professor of Recreation and Leisure Studies, University of Georgia, USA; Chiung-Tzu Lucetta Tsai, Associate Professor, National Taipei University, Taiwan; Walter van Beek, Professor of Anthropology and Religion, Tilburg University, The Netherlands; Sharon D. Welch, Professor of Religion and Society, Meadville Theological School, Chicago, USA; Leslie Witz, Professor of History, University of the Western Cape, South Africa.

More information about this series at
http://www.palgrave.com/gp/series/14823

Anju Beniwal • Rashmi Jain
Karl Spracklen
Editors

Global Leisure and the Struggle for a Better World

palgrave
macmillan

Editors
Anju Beniwal
Government Meera Girls College
Rajasthan, India

Rashmi Jain
Department of Sociology
University of Rajasthan
Jaipur, India

Karl Spracklen
School of Film, Music & Performing Arts
Leeds Beckett University
Leeds, UK

Leisure Studies in a Global Era
ISBN 978-3-319-70974-1   ISBN 978-3-319-70975-8   (eBook)
https://doi.org/10.1007/978-3-319-70975-8

Library of Congress Control Number: 2018933136

This Palgrave Macmillan imprint is published by Springer Nature
The registered company is Springer International Publishing AG
The registered company address is: Gewerbestrasse 11, 6330 Cham, Switzerland

Contents

List of Contributors

Aretha Oluwakemi Asakitikpi Dr has been a lecturer in various universities in Nigeria her home country as well as in South Africa where she has taught in the field of communication, gender as well as cultural studies. Her major area of research is media representations where she considers aspects such as leisure practices as depicted in various forms ranging from traditional art forms to more contemporary media forms such as the mass media.

Munehiko Asamizu Dr is an Associate Professor of Tourism Geography at Yamaguchi University. He received his PhD and MA from the Graduate School of International Studies, J. F. Oberlin University and BA from the Faculty of Education, Akita University. He currently teaches International Tourism Policy, Ethnicity, and Sociology. His major published works are "World Travel and Japanese Tourists (Gakubunsha, Tokyo 2005)", "Global Tourism (Kumpul, Tokyo 2010)", and "Tourists, International Students and Global Workforces (Saganoshoin, Kyoto 2017)".

Ertong Attar Dr completed her undergraduate studies in Bilkent University's Department of Economics in 2003 and her master's level studies in Ankara University's Department of Economics in 2005. She received her doctoral degree from the Department of Sociology in Ankara University. From 2007 to 2012, Dr. Ertong Attar worked in various units of the Ministry of Health and between 2012 and 2016 she worked at Scientific and Technological Research Council of Turkey. In June 2016, Dr. Ertong Attar was appointed to Mersin University's Department of Sociology as an assistant professor. She is currently a board member of the Sociological Association of Turkey and a member of European Sociological Association and of International Sociological Association. She is currently an editorial board member of the Journal of Sociological Research. Her research focuses on sociology of health and illness, trust, violence, and the relationship between technology and social change.

Giandra Anceski Bataglion graduated in Physical Education from Federal University of Santa Catarina (UFSC) (2013) and received her master's in Theory and Pedagogical Practice in Physical Education from Federal University of Santa Catarina (PPGEF/UFSC) (2016). She is a member of Leisure and Physical Activity Research Laboratory (LAPLAF/CEFID/UDESC/CNPq) and a member of the Nucleus of Research in Sports Pedagogy (NUPPE/CDS/UFSC) and the Adapted Motor Activity Programme (AMA/CDS/UFSC). She has experience in physical education in the subjects of adapted motor activity, ludic, play and playthings.

Anju Beniwal Dr studies are in anthropology and sociology. She is an Assistant Professor in the Department of Sociology, Government Meera Girls College. She has been actively engaged in community-based research, with over 14 years teaching experience. Areas of specialization include tribal welfare, rural development, women's issues and leisure studies. She is the coordinator of SPD-RUSA-DISHARI Scheme for Capacity Building and Employment Enhancement. Her work has appeared in 45 articles in various referred and professional journals and in 7 books. She is also a life member of various academic bodies. She has actively presented her views in conferences both in her country and abroad. She is a board member of Research Committee 13 (Sociology of Leisure) of the International Sociological Association.

Michael A. Elliott is Associate Professor of Sociology at Towson University (United States) and specializes in globalization, world history and social theory. He has published on the global expansion of human rights and world heritage as well as the development of monastic beer brewing in the Middle Ages and its connection to modern craft beer. Currently, he is working on a project about the sacred dimensions of fan communities and designing a survey of fan conventioneers in the United States.

Adriana Aparecida da Fonseca Viscardi graduated in Physical Education from State University of Santa Catarina (CEFID/UDESC) (2015). She was an extension and scientific initiation fellow at the Laboratory of Gerontology and had a fellowship of scientific initiation at the Leisure and Physical Activity Research Laboratory (LAPLAF/CEFID/UDESC/CNPq), participating in the project, "The playfulness and rehabilitation in public and private institutions of Florianópolis (SC)". She has experience in physical education, in concentrating on seniors and on nature adventure activities. She will begin her master's degree at the Federal University of Santa Catarina in 2017.

Damian Gałuszka is a PhD student at the Institute of Sociology of the Jagiellonian University in Poland, a graduate of Sociology at the Faculty of Humanities of the AGH University of Science and Technology, and a member of the Collegium Invisibile association, where he completed the tutorial on video games. An initiator and co-organizer of the national conference "Technological and Social Aspects of the Twenty-First century", an author of a book on video games in Polish families titled *Video Games in the Family Environment. Diagnosis and Recommendations,* and a co-author of two monographs: *Technoculture: Transhumanism and Digital Art,* and *Technological and Social Aspects of the Twenty-first Century.* He was awarded the scholarship of the Polish Minister of National Education and the Florian Znaniecki prize of the Polish Sociological Association for his master's thesis. He is interested in digital media and STS studies.

Jonathan Harth Dr studied sociology, philosophy and psychology at the Freie Universität Berlin and the University of Vienna. Since 2009 he has been working as a research fellow at the Chair of Sociology at Witten/Herdecke University. Harth's topics of interest are sociology of technology (especially computer games and virtual reality) and sociology of religion (Western Buddhism).

Saori Ishida is a project researcher at the Gender Center of the School of Information and Communication, Meiji University, Tokyo. She completed a PhD program at the Graduate School of Information and Communication, Meiji University. Her research focuses on Japanese subculture, particularly manga and anime female fandom.

Yoshi Iwasaki Dr has approximately 20 years of experience in community-based research, capacity-building, and knowledge mobilization. His areas of specialization include: (a) culture, diversity and community engagement; (b) active living and quality of life (e.g., meaning-making, mental health and leisure); and (c) participatory action research (PAR) to address social justice issues (e.g., human rights, social exclusion/inclusion, discrimination, marginalization/stigmatization and empowerment). With over $5 million external research support including federal grants from NIH, SSHRC and CIHR, his work has appeared in over 90 refereed academic and professional journal articles. Dr. Iwasaki's research teams have worked with and engaged indigenous peoples, culturally diverse 'high-risk' youth, and persons with disabilities, including psychiatric disability/mental illness, to address globally significant issues (e.g., social change through engagement, meaning-making and mental health) by giving attention to a local context while integrating the scholarship of engagement, social learning theory and social justice perspectives within a community of co-learning, power-sharing and practice.

Rashmi Jain Dr is Associate Professor in the Department of Sociology, as well as Director, University Grants Commission (UGC) Centre for the Study of Social Exclusion and Inclusive Policy, at the University of Rajasthan. Her interests are in leisure studies, development communication, gender studies, and sociology of law. She is also Deputy Coordinator in the UGC SAP DRS II on the theme "Society and culture of Rajasthan under the impact of globalization". She has regularly taken part in conferences and seminars both in the country and abroad, and she has been active in organizing national and international conferences. She has published three books and over 40 research articles. She is a Convener of the research committee on Sociology of Law of the Indian Sociological Society. Besides being an academician, she has worked to raise her voice for destitute women and citizen's issues by collaborating with civil society organizations of Rajasthan. She is also member of the Ethics committee for clinical trials at Monilek Hospital and Research Centre and a member of several bodies of the university and state government.

Daliana Stephanie Lecuona graduated in Physical Education from State University of Santa Catarina (CEFID/UDESC) (2016). She is currently a master's student in the Postgraduate Program in Human Movement Sciences at UDESC. She is a member of Leisure and Physical Activity Research Laboratory (LAPLAF/CEFID/UDESC/CNPq). She has experience in physical education concentrating on cooperative games, leisure and recreation, public health and health promotion.

KoFan Lee Dr received his doctoral degree of leisure behavior at Indiana University in 2013. He is currently an Assistant Professor of Recreation Administration at the University of Mississippi. His primary research interest focuses on quality of motivation, commitments and identity development, and positive experiences acquired from serious pursuits in adventure recreation.

Miraíra Noal Manfroi graduated in Physical Education from Federal University of Mato Grosso do Sul (2011), with a master's in Theory and Pedagogical Practice in Physical Education (UFSC) (2015). She is currently a doctoral student in the Postgraduate Programme in Physical Education at Federal University of Santa Catarina (PPGEF/UFSC), And she is a member of the Leisure and Physical Activity Research Laboratory (LAPLAF/CEFID/UDESC/CNPq), member of the Nucleus of Research in Sports Pedagogy (NUPPE/CDS/UFSC) and of the Observatory of Sports Media (LABOMIDIA/CDS/UFSC). She has experience in physical education in the subjects of child, ludic, play and leisure.

Alcyane Marinho Dr is a Lecturer in the Physical Education Department and in the Postgraduate Program in Human Movement Sciences at State University of Santa Catarina (UDESC) in Brazil., where she is leader of Leisure and Physical Activity Research Laboratory (LAPLAF/CEFID/UDESC/CNPq). She completed her bachelor's degree in Physical Education at São Paulo State University (UNESP) in 1995, her master's degree in 2001 and her PhD in 2006 at Campinas State University (UNICAMP) in Brazil. She is also a lecturer in the Postgraduate Program in Physical Education at the Federal University of Santa Catarina (UFSC), focusing on "Pedagogical Theory and Practice in Physical Education". Her research interests developed from professional experiences focusing on leisure and education.

Zuhal Yonca Odabaş graduated from the Undergraduate Program of Sociology Department of Ankara University in 2000, and received a master's degree in METU Sociology Department as well as a doctorate in Ankara University Sociology Department. Odabaş served as a Research Assistant at the Sociology Department of the University of Ankara between 2002 and 2010 and as Assistant Professor in the same department between 2010 and 2012. She worked as an academic staffer at Atatürk University, Sociology Department, between 2012 and 2015. Odabaş, who received the title of Associate Professor in 2014, is currently working on the academic staff in the Sociology Department of Çankırı Karatekin University. Her research interests are sociology of health and illness, sociology of disaster, disaster risk management, social problems, gender studies, children studies, youth studies, sociology of motherhood, sociology of education an methodology studies.

Alice Pacher is a PhD candidate at the Department of Clinical Psycho-social Science, Meiji University in Tokyo, Japan. She completed her master's degree at Meiji University in 2014, and her bachelor's at the University of Vienna, Austria, in 2011. Her main research focuses on Japanese couple relationships (married and unmarried) in contemporary times, with particular attention to sexual behavior and sexual consciousness among Japanese men and women from a sociological perspective. Past research refers to how sexual behaviour and consciousness of Japanese couples in the ages of the 20s and 30s has changed in recent years and in exploring the social influences behind this phenomenon. Since 2016, research expanded to comparative sociology regarding sexuality in Japan and in the German-speaking countries (with a main focus on Germany and Austria).

Juliana de Paula Figueiredo graduated in Physical Education from Campinas Pontifical Catholic University (PUC) (2009). She received her MA in Motricity from São Paulo State University (PPGCM/UNESP) (2012). She is currently a doctoral student in the Postgraduate Program in Physical Education at Federal University of Santa Catarina (PPGEF/UFSC). She is a Member of Leisure and Physical Activity Research Laboratory (LAPLAF/CEFID/UDESC/CNPq) and Leisure Studies Laboratory (LEL/UNESP/Rio Claro). She has experience in physical education, concentrating in the following subjects: leisure and recreation, adventure activities, technologies and media, environmental education, games and play environmental awareness.

Karl Spracklen PhD, is a Professor of Music, Leisure and Culture at Leeds Beckett University, and the author of over 90 books, papers and book chapters on leisure. He is the Secretary of Research Committee 13 (Sociology of Leisure) of the International Sociological Association. He is also a co-founder of the International Society for Metal Music Studies and the editor of the journal *Metal Music Studies*.

Yuki Tajima is a PhD and Postdoctoral Fellow at the Center for the Study of the Creative Economy at Doshisha University, Kyoto, Japan. His research fields are Media Studies, Popular Culture and Gender Studies. He is currently teaching Outline of Media Studies, History of Media, and Theory of Tourism and Media at universities in the Kansai area, Japan. His main publications are: *A History of Idol in Japanese Media* (shinwasha, 2017-3), Japanese Idol Culture for Regional Revitalization : A Case Study about the Performance of Regional Idols (*Social Science Review* (119), 2016-12).

Hiromi Tanaka is an associate professor at the School of Information and Communication, Meiji University, Tokyo. She received her PhD in Sociology from Ruhr University Bochum, Germany. She specializes in gender analysis of Japanese society and culture with a focus on media, leisure and popular culture.

Verônica Werle graduated in Physical Education from University Center UNIVATES, Brazil (2008). She has a master's degree in Physical Education from Federal University of Santa Catarina (UFSC) (2011). She is currently doctoral student in the Postgraduate Program in Education at Federal University of Santa Catarina (PPGE/UFSC), a Member of the Leisure and Physical Activity Research Laboratory (UDESC/CNPq) and the Education and Contemporary Society Studies Research Group (UFSC). She has experience in physical education, and her research interest is in leisure and recreation, pedagogical practices, gender and public policy.

List of Figures

List of Tables

1

Introduction: The Struggle for Leisure

Anju Beniwal, Rashmi Jain, and Karl Spracklen

The present collection highlights the diversity and reach of global leisure studies and global leisure theory, exploring the impact of globalization on leisure, and the sites of resistance and accommodation found in local and virtual leisure spaces. This edited collection brings together the best papers delivered at the Research Committee Thirteen (Sociology of Leisure, RC13) sessions at the International Sociological Association's Third Forum of Sociology in Vienna. The editors are members of RC13's executive board, and the lead editor, Spracklen, is RC13's Secretary and Vice-President for Publications. This volume, endorsed by RC13, is the

A. Beniwal (✉)
Department of Sociology, Government Meera Girls College,
Udaipur, Rajasthan, India

R. Jain
Department of Sociology, University of Rajasthan, Jaipur, Rajasthan, India

K. Spracklen
School of Film, Music and Performing Arts, Leeds Beckett University,
Leeds, UK

© The Author(s) 2018
A. Beniwal et al. (eds.), *Global Leisure and the Struggle for a Better World*, Leisure
Studies in a Global Era, https://doi.org/10.1007/978-3-319-70975-8_1

second coming out of RC13/ISA, published by Palgrave in *Leisure Studies in a Global Era*. The first collection in the series was edited by Benkő, Modi and Tarkó (2017). Unlike other edited collections on leisure studies, this one focuses strongly on leisure as a form of popular culture; also unlike other such collections, it represents a large and diverse leisure scholarship, one that is growing beyond the West—especially in India and Japan.

There is a long tradition of leisure studies in academic circles around the world and a strong history of edited collections, monographs and textbooks about leisure. Historically, leisure studies has had a multidisciplinary lens and a strong socio-cultural theory running through it, in parts; but its dominant mode of inquiry and theorizing has been positivist, scientific, managerial and practical. The older form of leisure studies, that which is associated with leisure sciences, leisure management and active recreation, continues to operate in some areas of the world, but it has been sidelined by the rapid growth in offshoots of leisure studies such as events management, sport management and sport studies. Yet, in the last ten years we've seen a renaissance of interest in critical leisure studies, drawing on interdisciplinary approaches owing as much to sociology, geography and cultural studies as to leisure studies. In July 2016, record numbers of delegates to the International Sociological Association's Third Forum of Sociology in Vienna attended sessions on the sociology of leisure. These were as likely to feature discussions of hyper-reality as physical fitness. New conferences are appearing, critiquing the notion of leisure vis-à-vis socio-cultural theory and historiography. Such a conference took place at the Sorbonne in November 2015. Despite once predicting the demise of leisure studies, Chris Rojek continues to write theoretical work on the intersections of leisure, sociology and culture, and, as an editor at Sage, he continues to publish such work (Rojek 2010, 2013; see also Bramham and Wagg 2014). Taylor and Francis run the highly successful journal *Leisure Studies*, which has a strong record of downloads and submissions; it has made a significant impact on the field. The T&F portfolio of leisure journals has increased in the last few years, taking on *Annals of Leisure Research, Leisure/Loisir* and *World Leisure Journal*. Additionally, Palgrave Macmillan publishes the interdisciplinary *Leisure Studies in a Global Era* book series, which, as mentioned, includes this collection.

Leisure studies, then, is expanding and growing even though the number of leisure studies degrees, courses and programs is falling: Leisure studies are now taught far beyond its original place in university structures. This collection captures the move from the discipline as being merely studies about recreation to those encompassing research on global, local and virtual leisure, shedding light on matters of philosophy, theology, anthropology, history, psychology, sociology and cultural studies. This drawing on leisure theory beyond leisure studies is happening at the same time as the increasing 'criticalization' of leisure studies degrees and related degrees in sport, events and tourism. Researchers in leisure studies and the related subject fields are applying complex theory to their work and to their teaching—as reflected in the present book.

After the Vienna conference, the editors of this volume invited each of the 120 presenters at RC13 sessions to submit an abstract to this collection. The result, seen here, demonstrates the strength of the sociology of leisure and leisure studies worldwide. This collection demonstrates the critical nature of the field and the growing maturity of theories of leisure in local, virtual and global spaces. The book concludes with a brief construction of a new theory of global, local and virtual leisure space in the ongoing counterhegemonic struggle for a better world. The thirteen chapters of the book serve as signposts for a new sociology of leisure—a new kind of leisure studies for a new century.

The book has three sections, loosely focused on local leisure (local leisure, meaning and resistance), virtual leisure (virtual leisure and pop culture) and global leisure (global leisure and responses). These organizing concepts run through each chapter, and the reader might view the structure as bringing similar research and theories close to one another, and not as a corset that constrains the book.

The Structure of the Book

Section One, Local Leisure, Meaning and Resistance, maps out how leisure is experienced and constructed in local spaces and cultures—which are in turn shaped by trans-local and global forms. Section Two, Virtual Leisure and Pop Culture, explores how leisure is shaped by trends in virtuality and in wider forms of popular culture. The final section, Global Leisure and Responses, shows how global leisure is being constructed under new conditions in the world.

Section One: Local Leisure, Meaning and Resistance

Chapter Two: Sexlessness Among Contemporary Japanese Couples

Alice Pacher
Meiji University, Tokyo, Japan

The research in the second chapter of our book examines the current situation of the sexless phenomenon among Japanese couples. The chapter first reviews the previous range of studies that dealt with the topic of sexual consciousness and sexual behaviour of men and women in contemporary Japanese society. In the second part, the chapter aims at a deeper understanding of the sexless phenomenon by using interviews conducted with 35 young Japanese adults, of both sexes, in their 20s to 30s. Most of the younger adults show a tendency to avoid sexual expression, primarily for three reasons: previous negative experiences, such as pain during sexual intercourse, lack of physical contact with their partners, and disinterest expressed by their partner. Interviewees who are sexless do not regard sexuality as an important form of communication within the couple relationship. Pacher argues that in Japan sex among couples is not seen as a recreational time activity. Men and women prefer leisure activities that can be enjoyed alone to activities involving sexual intimacy. Some interviewees of both age groups prefer to have sex outside of the relationship, such as by dating another person or through the use of sexual services, which is understood to be a leisure activity. The interviewees had in common exposure to an overabundance of pornography and to sexual services, as well as a lack of education regarding sexual health or sexual satisfaction.

Chapter Three: Singing Group: The Playful Present in Health Promotion

Miraíra Noal Manfroi[1,2], Adriana Aparecida da Fonseca Viscardi[2], Daliana Stephanie Lecuona[2], Giandra Anceski Bataglion[2], Verônica Werle[2], Juliana de Paula Figueiredo[1,2], and Alcyane Marinho[1,2]

[1]PPGEF/CDS/UFSC, Brazil
[2]LAPLAF/CEFID/UDESC, Brazil

The training, education and outlook of most health professionals does not collectively take into consideration educational and humanistic perspectives. However, through a more human-centred action, hospitals and other institutions whose focus is health promotion and rehabilitation may be able to produce knowledge, health and life quality improvement for the people they serve. This chapter is part of the authors' wider research aiming to investigate relations between the ludic component of health care and the rehabilitation process, treatment and health promotion. Their subject is a singing group made up of volunteers and professionals at a public health institution in Florianópolis (Santa Catarina, southern Brazil). As such, this study is configured as field research, presenting itself as descriptive and exploratory, with a qualitative approach. The participants in the study were responsible for the group, the assisted patients and their families. For data collection, the team used an array of systematic observation and semi-structured interviews. From the data, categories will be developed for content analysis. Preliminary data reveals that weekly visits by a group of social workers, nurses, volunteers and others to the homes of people with contributed to the recovery process. The group played instruments and sang. The effectiveness of this approach was evident in the grateful words, smiles and hugs by patients and family. In addition, the groups who performed this activity reported that they felt in a constant healing process. From this perspective, one sees the importance of reevaluating the educational process of professionals in health fields and the need to value a humanization of therapeutic initiatives.

Chapter Four: Celebration of Ramadan: The Case of Turkey

Zuhal Yonca Odabas[1] and Günnur Ertong Attar[2]
[1]Cankiri Karatekin University, Çankırı Merkez/Çankırı, Turkey
[2]Department of Sociology, Mersin University, Yenişehir/Mersin, Turkey

Ramadan is a holy month for Muslims around the world. During that month, Muslims aver that the God (Allah) is more forgiving than at the other times of the year. Among the many reasons for this belief is that the Quran, Islam's holy book, was revealed during this month. Ramadan entails much more than abstaining from food and drink: it is a time to purify the soul, refocus attention on God and practice self-discipline and sacrifice. It aims to teach the practitioner self-control, and it provides an insight into the light of the poor. Ramadan is also the month of celebration. Because of its religious importance, in social life it is possible to find different kinds of events that tie Muslims to each other in the name of Allah. It is the time of creating and re-creating the idea and the feeling of 'we' in both public and personal spheres. In Turkey, the meaning of Ramadan has been changing since the beginning of 2000s. During the time of the AK Party's power, conservatism in both public and private spheres has started to become more visible. Religion and all kinds of religious activities are no longer 'the other', different from past times of secular political power, when it was not accepted as normal in the public sphere but allowed in the private sphere. This transformation includes Ramadan. Its celebrations, which are in part taken from both Turkish and Islamic traditions, have been more legal in public than they were nearly 15 years ago.

This content of the fourth chapter is at the intersection of various subfields of sociology, such as the sociology of religion, of leisure and of celebration. Symbolic interactionism is the basic theoretical perspective, which is well suited to aiding the understanding of the fluid relationships between religions and social structures religions and cultural change, and the personal transformations experienced by the individual moving between religious systems of meaning. In addition to this theoretical perspective, Victor Turner's arguments and concepts of festivals and liminality serve as an aide to understand the construction of identity at a personal level. This paper describes Ramadan as 'a storytelling narrative' that helps people connect to their pasts, for example, to their own childhood. It is accepted that recent celebration activities of Ramadan in Turkey have an ideological face. Turning back to previous times through Ramadan celebrations fosters a feeling of 'we' and fills in missing roots, created and recreated by both AK (Justice and Development) Party. The personal mind has become a 'collective mind' again with the help of leisure activities such as Ramadan celebrations.

Chapter Five: Youth Well-Being and Leisure Time: An International Perspective

Anju Beniwal
Government Meera Girls College, Udaipur, India

The fifth chapter explores leisure time and the well-being of youth. It is rightly said that while children are the future of the country, youth are its present. The energy, enthusiasm, dynamism, innovative ideas and creative thinking youth possess make this population an important asset for any country's accelerated development. With regard to youth resources, India has a distinct edge over developed nations, most of which will be facing the burden of a fast-ageing population in the coming decades. India is experiencing a youth bulge. Around the world, young people are proving that leisure represents a prime opportunity not only for individual development but also for societal contribution and change. The amount of leisure time available to young people varies considerably according to age, gender and culture. How young people spend their leisure time is also linked to pressing threats to their well-being and to issues of globalization and interdependence. Given these interconnections, it is critical leisure be discussed in the context of development of young people and their participation in the development of community and society.

Participation in organized leisure and recreation by young people is seen as having positive benefits for society since it reduces the amount of time available for engagement in anti-social behaviour. It is important we understand the ways in which young people think about leisure—their beliefs about and attitudes toward leisure, the meaning of leisure to them and the forces that influence and shape their involvement in leisure activities. The purpose of this chapter is to examine the empirical evidence and describe theoretical perspectives that address under what conditions and in what way leisure activities are essential to youth's opportunities and well-being.

Section Two: Virtual Leisure and Pop Culture

Chapter Six: Japanese Idol Culture for Contents Tourism and Regional Revitalization: A Case Study of Regional Idols

Yuki Tajima
Doshisha University, Kyoto, Japan

The sixth chapter of our book explores idol culture in Japan. The popularity of idol culture in Japan is well represented by the Japanese media. Although idols in the past tended to focus their activities mainly on Tokyo, recent idols have become increasingly rooted in specific geographic areas. These modern idols differ from their predecessors in that they personify 'regional characteristics' and 'regional authenticity' in the modern context. NHK's wildly popular morning serial TV drama *Amachan* in 2013 illustrated this trend. This drama series received high audience ratings, and analysis of media reports related to *Amachan* revealed that the filming location for this series, Kuji-shi, as well as Iwate Prefecture, benefited economically from an increased number of tourists visiting the area. Research on this type of tourism, inspired by media content such as a TV drama series, is known as 'contents tourism'; it has been evolving in Japan since 2010. Idols are indeed contents, and tourism and regional revitalization based on idol culture can be one focus area for important discussions in the field of contents tourism research.

Contemporary Japanese idols in today's Japanese social context and media situation reveal that, starting from around 2010, many so-called regional idols have emerged whose activities focus on a specific geographical area. Most of these regional idols are groups of young females in their teens or early 20s that focus their activities in the region in which they were born and grew up in. Their main activities include performing live at local venues, participating in local festivals and other events and collaborating with local government and corporations to support community efforts. The new phenomenon can be called "regional idol boom"; it was born of a combination of the success of the pop group AKB48, the Japan earthquake and tsunami of 2011, the re-examination of the Japanese concept of community and the ideas symbolized in *Amachan*.

This chapter uses *Amachan* and explores the relationship between the media content in Japan and the residents of the community that serve as its stage—as well as the activities of Ama Club, which is the regional idol group born in its filming location Kuji-shi, Iwate Prefecture, in the Tohoku region. At the same time, by understanding the characteristics of regional idols using specific case studies as examples, this chapter discusses the potential of Japanese idol culture for contributing to contents tourism and regional revitalization.

Chapter Seven: 'Being There and Being Someone Else': Massively Distributed Virtual Reality Devices and Their Impact on the Concept of Body and Identity Management

Jonathan Harth
Witten/Herdecke University, Witten, Germany

At least since the emergence of queer studies, one must assume the body's potential abilities always exceed what the culture permits. Currently, this cultural limitation appears to be mainly negotiated in terms of technical advancements. In 2016, three major companies will have presented their first generation of virtual reality (VR) devices (Oculus Rift, HTC Vive and PlayStation VR). It is highly expected that the social impact of such multibillion investments in leisure technology will be enormous. In this seventh chapter, Harth focuses on two questions that should concern the sociology (of leisure): (1) What makes VR such a unique experience? and (2) What impact may it have on the user's perception of body and identity? The main principle of virtual reality devices is to produce a sensation of presence in the virtual world. This is achieved by sophisticated tracking systems and an almost borderless display. As a result the presented images are perceived to be real. But virtual reality may differ from common reality. And it is exactly this experience which allows certain new perspectives on the world and the individual within it. Clearly, when one literally sees the world through the eyes of another, or experiences impossible situations, one's perspective—both of self and others—changes. With this in mind, Harth presents the status quo of the technical standards of VR and its possibilities and uses. In addition, he intends to contextualize the technical point of view according to the following aspects: (1) From a sociological perspective one's body must always be considered as a (cultural) observed body. Therefore, the body has to be considered no longer static but 'poly-contextual'. (2) Computers in general, but especially the medium of computer games, present the opportunity for users to act as if they were someone else. The possibilities of VR are putting this to an even higher degree by creating an immersive full-spectrum 'space of presence'.

Chapter Eight: Video Games in the Family Context. How Do Digital Media Influence the Relation Between Children and Their Parents?

Damian Gałuszka
Jagiellonian University, Kraków, Poland

Video games in the family context are discussed in the eighth chapter. Video games are one of the most important cultural industries. Their role in contemporary culture is reflected in the attendant numbers: the population of gamers is growing and they devote an increasing amount of time to their hobby. This, in turn, significantly affects leisure activities from different social categories. Furthermore, this change has an impact on the global economy as evidenced by dramatically increased gaming market revenues. The growing population of gamers includes children, for whom video games are not only one of their favorite media but also a sphere of socialization, which mainly takes place in the family. The purpose of this chapter is to present conclusions from a study on the role of video games in the life of a modern family. The study particularly focuses on the issue of technological and cultural competencies of children and their parents. The research employed quantitative and qualitative methods—a questionnaire survey and an interview. Some disturbing phenomena were observed in the pool of 24 surveyed families, particularly in relation to the shortcomings in the cultural and technological competencies of parents, insufficient level of parental control, limited parent-child communication and the lack of support from the school. This chapter is an attempt to deepen the analysis of the impact that video games have on the family environment. This is particularly important from the perspective of the growing popularity of this medium as well as its specificity (significantly different from older media), which can be unclear to or disregarded by older generations of parents, educators and teachers.

Chapter Nine: Projecting Gender, Sexuality and the Body Through the Nigerian Music Industry

Aretha Oluwakemi Asakitikpi
Independent Scholar, Johannesburg, Nigeria

Our ninth chapter explores gender, sexuality and the body in the Nigerian music industry. The Nigerian leisure context has witnessed a significant transformation, and much has been due to the influence of the mass media. Unlike the 1980s–90s, when the Nigerian populace depended on their government to entertain them through the traditional media forms of television and radio, the coming of independent and private mass media stations opened the floodgates for diversity and choice. The mass media terrain did not only change in terms of number but also in terms of nationally produced programs and artists who introduced innovation to mass media entertainment. One such innovative change was in the area of music. Through music videos, Nigerian artists have not only entertained audiences within and outside Nigeria, they also have been able to significantly redefine what leisure should look like. In this redefinition, sexuality, gender relations and the body are projected.

Based on this phenomenon, the chapter considers two contemporary Nigerian music videos: *Collabo*, by P-Square, featuring Don Jazzy; and *JAMB Question*, by Simi, featuring Falz. Through these videos, the author explore gender, sexuality and the body. These videos were selected because they were produced by Nigerians with Nigerians featured prominently, they had gender relations as a major theme, and they had high public viewing and likes on social media platforms. The chapter uses qualitative data methods to analyze the lyrics of the songs as well as the visual projection of body movements, physical space and clothing to discuss the identified concepts within gender theories that speak about gender relations in terms of inequality and power. This chapter proposes that through such videos, subtle concepts of responsibilities and social norms are promoted for both genders.

Chapter Ten: The Meaning and Purpose of Leisure Activities of Manga/Anime Fans Called "*Fujoshi*": Contradictions and Ambivalences in Japanese Women's Fan Community

Hiromi Tanaka and Saori Ishida
Meiji University, Tokyo, Japan

Fujoshi refers to fans of female comics (*manga*) and related products such as animation (*anime*), who enjoy works that feature male homosexual relationships. What they consume are predominantly parodies of works in which originally male homosocial bonds are depicted. *Fujoshi* re-read these original works and replace homosocial bonds with homosexual ones, making parodies so that they can develop fantasies of male-male relationships, which, because they are female, they can never experience in reality. In this chapter, the authors examine the meaning and purpose of this unique type of leisure activity, which can be seen in Japan and other Asian countries today. Analyzing data collected through interviews with seven *fujoshi* women, the authors explore two themes. They identify what satisfies and fulfills these fans, what makes them happy ; and, they present their contradictory findings: how this type of leisure activity significantly contributes to the enhancement of quality of life for the people engaged in them while coexisting with tensions owed to differences among the *fujoshi* and with those outside their communities. In this tenth chapter, the authors address the importance of sociological perspectives of social difference in a fan community, even if such a community can offer space to its members for mutual exchange, learning, understanding and respect.

Section Three: Global Leisure and Responses

Chapter Eleven: The Globalization of Comic-Con and the Sacralization of Popular Culture

Michael A. Elliott
Towson University, Towson, USA

In 1970, the Golden State Comic-Con was held in San Diego, California, with about 300 people in attendance. At the time it was a relatively small convention of writers, artists and enthusiasts of comic books as well as science fiction and fantasy. Today, Comic-Con International: San Diego (as it is now called) is attended by over 130,000 people every July and is widely known as "the" premiere convention for fans celebrating the popular arts. Ironically, comic books are no longer the central focus. Rather, it is attended by a vast array of fans, vendors, celebrities and industry professionals representing movies, television shows, video games, novels and more. The four-day convention also features a vast array of activities such as costume contests, celebrity panels and autographs, art exhibits, vendor booths, industry awards and workshops. Indeed, Comic-Con has become a pop cultural phenomenon, spawning similar events across the United States as well as in Canada, France, India, Brazil and the United Arab Emirates. From the perspective of fans, in particular, Comic-Con and the celebration of popular culture also represents a thriving component of contemporary leisure activity. This eleventh chapter, the first of the final section, seeks to explore why Comic-Con has become such a popular event, particularly for fans, and why it has globalized in recent years. Contending explanations include cultural imperialism (CC is an example of U.S. hegemony and the exportation of American values and preferences), neo-Marxism (CC is driven by corporate interests and mass consumption), psychological perspectives (CC represents unnatural or harmful fan obsessions, writ large), and mainstream media (CC is mere entertainment and fun escapism). In addition, Elliott proposes a Durkheimian hypothesis: CC is a sacred ritual for devout fans and has globalized because key aspects of this event (e.g., the superhero) represent mythical archetypes that transcend national boundaries.

Chapter Twelve: Leisure and Environmental Education in Japan

Munehiko Asamizu
Yamaguchi University, Yamaguchi-shi, Japan

This twelfth chapter examines how leisure and tourism policy and education might promote social good in Japan. Rural activities as leisure pursuits are changing historical trends in Japan. Before the Green Tourism Law of 1994 was enacted, tourist-oriented agricultural activities such as fruit picking and livestock experiences on farms were popular among urban residents. Rental farmland near urban areas was also already popular. In addition, more remote rural areas such as Touno (Iwate Prefecture), Ajimu (Oita Prefecture) and Iida (Nagano Prefecture) developed rural tourism using farmers' houses. However, the enactment of this law spurred the nationwide spread of green tourism development. Educational rural tourism is also developing throughout Japan. Some small communities such as Ojika (Nagasaki Prefecture) and Suo Oshima (Yamaguchi Prefecture) already invite high school students to experience the rural way of life. After their success, many rural municipalities are following the same path. Exploring the rural way of life could attract international tourists as well. Ojika already accepts international excursionists from the US, Korea and Taiwan, and provides international volunteers to assist them. Suo Oshima accepts more than 4000 domestic excursionists each year, but in 2015 it also accepted participants from the World Scout Jamboree in Yamaguchi.

Chapter Thirteen: Using Serious and Internalized Outdoor Sport Participation to Enhance Well-Being

KoFan Lee
University of Mississippi, Oxford, USA

Outdoor sports (OS) have become popular exercise/recreation options for the public in recent years. By participating in those activities with inherent risks, participants not only fulfill the need of sensation seeking but also use those activities to create optimal leisure lifestyles and promote well-being. In this chapter, Lee uses the serious leisure (SL) perspective to explain the commitment to outdoor sports, to narrate the process participants undergo to become serious members in a recreation context, as well as personal and social enhancements associated with these serious pursuits. Furthermore, recent studies have shown that leisure commitment may parallel the process of internalization, which is a human tendency to continuously integrate external regulations in social environments with personal value. With high levels of internalization, human behaviors are based on a sense of volition and autonomy, rather than a sense of coercion. In SL, it is not uncommon to find that recreationists continuously assimilate themselves with norms, standards and subcultures of an activity in order to establish their capacities, identities and social networks, which, in turn, allow participants to use or breakthrough their potentials. On the other hand, previous studies reveal less internalized experiences discourage recreationists from engagements, such as peer pressure and gender expectation. A weaker sense of volition may lead to reduced well-being. Passion for sports driven by external regulations leads to negative emotions. Therefore, by borrowing the notion of internalization, this chapter will discuss how the process of internalization can be facilitated or hindered by social contexts in and out of SL.

Chapter Fourteen: Leisure and Meaning-Making: The Pursuit of a Meaningful Life Through Leisure

Yoshitaka Iwasaki
University of Alberta, Edmonton, Canada

Humans seek the pursuit of a meaningful, enriching life. 'Meaning-making' refers to a process by which a person derives meaning(s) from leisure activities that provide such opportunities, for example, creative leisure and spiritual leisure. This chapter critically summarizes the current understanding of the ways in which leisure promotes meaning-making, with implications for the field of leisure studies and services globally.

A recent literature review based on 363 research articles linking leisure and subjective well-being (SWB) identified meaning-making as a core mechanism for promoting SWB. Meaning-making through leisure represents a liberating source of experiencing "infinite, liberating effects of leisure," while artists showed experiential (e.g., expressive) and existential (e.g., meaning, vitality, identity and achievement) meaning through construction of flow. An integrative review of the literature highlighted culturally contextualized processes of meaning-making through leisure that involve both "remedying the bad" and "enhancing the good" in people's quest for a meaningful life. Broadly, the role of leisure in meaning-making is in line with an increasing emphasis on 'positiveness' in the social sciences. Importantly, the role of leisure in meaning-making has practical implications. Creating a life of meaning was identified as a primary role of therapeutic recreation in supporting clients with challenges/limitations. Living a life of meaning was a key theme found in research on leisure and successful ageing and on post-traumatic growth for people with spinal cord injury. Not only was the role of leisure in meaning-making identified among elders with dementia (through enhancing enjoyment, identity and autonomy), but such a role was also shown among immigrants (through promoting self-realization, self-expression and connectedness).

A recent study with adults with mental illness found "an inspiration for an engaged life" as an overarching leisure meaning-making theme. Such leisure-generated meanings appear particularly salient to marginalized populations, including persons with disabilities and ethnic minorities globally.

References

Benkő, Z., Modi, I., & Tarkó, K. (2017). *Leisure, Health and Well-Being: A Holistic Approach*. London: Palgrave.

Bramham, P., & Wagg, S. (2014). *An Introduction to Leisure Studies*. London: Sage.

Rojek, C. (2010). *The Labour of Leisure*. London: Sage.

Rojek, C. (2013). *Event Power*. London: Sage.

Section I

Local Leisure: Meaning and Resistance

2

Sexlessness Among Contemporary Japanese Couples

Alice Pacher

Introduction and Overview

Since sex in the Europe is neither confined to its functional task of reproduction nor bound by rigid moral regulations, discussions about sex and sexuality among European couples mostly pertain to pleasure, recreation or relationship-fostering sexual communication (Bänziger et al. 2015, Lewandowski 2008). Sex is most often regarded as recreation, an activity for leisure. It is seen as detached from daily nuisances and everyday duties, done for enjoyment, fun and pleasure. In modern times, leisure activities generally serve to achieve self-fulfillment. The same is true for sexuality within couple relationships. Popular media and scholars, such as counseling literature (therapy books), started increasingly reporting on an aspect of sexuality (which mainly focuses on issues like pleasure, intimacy). The use of psychological discourse as a tool to help advise on enhancing sexual communication with beloved ones, with the ultimate

A. Pacher (✉)
Meiji University, Tokyo, Japan

© The Author(s) 2018
A. Beniwal et al. (eds.), *Global Leisure and the Struggle for a Better World*, Leisure Studies in a Global Era, https://doi.org/10.1007/978-3-319-70975-8_2

goal of increasing relational satisfaction, are increasing. This dominant perception of sexuality is gaining popularity among the European countries. However, such a discourse may not be applicable to all societies, whether in Europe or in other regions.[1] This is so because the way sexuality is perceived is not only a result of biological functions (all humans naturally possesses sex drive), but also of culture influences. This article examines this in the case of Japan.

In Japan, there is hardly any discourse involving sexual pleasure in couple relationships. On the contrary, debates center around sexless relationships, a phenomenon which has been rapidly increasing in recent years. The issue of sexless couples started to gain attention in the popular media when the psychiatrist Teruo Abe first made not of it in 1994 (Abe 2004). Beyond sexlessness, we observe a trend that the age at which young adults in Japan experienced first coitus increased between 2008 and 2014. The experience of kissing and dating and interest in sexual intercourse seems to be rapidly decreasing among younger Japanese. Another dataset shows that 60% of women and 76% of men in their 20s are currently not in a partnership, and 23% of female and 41% of the male respondents have never experienced intimate relationships. The main reason they give is they give not wishing to be in relationships is that falling in love is bothersome (Ushikubo 2015).

Nevertheless, while the share of people who do not exhibit any interest in 'being in love' has been increasing, 89.4% of the women and 86.3% of the men still nurture the wish to marry in the future. This first part sheds light on some of the salient reasons for sexlessness in contemporary Japan as well as on related aspects, including how (extramarital) sexuality is perceived as a leisurely activity. The rest of the chapter is in three parts. Part one provides a literature review of sexlessness in contemporary Japan. Part two charts a change in the direction of the literature review of leisure and sexuality. Due to a lack of discourse about sexual recreation in Japan, it will mainly focus on European discourses as to enable comparisons, but it will also analyze the meaning of sexual leisure in contemporary Japanese society. Part three covers interviews which were conducted between August 2012 and July 2013 with 35 young Japanese adults of both sexes in their 20s and 30s. After discussing the results, some conclusions are presented.

This paper uses the term 'couple relationship' and 'couple' to denote "a permanent and sexually founded connection between two persons with a particular form of institutionalization (sexual partnership, residential community, marriage) and an intimate everyday practice" (Burkart 2018:29). This means that the term 'couple' as used in this paper refers to married connections between two persons, but also to unmarried ones which aim to attain a higher degree of social institutionalization and intimate practice; however, the term does not denote extramarital sexual relationships that do not aim to obtain institutionalization. This is distinction is important in particular for Japanese readers because the common Japanese understanding of the term 'couple' covers a different scope than in the Western semantics, often integrating rather loose and superficial interpersonal relations, but not married persons.

Literature Review

Literature Review Regarding Sexlessness

The discussion around the sexless phenomenon gained momentum in 1991—when the psychiatrist Teruo Abe published his paper on, "sexless couples and avoidant personality disorder" (Abe 1991). In 1994, Abe defined as 'sexless' those couples that "do not engage in consensual sexual intercourse or sexual contact for more than a month—and an even longer period is to be expected—even though special circumstances cannot be observed". In this case, 'sexual contact' refers to kisses, caresses, lying together in bed naked and so on (Abe 2004).

This definition became widely used, and numerous subsequent studies on sexless couples were based on this definition. However, 'sexless' as defined by Abe in contrast to how it is imagined by the general public differ. For example, in his definition, Abe includes not only sexual intercourse as such, but also the lack of other kinds of sexual interaction outside that situation. I would argue that Abe's definition deviates too much from what one would reasonably understand of 'sexlessness'; his definition is overly extensive and encompasses elements that are outside the definitional halo of the words used. For the purpose of this paper, I follow a narrow interpretation of 'sexlessness', which I deem to be on par with the general public's reference of sexlessness to couples that do engage in 'weaker' sort of sexual behavior in daily life—such as flirting or kissing—without exercising actual sexual intercourse with one another for long periods.

Previous Surveys

The Japanese Ministry of Health, Labor and Welfare and the Japan Family Planning Association (JFPA) conducted a survey of 3000 men and women aged 16 to 49, between 2004 and 2016, and found that the number of married couples, who were 'disinterested in sex' increased from 31.9% to 47.2%. The survey found that the most common factors contributing to this disinterest were childbirth, overtiredness from work and the perception of sex as something bothersome (Japan Family Planning Association 2016).

Most similar surveys about sexual behavior focused on married couples. A survey published in 1999 by NHK, Japan's national public broadcasting organization, however, deviated from this to target respondents regardless of whether they were married or unmarried, who were in their 20s, 30s and 40s. It revealed that 43% of the women who were unsatisfied with their current sex life and who were 'sexless' in their relationship (NHK 2002). This brought due attention on the sexlessness prevailing among young couples in contemporary Japan, which ought to be discussed as a social problem due to a decrease in the young population and low birthrate.

Western countries started to take notice of this Japanese phenomenon of sexless young couples owing to a sexual well-being survey conducted by Durex in 26 countries, which was published in 2005 (Durex 2005). In its findings, Japan was cited as the country with the least frequent sexual contacts among all the countries surveyed. Not only was Japan the country with the lowest frequency in sexual contacts, but it also ranked lower than other Asian countries regarding satisfaction in sex life. In 2006, another international survey on sex life and satisfaction levels was conducted in 29 countries (Laumann et al. 2006). Here, too, Japan ranked lowest.

Western media have depicted the Japanese phenomenon of sexlessness as a problematic situation and an anomaly (Haworth 2013; Thompson 2016). They assert that Japanese young adults feel a strong aversion to sexuality. Most Western media discussions attempt to identify reasons for the absence of frequent sexual intercourses among Japanese couples.

Literature Review Regarding Sexuality and Leisure

After having discussed the current situation of sexlessness in Japan, the chapter will now focus on sexuality as part of recreation and pleasure in contemporary Japanese society. This subsection will first give a brief description of the history of sexual recreation in Western countries, which then will be compared with the way Japanese informants think about sexual pleasure. This will demonstrate that sex as recreation has not always been evident in Western countries. The current meaning of sex and recreation is a recent phenomenon. It also highlights that sexuality among romantic couple relationships is perceived differently in different cultures.

In contemporary European society, sex is clearly and most often regarded as a part of recreation. Recreation is an activity for leisure, detached from daily nuisances and everyday duties and done for enjoyment, fun and pleasure. In modern times, leisure activities generally serve to achieve self-fulfillment. The same is true for sexuality within couple relationships. Sexuality in Western countries is often considered in terms of self-expression, achieving satisfaction, sharing sexual enjoyment and gratifying personal well-being. 'Sexuality' naturally has various meanings, and its perception is diverse, but the dominating discourse revolving around pleasure and recreation is the focus: "Individuals are today more willing to design their own intimate arrangements to suit their singular needs and value" (Seidman 1991).

A Short History of Sexuality and Recreation

The historical function of sex has been to allow humans to reproduce. Today, sexuality has largely been emancipated from the rigid boundaries of functional reproduction and moral regulations, and it increasingly a related to the wider area of lifestyle. Before the sexual revolution, sex was regarded in terms of the social and interpersonal functions it fulfilled. It was comparatively rare that one should hear sex discussed within a context of pleasure. (Sex as pleasure was something encountered mainly outside of the marriage relationship.) A quick look at how sexual ideology was transformed by the Sexual Revolution in the 1960s and 1970s is illustrative.

In the 1960s, the publication of sex manuals[2] soon caught up to marriage manuals (Seidman 1991, p. 126). Although sex in a couple relationship has various meanings, discourse about sexual pleasure became highly valued, and erotic pleasure came to be understood as an expression of one's autonomy. The 1970s introduced notions of lust and desire into the discourse.

In the 1980s and 1990s, the dominant understanding of sexuality underwent a further transformation; increasingly, individualism underlined the discourse, and notions of recreation and the reproductive function of sexuality became less central (Matthiesen 2007). Especially in comparison with the beginning of the twentieth century, we can indeed witness a revolution in the understanding of sexuality, a complete modification that departed from a functional, reproductive view, often in terms of effective methods to control fertility (Seidman 1991, p. 53), to one that was more recreational and pleasant.[3] The individualistic approach that saw sexuality as a type of pleasant recreation also attracted the attention of both academic and popular writers.

We can see the change in sexual consciousness in the survey by Schmidt (Schmidt 2000). It demonstrates gender differences and social changes in sexual behavior and consciousness among students in 1981 and 1996. In 1981, sexuality in couple relationships was more valued as providing psychological satisfaction and intimacy, whereas in 1996 students more often defined sexuality as fun and an opportunity for novel experiences.

Benagiano and Mori (2009) answered the question about the origin of human sexuality, 'Procreation or recreation?' with: 'Both and much more'. As Abramson and Pickerton (1995) explained, "Sex isn't just for reproduction anymore. It's also for pleasure… the motive behind the procreation (1995:5)".

Consciousness About Sexual Pleasure: German and Japan

Sex in couple relationships has various meanings, among which the understanding of pleasure is broadly conceived of as an autonomous value. This view renders the activity of sex as something more acceptable within a couple relationship, a view that is widespread in Western countries. In Japan, the discussion about procreation in the couple relationship is not as strongly considered and is often overlooked in theoretical discussions in Japan.

Pacher (2016) compared the sexual behavior and consciousness between men and women in Japan and in German-speaking countries. In an interview research of 27 German-speaking informants in their 20s and 30s, Pacher showed that the meaning of sex for women strongly relates to the feeling of pleasure and fun. On the other hand, men tend to compare sex in the couple relationship as an important leisure activity that must not be missed. As a respondent said, (Pacher 2016:119), "Sex is as important as a soccer game. Since my childhood, I play soccer, and I can never miss a game to play". He then compared sex within a couple relationship to soccer in his leisure.

Interviewees also expressed that maintenance of intimacy via sexual pleasure was regarded as a way to foster relationships, who viewed enjoyment by both partners as highly important. This was in stark contrast to the statements of Japanese informants none of whom averred the sex in couple relationships to be related to recreation.[4] But surprisingly, most male informants mentioned that using sexual services was more related with pleasure than having sex with the partner (more on page 16–17).

For women, enjoying sexual affairs outside of the couple relationship was perceived more as leisure. Extramarital affairs for both sexes (but especially for women) increased between 2000 and 2012. The trend of extramarital affairs between single females and married men often observed before 2000 changed in 2000, when both groups involved in extramarital affairs had spouses. The interviewees expressed that as long as family life is not destroyed, it is acceptable to have fun and enjoy love relationships outside of marriage. Outside of married life, they believed they could enjoy being a genuine man or woman (i.e., a role seemingly associated with the freedom to express sexual desire), which is not the case when they were confined to the role of a mother and wife or father and husband. It seems that the social expectations that are attached to the role of mother and wife or father and husband (as opposed to the roles of a 'genuine' woman and man) are devoid of sexuality.

Japanese Sexual Service

Fūzoku (or *sei-fūzoku sangyo*) is the Japanese term for the sexual service industry and its wide ranges of services (Sakatsume 2016). In contrast to the adult industry (i.e., prostitution) in Western countries, the variety of

Japanese sexual services is very wide and includes those that offer sexual intercourse or those that forbid sexual intercourses but provide oral satisfaction. There are also services that only allow cuddling or mere touching. The main services are termed soap land,[5] pink salon, delivery health (*deriheru*) and erotic massages. Since 2000, the sexual service industry witnessed a significant change. A new law regulating sexual services was amended, which led to declining number of shop businesses as opposed to the increasing amount of sexual services that are offered outside facilities such as shops or salons. In contemporary Japan, therefore, the popularity of soap lands suffers while delivery health or *deriheru*, in which women can work flexible (any time, any place) has gained traction. "Delivery health" refers to a call service. The ordered women goes to the hotel or to the room of the customer and gives him the service he wants (Nakamura and Teshigawara 2015, p. 68).

Along with this new trend from shop businesses to non-shop businesses, the consciousness of women who work in the adult industry also changed. Women are not employers in their shops anymore; instead, they find the customer on their own (mostly via a website or a dating app) and try to give the customer the service they desire. Because of high competition with other women, the girl's hospitality is highly valued (the women have to be very kind, try to make the men feel loved). Nakamura (2014) mentioned that more women, especially those in their 20s (born in the 1990s), are open to sexuality and see this work more positively. To work in this adult industry is also seen as a high status for women (Nakamura 2014, pp. 12–19). However, one might doubt this perception in light of the recent proliferation of these services, prompted by the economic crisis around 2008. Many women became engaged in the sex industry due to their fundamental economic needs and out of desperation. It remains to be explored how much room for high status there can be under such circumstances.

For male customers, using sexual services is seen more as pleasure and a form of recreation as compared with sexual life with their partners. This is partly based on a perception that the women in the sex industry provide them with a high quality service and with a wider range of options. They can try more things with these girls than with the wife. Another facet of sexlessness is that some men who are sexless with their wives prefer using sexual services rather than having sex with their own partner. In some cases, they also prefer the sexual service more than dating a partner outside the marriage relationship. A generic reason given is as follows: "If

I fall in love with someone, it could be bothersome and can destroy the family. But using a sexual service is only a service. It means I pay money for the service. So there is no feeling between the person and the customer" (Kameyama 2003, p. 75). Or, the men seek to enjoy obtaining pleasure without any preceding courteous activities towards the woman (such as flirting or actively giving them pleasure).

Significance of the Research

Criticism Regarding the Problem

Since the 1990s, sexless couples have become a growing concern in the media, and researchers have been exploring causes of the phenomenon. Some criticize the very problematization of this phenomenon. To the sociologist Akagawa (1999), the very fact that being sexless is generally approached in a pathological sense brings negative attention to the issue. He claims that precisely because "it is seen as a deviation from the norm in terms of marital sexual behavior", being sexless is perceived as a "disease that needs to be cured, as a social issue (Akagawa 1999, p. 385)".

In Akagawa's opinion, there is no need to explore the causes of the phenomenon of sexlessness because most such questions seem to completely ignore the sexual discourse that came out of the 1970s. He pointed out that why does someone get treated as an 'ill person' if someone has less then one-month of sexual contact, or why does someone get treated as a 'healthy person' when a person has sex more than one time in a month. He contends that the real sociological inquiry should be "Why is the sexless phenomenon being noticed, discussed and problematized?" (Akagawa 1999, pp. 384–386). Criticizing the problematization of sexlessness may have appeal to people for whom being in a sexless relationship does not create any frustration, people who do not perceive it as a "problem". However, there are people for whom the prolonged lack of sex creates frustration and distress. Thus, I propose that sexlessness be conceptualized as 'problematic' in those situations in which one of the partners desires sex but the other does not respond. In these situations, the partner who desires sex feels frustrated, and because their need for emotional desire is not satisfied, they will live in perpetual anguish. Having their feelings hurt, it is plausible their emotional life and therefore their livelihood will be affected. If this assumption about sexlessness' impact on psychological well-being and psychological health holds, then it is indeed a reason for scholars to explore the causes and find potential remedies for the (at least subjectively) problematized phenomenon, rather than passively accepting that this situation continues. Other authors consider that "having or not having sex is not the issue. The issue is more that communication works between couples and quality of a relationship should be re-examined" (Ataka 1995, p. 21).

To gain a deeper understanding of the background of the sexlessness, the following section analyzes conducted interviews; the analysis is guided by two questions:

(1) What are the reasons for sexless couple relationships?
(2) Do sexless couple relationships lead to higher use of sexual services as a form of recreation?

Methodology

The semi-structured interviews (conducted between August 2012 and July 2013) allowed informants to speak as freely as possible. The paper is based on interviews with 21 informants in their 20s and 14 informants in their thirties. While it cannot be claimed that 35 interviews reflect the behavior of all Japanese, the study can nevertheless highlight some general tendencies in contemporary Japanese perceptions about sexual values.

The interviews lasted from one to one and a half hours. They were conducted at a place of the respective informant's choice. Most were conducted at coffee shops, restaurants or the informant's workplace.

Questions

(1) Context: Age, job (present or absent), working hours, leisure time, family structure, etc.
(2) Attitudes towards sex: Meaning of sex, interest and importance, presence/lack of sexual education, contraception, etc.

(3) Sex-life situation: Reason(s) for having/not having sex with partner, frequency, satisfaction level, conversations about sex, etc.

(4) Relationship with the partner: Time spent together, time/lack of time spent as 'a man and a woman', sharing housework, satisfaction level in the relationship with the partner, etc.

(5) In the case of 'sexless' couples: period spent being 'sexless' and reasons, changes in lifestyle (or lack thereof), presence/lack of other type of physical contact, satisfaction level, etc.

(6) In the case of a childbirth experience: delivery in the presence/absence of the father, presence/lack of episiotomy, overall physical condition after delivery

I mention the interviewees in the following form:
(F20.XX), (M20.XX): F=female, M=male, in their twenties
(F30.XX), (M30.XX): F=female, M=male, in their thirties

Findings

Talking About Sexuality

Although, informants were able to answer most questions, many men and women in their early 20s and thirties found it difficult to express the reasons behind their answers. Especially difficult were the questions about what sex means to them, sexual interest, the importance attached in their relationships . One major factor is that until the interview they never had a chance to think or talk seriously about sexuality. Another reason may have been the lack of extensive sexual experience. As they were not used to this topic, many of the informants were very careful about the language they used to answer. The informants constantly tried to find appropriate words to explain their sexual experience and not to make it sound like a 'dirty joke'.[6] It became clear that, unlike the informants in their early twenties, those in their late 20s and 30s had more content to report on and they could express their ideas more clearly and minutely.

Nevertheless, although most said they do not normally discuss this topic, some informants interestingly used the opportunity to talk for a long time about sex. However, they talked more about other people's sexual experiences than their own.

Causes of Not Having Sex in the Couple Relationship

Informants of Men and Women in 20s

I interviewed eleven men and ten women in their 20s. Three men and three women among them were in a sexless relationship at the time of the interview. Additionally, one male and one female informant were not in a relationship but they had experienced a sexless relationship in the past. The most salient reason why they were sexless reported:

Women

Bad sexual experiences in past relationship, lack of pleasure during sex, lack of physical energy, the partner has more sexual desire, feeling duty, no fun in having sex, refusal of sex from the partner (no sexual attractiveness to the other partner).

Men

Bad sexual experiences in past relationship, refusal of sex from the partner (no sexual attractiveness to the other partner), the partner made fun about sex with him.

Case Examples: Bad Sexual Experiences in Past Relationship, Painful Intercourse, Lack of Pleasure

Example of Female Interviewees

More women than men in their 20s perceived sex as stressful. This was especially the case when they had negative past experiences including sex performed from a strong sense of obligation, painful intercourse, a non-enjoyable experience, lack of pleasure, lack of physical strength and a stronger sexual desire on the part of the partner. This led to a gradual reduction in their desire. Despite this, women often perceived sex as a necessary duty among couples; the sense of obligation was therefore very strong. In this case, even if they experienced pain during intercourse, women tended to avoid expressing their opinions or intentions.

Example of Male Interviewees

Additionally, there was also a man who said he could "no longer engage actively in sex because of past experiences". In this case, too, it became apparent that the topic of sex had been eliminated from the couple's conversations. He stated: "When I was going out with my previous girlfriend, she told me that she doesn't like this stuff. She said it was painful. And I said ok, I understand. We went out for a year or so, without having sex. It's not like I didn't want to have sex, but because she seemed to hate it, we just [hung] around together. And the sex—well, I said it's OK. So I said we can still be together even if we didn't have sex." When I asked about why it was painful for her to have sex or what kind of pain it was, (M20.05) said: "I don't know exactly." When asked whether the lack of sex had frustrated him, he said it did not; "I think that sex is tiring anyway, and it's a waste of time (he laughs), and you can always do all sorts of other things."

Even if this example is embodied in a male interviewee, the reason for his lack of sexual interest was initiated from the female's side. But here we witness that he has neither capability nor knowledge of to constructively deal with the problem and solve rather than avoid it. In Japan, there is a lack of relevant knowledge and sexual education, and few psychological or other helpful guides that would explain how to handle such situations.

Case Examples: Feeling Negative Duty

One example of a female informant perceiving sex as a mere duty was (F20.9), who was in her second relationship. Ever since her experience with her first boyfriend, she stopped feeling pleasure in sexual intimacy. During the first sexual intercourse in her previous relationship, she reported: "I had a lot of pain and from that time I feel traumatized. From that time, I have a bad image of sex. I told him about my pain during sex, but that time, I had no experiences to talk about that. So I could not explain him what I want, what he could do to make it better, and why I have pain. He also has not so much sexual desire and no knowledge. So after that, we had no sex for two years and then we broke up."

Now the informant is in another relationship but she has still a negative image about sex in the relationship. She suffers from knowing the current partner has more sexual desire than she does. She explains that in her mind, sex is a kind of a duty: "On the one hand, there is a sense of obligation, but on the other hand, it is a way to obtain kinship. I like him, and I also enjoy kinship."

Similar to other female interviewees, she did not feel pleasure in the sexual intercourse, but she nevertheless craved to have kinship. When I asked her why she does not tell her partner when she is not happy with the sexual life, she responded:

> "I don't tell because I don't want to hurt him. So I bear it […].
> I really suffer. This is why I lie like a fish (like a maguro fish) and open my legs. Then I wait until he is finished. I really don't know how to enjoy sex. I always think let's enjoy this time but I cannot." (F20.9)

Case Examples: No Fun in Having Sex (Sex Is Bothersome)

Another big reason Japanese become sexless is that sex is 'bothersome'. Various reasons were given for this perception:

Example of Male Interviewees

- The previous girlfriend made fun of him during sexual intercourse. Since then, the male informant (M20.10) avoided sexual intercourse and believes sex is bothersome. He wishes a relationship without sex. The only time he wants to have sex is when he wants to have a child.

– Because of lack of sexual attractiveness to the other partner, he refuses sexual intimacy with the partner. (M20.11) does not feel any sexual desire for the partner since they got married. But, he mentioned that he loves his partner and he would not think of divorcing her. But he feels more sexual desire for other women, and he also has extramarital affairs. He also said, due to the feeling of love he has towards her, he cannot have sex with her. He can only have sex only with someone he does not love (as if it sex was merely lust-oriented).

Example of Female Interviewees

– Sex is bothersome because of the lack of pleasant feelings.
– A female informant (F20.07) mentioned that sex is not important for her because she does not see it as a way of communication. She furthermore never feels fun or pleasure during the sexual act. She therefore feels better when there is no sexual intercourse with the partner.
– Feeling tired: Another stated fact is that some informants, especially women, feel physically tired. This is true not only during sex but also in daily life. After having sex, they feel more exhausted. So they want to avoid sex (F20.09).

Summary

We can see that bad sexual experiences in past relationships influence current sexual consciousness and behavior. The negative first sexual contact is not a phenomenon isolated to Japan; it occurs all over the world. However, what is particular to Japan is the fact that women embrace the fear that they will continue to experience negative sex again. I question if this is the reason they avoid sexual contact with their partner—because they start equating 'pain' with sexual contact after their first sexual experience and thus start to enjoy it less and less. Moreover, it often happens that men respond to this avoidance of sexual contact and thus couples become gradually sexless. This is why social support (e.g., sex education) for couples is different in Europe and Japan. Traditionally, women were stereotypically considered 'a passive presence' during sex.

There are many cases in which women do not talk about their sexual desire or they do not attach importance to female sexual pleasure, especially when they see themselves as a 'passive presence' and 'unmotivated'. This perception of women as a passive presence has decreased significantly in Europe, but in Japan it is still an enduring stereotype. It is possible that this still applies to the two informants (F20.09) and (F20.7)—the idea that a woman does not feel pleasure during sex; she just 'lends' her body to her partner. The author believes these preconceptions and stereotypes need to be changed.

There is still not enough information about strategies to cope with sexual problems in Japan (such as painful contact), and opportunities to learn about sex are limited, for both men and women. Thus, it is possible that women do not fully understand how to cope with pain during intercourse. Moreover, it is also possible that men and women do not have a good understanding of each other's bodies, of sex and of their own bodies. Therefore, it is important for them to deepen their understanding about their bodies and about sexual desire.

Interviewees of Men and Women in Thirties

I interviewed eight women and six men in their thirties; among them, twelve informants (six women and one man) are married, whereas one woman and three men are not in a relationship now. Four women and one man are currently in a sexless relationship. One woman and two men had a sexless relationship in the past.

The most salient reasons they were sexless were reported as follows:

Women

Losing sexual desire after a special life event such as marriage, living together and/or childbirth, a sense of family has been developed which made the partner less desirable, not taking time for each other (having dinner or going out together, lack of romance, etc.).

Men

Losing sexual desire after a special life event such as marriage, living together and/or childbirth, a sense of family has been developed which made the partner less desirable, not taking time for each other (having dinner or going out together, lack of romance, etc.), tired from work, sexual routine.

Case Examples: Losing Sexual Desire After Living Together

The following applies to both men and women. Before living together with a partner, sexual desire for the partner exists. But after living together, sexual desire slowly decreases. "I don't know why it happened. Suddenly we stopped having sex." (M30.3)

A male informant (M30.04) who experienced a sexless relationship in the past stated that he started to live with the partner three months into the relationship. After six months living together, they stopped having sex. I asked the reason why they no longer had sex anymore and the answer was: "I don't know. But I think at that moment I was too busy with work compared to now. I went home every night at 22:00, I ate my dinner and slept. I didn't have any problems having no sex, but I think my partner had a problem. This is why she broke up with me." (M30.4)

Females often mention that they no longer feel love for the partner when they start living together, getting married or after having a child. Also, (F30.05) and (F30.6) both mentioned that the relationship to the partner changed after marriage. After marriage, when they started to live with the partner and after living together they stopped having sex:

> My husband kisses very bad. So, I don't get sexually excited. Before marriage I was falling in love with him, so I wanted to have sex. But now, after three years of living together, we are like friends. I don't feel any love for my husband anymore. (F30.05)

> I don't think I want to have fun with my partner (sexually). When I think I want sexual fun, it's so unnatural. Usually I don't hug him, I don't give

him a kiss. We are like a family. It's like, you don't hold hands with your siblings, right? In Japan, we don't hug each other (in a relationship). But, it's normal that we are together. (F30.06)

Surprisingly both informants wanted to have a child. So to conceive a child, they started to have sex again, but after the woman became pregnant, they again stopped.

Case Examples: Like a Brother and Sister Relationship, Which Made Them Less Desirable

A male interviewee mentioned the following: "I am pretty busy. Because I am busy with work and I am tired, I do not feel like having sex. I have not done it (sex) even for half a year before I got divorced with my wife, because I did not feel like it. Perhaps if there were time where we could regain feelings, then it would work. If you are a couple (and not a married couple) you sometimes meet the person, go out on a date, have a nice dinner together, and you would do that kind of thing (sex). But if you become wife and husband, you start living together. You live with the person under one roof and become a single life, I became part of a family, not a lover. It's the same like: You don't want to have sex with your mum or sister. So it's the same with a wife. My wife is like a family member. I don't feel like having sex anymore." (M 30.04)

Although above (M30.04) states that not only "tiredness" is the cause of sexlessness, in fact it is understood that multiple factors are related to this phenomenon. Not only the element of tiredness (fatigue) but also the fact their significant other no longer has sexual appeal can be seen in the changing of a 'love relationship' into a 'family relationship'. In addition, in order to prioritize work he did not make the time and space in which he could dare to be with the partner.

Case Examples: Sexless After Childbirth

Also, after childbirth the role of 'man and woman' becomes more a role of 'father and mother' . As couples focus on childrearing rather than on their relationship, the tendency to avoid sex increases (Fig. 2.1).

Fig. 2.1 Made by the author

It is a common belief in Japan that sex is meant for unmarried young couples and not for married couples. Interviewees in their thirties, especially women, say that before their marriage, their preferred way of showing affection was the sexual act.

I give one particular example from a female interviewee (F30.01), who is married and has a child. For her, marriage, living together and being pregnant happened in the same time period. Therefore, she doesn't know exactly what factors lead to her 'sexlessness'. Before her marriage, she and her partner had sex on a regular basis. In her opinion, sex is important before marriage, as it is the only way to show affection towards your partner. Whereas marriage itself is a sign of love; as a result, there is no need for sex anymore. Moreover, she feels tired and exhausted after work. Nevertheless, she feels sorry for her husband because she is not putting any effort into their sexual relationship. She wants to resume her sex life once their child is a bit older.

After marriage or childbirth, the process of becoming a family leads to a decrease in sexual contact, because after giving birth the child becomes the couple's center of attention. Moreover, most of the informants answered that sexual intimacy is not an important way of communication in a relationship. The feeling of being together was enough to keep a relationship going, and they do not feel sex plays an important role anymore. This 'satisfaction' leads to sexless situations.

Also, the results of this interview showed that most of the interviewees do not know each other's sexual preferences. They do not talk about sexual desires and fantasies. In general, informants feel unsatisfied with their sex lives. They do not talk about it even with friends or their parents. Most of the informants do not talk about things related to sex at all.

Summary

Women in their thirties mention reasons for refusing sex different from those of the women in their 20s. For example, not feeling any pleasure during sex, husbands not very skilled at kissing or touching their bodies, or they do not create a romantic mood. Another aspect is that they start feeling too old for sex or lose energy for sexual activity. One informant said she feels constantly exhausted and tired after work and doesn't want to put any effort into having sex with her partner. However, she feels sorry for her husband because she avoids having sex. She believes she will be able to resume her sex life once their child is a little older.

In this interview, men blamed specific mannerisms/routine of their partners during sex as one of the main causes of their sexlessness. Men feel that women always repeat the same sexual pattern, whereas they themselves want to try new things during sex. However, men do not want to talk about this problem with their partners. Another major factor is stress caused by overwork or a bad environment at their workplaces.

For interviewees who have experienced sexlessness, sex is getting systematically excluded from everyday life; for the Japanese, it is increasingly unimaginable that sex might play an important role in their daily routine; especially, the thought of having sex at home, where they live, eat and sleep, gets rather bothersome. This is one reason married couples in Japan struggle with their sexual relationship.

Therefore, it can be said that the importance of sex between couples has gone down. For example, couple don't go out on a date, such as a romantic dinner or going to the movies and so on. Some interviewees also try to avoid being together in one room. Or, some interviewees only eat once a year with their partner (for example ,for birthdays). Some interviewees believe that it is important to make time for their partner, but they don't know how. Or, they believe it is already too late to actually resume their relationship. In a long-term relationship, some couples become 'more like roommates' for each other, so it becomes even more difficult for men and women to consciously feel their relationship (as they cannot imagine having sex with each other). It is interesting that informants who experienced sexlessness in their relationship did not find a solution for the situation, or they did not try to actively change the situation.

Sexual Pleasure and Sex Outside the Couple Relationship

Significance Regarding Perception of Sexuality as Recreation

In this interview there were two types of interviewees:
Interviewees (men and women) for whom interest in and importance of sex in the couple relationship is low:

1. "I am not really interested in sex. There are other things I can do or think about." (F20.02), (F20.03), (M20.05) (e.g., traveling, going shopping, reading books).
   "I don't think sex is necessary to show love to the partner. There are many other way to show love to the partner." (M20.03, M20.06, F30.01, F30.05). (After being asked how they show a partner their love, they said: "I don't know, but in many ways, like having a good communication or kissing each other, or the fact, that we are living together, sleeping in one bed together [and not in separated bed like in many Japanese households].")
2. Interviewees for whom interest in sex exists, but not in the current relationship:
   "I am interested in sex but not with my partner. I can't imagine to have sex with him/her. He/she is like my roommate or my friend." (F30. 06, M30.01, M30.04)
   "I don't think sex in a relationship is necessary, because you can also have sex outside the relationship for [one's] own pleasure." (M20.9, M20.11)

We found interviewees who experienced a sexual relationship outside the couple relationship (M20. 08, M30.01, M30.4, F30.03, F30.06) and also male interviewees who used sexual services though they had a partner (M30.04). They enjoy dates, a romantic atmosphere and being loved. Especially (F30.06),(M30.01) and (M30.04) mentioned that "family and sex is a different sphere. Family is family. But fall[ing] in love happens outside the family."

In this interview what was interesting was that even if some interviewees didn't experience a sexual relationship outside the couple relationship, some male interviewees could imagine having an affair or having sex with someone else if they had more time and money.

Another fact is that, some female interviewees would not accept when the partner has an affair outside the relationship, but they would understand when the partner would use a sexual service: "When a man can not satisfy his sexual desire, it would be better to go to the fūzoku." (F20.04), (F20.05), (F20.06), (F20.07) "I don't want that my boyfriend likes another girl and fall[s] in love with her. But going to *fūzoku* is ok, because it's only a physical relationship and not emotional."(F20.04)

On the other hand, there are male informants who are not interested in having sexual contact outside the couple relationship. For example, (M20.03) was living abroad for one year. During that time he talked a lot with foreigners about sexuality in a couple relationship. He said because of this experience overseas, he felt sexual intercourse to be more important than before. Another male interviewee (M20.05) could not imagine having sex outside the main relationship. In the past he had a bad experience with his girlfriend. Also, for (M30.03) the interest and the importance of sexuality were very low. He mentioned being too tired from work and that interest in having sex generally decreased.

Some interviewees who are sexless but enjoy extramarital sexual relationships said they enjoy pleasure they could not find in their own couple relationships. On the other hand, some interviewees were not interested in having sex, either within or outside their relationships. They believe sex is not for recreation. They enjoy other leisure activities (such as shopping, reading books, traveling) rather than having sex. It therefore would be not right to conclude that sexlessness leads to a higher use of sexual services as a form of recreation. But, we also cannot say like Abe (2004) that the reason for sexlessness is merely sexual aversion. This point needs to be analyzed in greater depth.

Common Ground of the Interviewees

Sexual Education

It is safe to say that many of the informants lack a role model in terms of sexual awareness and sexual behavior. Moreover, the informants knew nothing about their parent's sex life. Essentially, most informants received little or no sexual education from their parents. For example, (F20.10) said she wanted to talk to her parents about sex, but continued: "They never did. I would have wanted to talk about it [sex] with my parents and friends. Because I'm one who has never talked about it, I would like to talk to my children about it, because my parents never taught me." (M20.09) also said: "I would have liked my parents to teach me about sex."

In addition, the interview also revealed that sex was not only absent in the family, but physical contact between the parents was also scarce or altogether absent. When asked if their parents ever flirted (kissed or embraced) in front of them, most of the 20-year-olds responded "no"; "they don't"; "they only do it occasionally, in a playful manner".[7] When asked how their parents expressed affection towards one another, they answered, "They give each other presents for one event or another"; "I don't know, there is a certain atmosphere." In other words, there are cases in which the informants assume affection from the fact that their parents do not fight. In that sense, we can say that their parents may not have given them the idea that "sex is an expression of affection". They reported a tendency of not talking to their parents or asking them for advice about sex.

It became clear that sexual education received in school was also limited. When asked about the meaning of 'sexual education,' the 20-year-old informants answered, "the structure of the body" and the 30-year-olds answered "the structure of the body" and "I haven't received a sexual education". At school, they usually learned about the bodily mechanisms, pregnancy and sexual diseases. However, sex as a form of communication between men and women was not part of the sexual education offered by parents or by the school. Because they did not learn about sexual communication between the members of a couple, they also eliminated conversations about sex in their own couple relationship. Alternately, it may be faulty communication results in relationships in which men and women fail to understand each other.

Sexual Communication

This interview's results revealed that most informants do not talk about sex with their friends or others. In other words, a tendency to completely exclude the topic of sex from daily life could be observed.

Thus, even if in daily life they have trouble or questions about sex, they have no party to consult with, and they do not exchange information about sex with friends. Because neither member of a couple conveys their desire to their partner, most informants said they don't know their partner's sexual preferences. Furthermore, they do not touch upon this topic in daily conversations because there is no opportunity to do so. This tendency is found not only among women, but also among men—as in the case of the young man who was trying to avoid 'dirty jokes'. In other words, we can conclude that couples do not communication about sex .

Conclusion

The sexless phenomenon in Japan is multicausal: bad sexual experiences in past relationship, pain during sexual intercourse, lack of pleasure and perception of sex as a negative duty are the main reasons thereof. Whereas these factors were frequently brought out by interviewees under the age of 30, interviewees above the age of thirty predominantly pointed out other reasons, namely a decline in interest after marriage and childbirth. At the same time excessive overtime work and other exhausting working conditions act as a catalyst for the avoidance of sexual intimacy.

However, it can be argued that most of these factors are merely facets of deeper causes such as a lack of communication within the couple relationship along with insufficient knowledge about each other's sexual desires, an inadequate state of sexual education and a socially related separation between family and romance. In general, sex among married couples is not perceived as a recreational time activity, which leads to a weakening will to maintain a joint sexual life after a certain period in the relationship.

Some interviewees were not interested in having sex, both within and outside their relationships. For these interviewees, not having a sexual relationship is not a problem. They are satisfied with not having sex. On the other hand, we could find interviewees who are sexless but enjoy extramarital sexual relationships and enjoy the pleasure they cannot find in their own couple relationships.

In contemporary Western society, sexuality in the couple relationship is most often regarded as a part of recreation, as an important, even necessary, part of joint leisurely activity. It is perceived as detached from the daily nuisances and everyday duties, and it is done for enjoyment, fun and pleasure. The enjoyment of recreation together is highly valued in couple relationships, and sexual pleasure is an inherent part of this leisure. This is also embodied in the fact that the West provides various societal means that enable people to reflect upon and to enhance their joint sexual life – such as sexual education in school, therapeutical measures in case people need help, the widespread distribution of advisory brochures, etc.

In Japan, discourse about sexual recreation does not exist. There are only a few opportunities to learn about sexuality in a relationship (plus, there is a severe lack of sexual education in general).

The author believes the difficulty Japanese men and women meet in verbally conveying sexuality is also connected to an insufficient social support (books for couples, sexual education at school, therapists, etc.). Not being able to properly communicate desires and opinions related to sexuality is not solely a personal problem, but rather a social issue.

Notes

1. In every culture and society, if we see it from micro-level, they have their own sexual script, pattern, norms, etc. After all, sexuality in European society discussed often as macro-level, as 'global culture'. In this paper, the author is using the term 'Europe' (or Western society) to make the Japanese sexual phenomenon more understandable.

2. The main two were *Everything You Wanted to Know About Sex,But Were Afraid to Ask* (Reuben,1969), and *The Joy of Sex* (Comfort,1972).
3. The author uses the term 'leisure' as the meaning relevant to 'recreational' and 'pleasure'.
4. Some informants said reading books, going out for shopping, going out with friends and traveling are more related to feelings of pleasure and fun than having sex with a partner.
5. A soap land—also called a Turkish bath or sauna house of prostitution—has a long, if not the longest, history among all Japanese sexual services. It refers to a bathhouse where the customer is provided with a sexual service called 'soapland'. Pink salon, on the other hand, is a type of brothel that offers oral satisfaction.
6. Although some of the informants were indeed uncomfortable talking about sex, there were some who did not feel reluctant at all. For example, one informant who had studied abroad (in Sweden) for one year provided more coherent and clear answers. He was much more open about sex than the others. He himself stated that he was able to speak more freely about sex because during his exchange year, there were more people talking about sex, thus he had been able to think about it.
7. Only one informant answered "yes" (F20.01). She said that her parents hold hands and kiss in front of her (she also said that, even if she gets married, she will enjoy physical contact with her partner and that she wants to become like her parents, who drink alcohol and enjoy themselves) (F20.01).

References

Abe, T. (1991). 'Sekkusuresu kappuru to kaihigata jinkaku shougai' [Sexless Couples and Evasive Personal Disorder]. *Japan Society of Sexual Science, 8*(2), 10–23.
Abe, T. (2004). *Sekkusuresu no seishin igaku* [The Psychiatry of Sexlessness]. Tōkyō: Chikuma Shinsho.
Abramson, P. R., & Pickerton, S. D. (1995). *With Pleasure: Thoughts on the Nature of Human Sexuality*. New York: Oxford University Press.
Akagawa, M. (1999) *Sexuality no rekishigaku* [The History of Sexuality] (pp. 384–386). Tōkyō: Keisoshobo.

Ataka, S. (1995) *Sekkusuresu. Shitakunai tsuma, dekinai otto* [Sexlessness. The Wife Who Does Not Desire It. The Husband Who Cannot Do It]. Tōkyō: Shufu no Tomo.

Bänziger, P., Beljan, M., & Eder, X. F. (Eds.). (2015). *Sexuelle Revolution? Geschichte der Sexualität im deutschsprachigen Raum seit dem 1960er Jahren.* Bielefeld: Transcript Verlag.

Benagiano, G., & Mori, M. (2009). The Origins of Human Sexuality: Procreation or Recreation? *Ethics, Bioscience and Life, 4,* 50–59.

Burkart, G. (2018). *Soziologie der Paarbeziehung-Eine Einführung.* Deutschland: SpringerVS.

Comfort, A. (1972). *The Joy of Sex.* New York: Crown Publishers.

Durex Network. (2005). *2005 Global Sex Survey Results* [Online]. Available: http://www.durexnetwork.org/en-GB/research/faceofglobalsex/Pages/Home. aspx [12 Feb 2017].

Haworth, A. (2013). Why Have Young People in Japan Stopped Having Sex? *The Guardian* [Online]. Available at: https://www.theguardian.com/world/2013/oct/20/young-people-japan-stopped-having-sex. Accessed 29 Mar 2017.

Japan Family Planning Association. (2016). Haigūsha to no sekkusuresu wariai [The Rate of Sexless Married Couples]. [Online]. Available at: http://www2. ttcn.ne.jp/honkawa/2265.html [29 Mar 2017].

Kameyama, S. (2003). *Tsuma to ha dekinai koto* [Things I Cannot Do With My Wife]. Tōkyō: Wave Bunko.

Laumann, et al. (2006). A Cross-National Study of Subjective Sexual Well-Being Among Older Women and Men: Findings from the Global Study of Sexual Attitudes and Behaviors. *Archives of Sexual Behavior, 26,* 399–419.

Lewandowski, S. (2008). Diesseits des Lustprinzips–über den Wandel des Sexuellen in der modernen Gesellschaft. *SWS-Rundschau, 48*(3), 242–263.

Nakamura, A. (2014). *Nihon no fūzokujō* [Japanese fūzoku]. Tōkyō: Shinchosha.

Nakamura, A. & Teshigawara, M. (2015). *Shokugyō toshite no fūzokujō* [Fuzoku as a Work]. Tōkyō: Tamashimasha.

NHK Databook. (2002). *Nihonjin no seikōdō seiishiki* [Sexual Behavior and Consciousness of Japanese]. Tōkyō: NHK Shuppan.

Pacher, A. (2016). '20 dai doitsugo ken no danjo ni okeru sei ishiki seikōdō no genjō. Nihonjin to no chōsa hikaku kara' [Sexual Consciousness and Behavior of Men and Women in Their Twenties in German-Speaking Countries: Comparison with Japanese Couples]. *Journal of Psycho-Sociology*, Meiji University: Tokyo, *12,* 113–133.

Reuben, M. D. (1969). *Everything You Wanted to Know About Sex, but Were Afraid to Ask*. New York: Random House, Inc.

Sakatsume, S. (2016). *Seifūzoku no ibitsuna genba* [Twisted Site of Sexual fūzoku]. Tōkyō: Chikuma Shobō.

Schmidt, G. (2000). *Kinder der sexuellen Revolution. Kontinuität und Wandel studentischer Sexualität 1966–1996. Eine empirische Untersuchung*. Gießen: Psychosoziologie Verlag.

Seidman, S. (1991). *Romantic Longings. Love in America, 1830–1980*. New York: Routledge.

Silja Matthiesen. (2007). *Wandel von Liebesbeziehungen und Sexualität. Empirische und theoretische Analysen*, p. 80. Gießen: Psychosozial-Verlag.

Thompson, N. (2016). With Its Population Contracting, Is Japan Having Enough Sex? *The World Weekly* [Online]. Available at: https://www.theworldweekly.com/reader/view/magazine/2016-03-03/with-its-population-contracting-is-japan-having-enough-sex/6950/ [29 Mar 2017].

Ushikubo, R. (2015). *Renai shinai wakamonotachi* [Young People Who Do Not Fall in Love]. Tōkyō: Discover Twenty-One.

3

Singing Group: The Playful Present in Health Promotion

Miraíra Noal Manfroi, Adriana Aparecida da Fonseca Viscardi, Daliana Stephanie Lecuona, Giandra Anceski Bataglion, Verônica Werle, Juliana de Paula Figueiredo, and Alcyane Marinho

M. N. Manfroi • A. A. da F. Viscardi • J. de P. Figueiredo
Physical Education Postgraduate Program, Federal University of Santa Catarina, Florianópolis, SC, Brazil

D. S. Lecuona
Human Movement Sciences Postgraduate Program, Santa Catarina State University, Florianópolis, SC, Brazil

G. A. Bataglion
Human Movement Sciences Postgraduate Program, Federal University of Rio Grande do Sul, Porto Alegre, RS, Brazil

V. Werle
Federal University of Parana, Curitiba, PR, Brazil

A. Marinho (✉)
Santa Catarina State University, Florianópolis, SC, Brazil

Introduction

This chapter focuses on an area of public health characterized by the association of the technical, social and political aspects of health care. It is necessary for health care professionals to understand practices which aim to improve the quality of life and public health by understanding the nature of human beings. The term 'public health' here does not signal a specific socioeconomic group as assisted by the public health system, but more broadly refers to the physical, mental and social well-being of the general population (Mota et al. 2017; Velloso et al. 2016). In addition, in the process of improving health, practices such as prevention, promotion, care and recovery should be developed (Velloso et al. 2016).

Public health improvement is characterized by a collaboration of society and government, whose aim is to promote public policies that contribute to the quality of life and equitable health among its citizens. It fosters the empowerment and autonomy of public healthcare users (Bezerra and Sorpreso 2016). However, according to these authors, there are still challenges in putting these assumptions into practice when the predominant conception is that 'treatment' refers only to simple ways to cure diseases with an individualistic focus. In an attempt to overcome these challenges, vision studies have been organized that seek to measure the general well-being of a population based on a set of indicators not limited to a single aspect. The human development index (HDI)[1] is an indicator based on experiences and personal parameters that diverge from a direct association between the well-being and resources or income of a population, as noted by Nahas (2013). According to Nahas, the concept of human development is associated with "… happy people…[who are] socially productive and able to reach their goals [more fully] in life" (Nahas 2013, p. 17).

However, well-being is a category that varies according to sociocultural conditions; we need to establish specific indicators for each country. In this sense, studies conducted by Bryan Smale have developed and improved the levels of well-being that are appropriate to the context. The Canadian Index of Wellbeing (2016) is made up of eight areas: community vitality, democratic engagement, education, environment, healthy population, leisure and culture, living standards and time use. The latest research, published in 2016, suggests the Canadian Index of Wellbeing provides important results. Although the economy has been recovering since the recession of 2008, even with a significant increase in gross domestic product (GDP), the indices of well-being have not increased in the same proportions (Canadian Index of Wellbeing 2016). Living standards (such as those related to housing, work and consumer goods) are among the areas most affected. Also, leisure and culture suffered from fewer investments. With regard to the health field, despite evidence of increased life expectancy, Canadians do not assess improvement in public health (Canadian Index of Wellbeing 2016).

As for the Brazilian context, there is no statistical index for assessing well-being; however, studies have been conducted to address issues regarding quality of life, which is defined as "the perception of well-being resulting from a set of individual parameters and, changeable or not, which characterize the conditions under which the human being lives" (Nahas 2013, p. 15). Environmental parameters in this context include housing, transport, security, medical assistance, working conditions and remuneration, education, leisure options,[2] environment and culture. Individual parameters include heredity and lifestyle, the latter of which includes diet, stress control, habitual physical activity and relationships.

Thus, recent expanded definitions of health and well-being have led to the development of actions that promote health, including playful activities, especially those involving the forms, manifestations and resonances of the lives of different social actors who contribute their expertise to public health in Brazil. Because it is a source of development and of fundamental importance to the physical and mental health of any individual, playfulness may be considered an important element in different contexts, whether in education, leisure and even health environments (Isayama et al. 2011; Moran 2016; Simon and Kunz 2014).

As Huizinga (1971) argues, playfulness is an element characterized by qualities such as joy, fun, pleasure and spontaneity. Applied to the arena of health, playfulness can bring about more humanized professional practices, based on the valorization of users. This more welcoming approach regards patients as having more than merely biological needs (Bezerra and Sorpreso 2016).

Humanized actions in the context of public health are based on the capacity of providers to listen to people's needs, to apprehend these needs and attend to them as fully as possible. Fundamentally, we believe the promotion, invigoration and implementation of the human dimension can benefit every mode of health practice. Knowing the nature of such actions and the development of attitudes that embody such values is essential to the process of humanization (Casate and Corrêa 2005). Health services should not reduce people to objects of purely technical intervention. The subjectivity inherent to human actions is important in all areas of health practice (Brasil 2005).

In this context, a wide-ranging project entitled "Playful Possibilities in Health Institutions of Florianópolis (SC)" was approved by the National Council for Scientific and Technological Development (CNPq 2016),[3] with the objective of analysing the potential of playful activities in the promotion of the population's health in Florianópolis (SC, Brazil). Municipal public health institutions, referred to as 'health centres', were the focus of the study. They hosted projects and activities related to different areas of health development (e.g., combating smoking, gestational monitoring, child psychology, physical activity), including artistic and cultural practices such as art therapy, horticulture, handicrafts and singing, in which a playful dimension was a major component of the service provided. In this paper, the results are presented with regard to the investigation of one of these activities, the singing group. The purpose of this singing group is to service people with comorbidities that interfere with, or prevent, travel; many of these conditions are associated with physical or intellectual decrepitude processes related to old age. The specific objective of this study was to analyse the meaning of the group's activity for the participants (professionals, volunteers, family members and users) and the effects of the activity on the health of those receiving the service.

Public Health in Brazil

Brazil's public health system, the Unified Health System (Sistema Único de Saúde, SUS), has been in force since 1988 through the country's Federal Constitution. The main objective of the SUS is to improve the quality of healthcare in Brazil, equally and adequately, according to national and unified[4] principles and guidelines (Brasil 1990). Among the guiding elements of SUS is the principle of *integrality*, which is characterized by the recognition of the human being in its completeness, treating it as a biopsychosocial structure that requires diverse forms of healthcare. To do this, it must provide the user with the appropriate resources for health promotion, risk and injury prevention, care and recovery, as well as giving the user access to the suitable establishments, trained personnel and resources necessary to realize each action (Brasil 1990; Kalichman and Ayres 2016). That is, for the principle of completeness to be effectively fulfilled, it is necessary to regard users not only from the biological perspective but also from a perspective that allows alternatives for their health care, such as those related to other spheres of human life.

The SUS is composed of three levels of healthcare, as follows: (a) *primary care*: ambulatory care and family health monitoring in health centres; (b) *intermediary*: specialized care and the use of technological resources for diagnosis and treatment, which can be obtained in polyclinics and emergency care units; and (c) *advanced*: specialized treatment services, hospitalization and surgeries in large hospitals. The services are free and articulate the three levels of government: federal, state and municipal.

Health centres are institutions that include basic medical specialties as well as the engagement of health professionals. In addition, the centres promote projects and activities that are related to disease prevention and health promotion (Brasil 2000), which includes the activity represented by the singing group. Although the SUS is recognized for its breadth and organization, its users face difficulties, such as delays in making appointments, especially for specialty care, as well as in service and return of results, medication costs, and the unpreparedness of professionals and society to act collectively (Azevedo and Costa 2010), inadequacy and instability of public funding, management problems, administrative discontinuity, fragmentation of services, infrastructural problems, bureaucracy and corruption in the public sector (Paim and Teixeira 2007).

Despite these difficulties, important mechanisms have been developed to materialize the principles of the SUS. One such mechanism, the National Humanization Policy, was created in 2003 (Brasil 2013). The policy aims to qualify management practices and health care that give priority to the human being and offer a setting for subjectivity. In this sense, this policy seeks to encourage forms of intervention that offer an integral approach to user health. In 2006, the Ministry of Health created the National Policy for Integrative and Complementary Practices (PNPIC), which by means of alternative treatments such as acupuncture, homeopathy and phytotherapy, sought to support users in the prevention of injuries and promotion and recovery of health, with a focus on continued, humanized, integral health care (Brasil 2006).

It is in this context of appreciation of the extended clinic and humanized practices that ludic activities have become a part of basic health care in Brazil, although research related to this subject is still more focused on the complexity of health care. That is, research has focused on cases of treatment that are directly related to hospitalization, as we will show next.

Playfulness and Health

Huizinga (1971) defines 'playfulness' as an element from primitive societies; some of its features can be expressed in a game format, such as: pleasure, fun, freedom, spontaneity and solemnity, enthusiasm, joy, satisfaction and well-being. Because it is an element that can only be understood through its enjoyment and its various manifestations, it can be said that playfulness is a complex, holistic phenomenon and therefore difficult to understand and conceptualize (Ferland 2006; Marinho 2004). This is because playfulness refers to a type of behaviour, a valuation, a sense, or a human intentionality that is directly related to subjective experience (Marinho 2004).

For Ferland (2006), playfulness is part of being human, but, one which is difficult to provide a theoretical explanation for; attempting to do so often leads the loss of its characteristics, since the components that motivate or move a game or play are part of the intrinsic nature of human beings. That is, "it is a subjective attitude in which pleasure, curiosity, sense of humour and spontaneity are in touch; such an attitude is translated by a freely chosen behaviour, from which no specific income is expected" (Ferland 2006, p. 18). In this way, a playful moment is an end in itself and a part of primordial human development. As Saura (2013, p. 6) notes: "We observe that to participate in a play is, for children and adults, unlike the idea of entertainment and fun inconsequential and without further damage, something deep, transformer, transgressor and formative of human nature."

It is believed that playfulness can be experienced through toys, games, plays, music and other activities that involve the core qualities of spontaneity and pleasure; however, these terms are not used as synonyms for playfulness but as potential means of playful enjoyment to be established; that is, they are recreational activities. For people to be able to express themselves and obtain pleasure through these activities, human values such as creativity, sensitivity, ethics, solidarity, altruism and joy must be added, as is clarified by Beuter and Alvim (2010). The authors add that the total involvement of the individual is necessary because, regardless of the activity, whether it is a game, a painting, a toy, or any other object or activity, such activities have no life independent from human interaction.

Although leisure can be a privileged time/space in which to manifest playfulness, it is not the only context for it to occur. Even within health institutions there may be opportunities for its occurrence, through playful activities that become strategic tools for humanized work, as has been shown by certain studies. Through a review of articles that were published between 2003 and 2013 with the use of The Virtual Health–Nursing Library and Scientific Electronic Library Online (Scielo) database, Ribeiro et al. (2014) found the use of playful activities in the reading of children's tales and songs as humanitarian strategies. With regard to the influence of these activities, the studies indicated greater attention to the participation and joy of hospitalized children (Albano and Correa 2011), as well as a greater response to treatment and the generation of affective bonds between patients, medical staff and family members (Marques et al. 2016).

Among other factors that have an impact on treatment processes, playfulness can be an important element for the reduction of stress and feelings of sadness, as it facilitates recovery (Mello et al. 1999). From this perspective, Souza and Mitre (2009) focus on the importance of providing appropriate assistance projects in health institutions that aim, through playful activities, to minimize and/or prevent the negative effects of the treatment period and to thus promote improvement in the quality of life of public health care users.

Along these lines, the presence of playful experiences in health environments is justified by the permanence of the 'human' in health practices that even today are circumscribed by preventive and biological actions, which, although important for health, do not enrich the elements that constitute their conception (Bezzerra and Sorpreso 2016; Prado 2016). This argument is pertinent to other systems that are also increasingly unbalanced by the decline of the playful spirit, such as the family system, educational system, economic system and scientific system (Federici 2015).

It is not possible to deny the existence of contradictory aspects in the understanding of the potentialities of playful activities. One such understanding is the idea that such an activity is 'used' as an 'instrument', as opposed to the conception of play, which is at the core of how children experience the world. For children, adults and the elderly, as well as for many professionals, play is more than an instrument: it represents how individuals find meaning in the world around them. In this way, the contradictions and tensions that surround this topic have led to an even greater desire by professionals to understand its role and value, especially in health care. Given that the subject of the current study, the singing group, promotes playful actions, meaning and effect for those involved are investigated.

Methodology

This research, which is part of a more comprehensive study, was carried out by descriptive-exploratory field research with a qualitative approach to data.[5] Descriptive research, according to Gil (2002), describes the characteristics of the object of study in depth and in detail. This type of research presents a detailed description of phenomena; however, it does not attempt to test or build theoretical models (Thomas and Nelson 2012).

The context of this research was a singing group, in which professionals from the area of social assistance and nursing, in addition to volunteers, visit the residences of patients with different illnesses to play and sing songs. This group performs once a week, for approximately one hour, and they are part of the activities that were developed by one of the 49 health centres of Florianópolis (SC, Brazil). Thus, the participants of this survey were professionals and volunteers as well as users and their family members who participated in the singing experiences. Eight observations were conducted involving eight users, five volunteers, two social workers, a nurse and six family members. The names of the participants of this study have been replaced by fictitious names to preserve their identities. Systematic observations were made over two months and consisted of monitoring the group between the health centre and users' homes.

Semi-structured interviews were conducted at the homes of users, with both users and their families, with an average duration of 10 minutes per interview. At the health unit, interviews were conducted with one of the responsible professionals, with an average duration of 30 minutes, and with volunteers, with an approximate duration of 10 minutes each. The interview was recorded with an audio recorder and later transcribed in full, following the guidelines of Bardin (2010). Many of the participants were not able to communicate verbally, and they were often bedridden, making interviewing difficult. So, observation of body movement and facial expression enabled a deeper understanding of the effects of the singing group on them, and subjects' bodily expressions were strong and significant.

Data was organized and descriptively analysed according to the elements of the content analysis technique recommended by Bardin (2010). According to this organization, based on the guidelines of the above-noted author, the categories of analysis were elaborated to guide the technique by employing systematic procedures and objective descriptions of the contents of the messages and indicators to allow for inferences of knowledge through production and/or reception conditions (inferred variables).

About the Singing Group

The singing group is composed of ten people and includes nurses, social workers and volunteers who go to houses to play instruments (guitar, tambourine, rattle, drum and triangle) and sing. The group performs once a week in various residences for one hour.

Although there are no restrictions regarding age and sex for care, Neuza, who has been a social worker for 15 years and is one of the founders of the group, explains that in over five years of operation, they have only attended to the elderly, especially those with diabetes and depression, among other less frequent cases. Also Neuza says the early patients were visited because of her and the group's effort, after the intervention of the first home visit. Currently, because the project has community recognition, community members travel to the health centre to ask the singing group to visit their homes. In this dynamic, after receiving requests, Neuza goes to homes, talks with relatives and users (when they are able), explains the service that they perform and schedules a visit.

Every Tuesday, at approximately 10 a.m., the group leaves the health centre wearing their uniforms of matching yellow tee shirts. They converse and walk together to the homes of the sick. Usually, they are well received, as this project has been going on for a few years. The songs have been selected over time by the group members and by the users, and group members carry folders that contain song lyrics. They specifically choose songs composed by Brazilians and written in Portuguese; the majority of the songs are old, focusing on themes such as love, life and joy. The group begins each visit with a specific song of greeting and end with a particular song to say goodbye.

In general, the visit begins by acknowledging the user. Then they make a circle around the user and begin to sing. The songs are numbered to facilitate identification and, during the singing, Neuza suggests the next song so everyone can accompany and sing; the participants are free to choose other songs. Usually Gilda (a social worker) plays the triangle and rattle and Elias plays the guitar, while Heitor plays the drum and Adir the tambourine; the others form the choir.

This initiative fits into a basic health care paradigm, such as home care, that has therapeutic, preventive and health promotion goals (Galiassi et al. 2014). In addition to these goals, the authors emphasize a revaluation of the home, the family and society in terms of health care. This initiative respects individuals and involves the health professional in the socio-economic and cultural context of the user, in which they consider their family and social relationships.

To form a better understanding of the actions taken by the group and the results obtained, an analysis of the data is presented according to the following categories: (a) family service capabilities; (b) expressions of 'life'; (c) dates and coexistence; and (d) collective 'cure'.

Results and Discussion

The Potential of Home Care

The first notable aspect of the group's investigation was the flexibility that the home care model favours, which allows sensitivity and respects the routines, times and feelings of the users as well as facilitates participation and care of the family at the time of service. This dynamic is evident in the visit that was carried out for the user, Rosa:

> When we arrived, they warned us that Rosa was taking a shower. We waited in the living room. When she arrived, Rosa said: "*Today my stomach does not feel well, I do not know what I ate yesterday*", demonstrating spontaneity in the relationship with the members of the Group. We began to sing, and after a while, her son arrived and stayed until the end, demonstrating that he was familiar with the visits because he soon realized that Neuza sang a lot and needed some water. Rosa accompanied some songs, but at the end she apologized, saying: "*Today I'm not good with people, so I did not sing them all.*" Even so, in the end, she served cookies and juice, demonstrating her gratitude to the group for the visit. (Field Journal, Sept. 29, 2015)

In addition to the group's waiting for the user to end her personal activities, as is illustrated above, the group also waits for the user to feel good and will stop their activity in specific cases. When needed, they anticipate or reschedule their visits. That is, the dynamic is performed with a focus on the person, in contrast with care given in health care institutions, which is characterized by measured time and is impersonal.

It is understood that the singing group's work is based on the concept of care, as was elaborated by Leonardo Boff (Silva et al. 2005). In addition to a singular act, the author expands the idea of 'care' as a way to be, as well as describing the way one relates to the world, to oneself and to others. To relate the concept of care with the work of health professionals, specifically to nursing, Silva et al. (2005) note that 'care' refers to helping people find ways to take care of themselves, seeking an understanding that life is full of meaning, which is similar to the observations of the work developed by the singing group. Still, the gesture of Rosa's son to provide water to Neuza and the offering of a snack demonstrate that in these situations there is reciprocity in care.

The difficulties faced by health professionals in approaching patients in a sensitive way due to their biomedical training have been recognized (Bergold and Alvim 2009). In addition, the rigidity that permeates hospital environments 'requires' objectivity in procedures and little affective involvement. By contrast, the home care investigated in the current study seems to favour the planning and execution of activities from the perspective of humanized work and involves greater freedom to develop playful activities. This is noted when Neuza (Interview, Oct. 30, 2015) describes the group's dynamics with affection: "*We work with joy and sing and write poetic compositions that are accompanied by music and folk songs. We make the person surrender to the music so they can be cheered up.*" She also clarifies the care she takes in planning: "*Another social worker and I sit together and plan where we will go and the songs we will sing. We used to schedule rehearsals, and it was like that for a long time, but now that the group is experienced, we almost never rehearse.*" With respect to the aims of the group, Neuza states that it is "*improving the health of the people who are served as a whole*".

In Neuza's statements, lightness and tranquility are evident as the group plans and carries out their visits. The emphasis is on the visit itself and the joy that is experienced, without concern for the musical performance. In this case, the songs are paths to fun, mutual exchange, recollections of the past and expressions of feelings that are developed under a dynamic that balances easeful visits with the improvement of health conditions.

In addition to the involvement of the health professionals with the users and their families, there is also community participation. Neighbours and small shopkeepers in the neighbourhood know about the singing group and ask about the people they visit and inform them about others who could benefit from their service. The network of people, information and care that is generated by home care seems to 'reposition' the user within his or her own community, minimizes their suffering, makes the process of care less traumatic and strengthens family, professional and community ties.

Expressions of 'Life'

Playful activity developed through music can contribute to the expression of emotions and corporeal manifestations. Singing, dancing and verbal exchanges can accomplish the same result. This situation can be linked to the fact that through music there is a possibility for transcending obstacles and facilitating the exchange and contact between people as well as for building paths of communication (Souza 2005). According to this concept, it is possible to accompany people, who participated of the research, after they return, who then talk, dance, cry and express their feelings through corporeal expressions during the group's visit:

> When [they were] singing, the group was very happy and looked happy "*[The user] didn't say anything, but he started to talk when he heard the music.*" Several songs made him cry and others made him laugh. His wife, Sara, at the end of the performance chatted briefly with us and told us her impression of the Group: "*I really like your group and he likes it too. It was a shame that I couldn't stay with you from the beginning. I like when you guys come and sing, because he likes to listen to you and he dances a little. This group is very good.*" (Field Journal, Sept. 15, 2015)

This example has similarities to the study by Noordhoek and Jokl (2008), which considered the effects of music on treating rheumatic (mostly elderly) people, of the possibility that the musical process helps users recognize themselves as protagonists for the way it brings out their rhythm and musicality, contributing to an awareness in them of a new body as well as a recognition of their limits. It also can help them discover the possibility of overcoming the challenges imposed by age and/or illness. So, although the goal of the singing group is to provide moments of joy, as noted above, its aim is not to deny the restrictions, limits and pain caused by disease or age. Thus, respect and courtesy are components of each visit. This situation was evident during a home visit to a man, as described by a member of the group:

> *[He'd] had a stroke and a number of subsequent strokes and had difficulty speaking. His leg was amputated due to a very serious injury."* This gentleman sat on his bed and the group stood around him. As we started playing, he had a sad and distant look and looked out the window behind his bed, avoiding looking at the visitors. Over time, as the group performed, he, even with difficulty, began singing, drumming and moving his body with the rhythm of most of the songs. (Field Journal, Sept. 15, 2015)

In this respect, expressions of sadness and distance were not discouraged by the group. Therefore, it was observed that the group was careful to be respectful of users' lives and their pain, not requiring of them a standardized response nor the obligation of joy. This versatility of feelings that differ for each user can be linked to the fact that music is a universal language present at different times and in different cultures. Thus, music can be accepted by human beings because it supports a range of psychological reactions within each individual (Oliveira et al. 2012). Additionally, music enables "the person [to] orchestrate the mind, body, heart and soul, rescuing their identity and making the individual…become the conductor of their own life" (Gomes and Amaral 2012, p. 112).

From this perspective of strengthening users to exercise the mastery of their lives, Rosana, a woman who could not get out of bed, was visited. After two songs, she began to participate in a humorous chorus that Neuza had invented and let out a little shout at the end of each song. This continued until the end of the performance, when she gave an enthusiastic shout (Field Journal, Sept. 8, 2015). This growing involvement of the user, which occurred with the singing, led to the reflection that the area of geriatrics and gerontology, in combination with the field of music, has provided significant, excellent effects in the psycho-emotional, physical and social spheres of human care and has led to improvements in self-esteem and socialization (Gomes and Amaral 2012).

Based on the reported experiences and on studies by Bergold and Alvim (2009), it can be seen that the use of music in health care enables the expression of emotions, desires and subjectivities, as well as facilitates interpersonal communication. Music also represents a sensitive approach that professionals can take with patients and their families, and it promotes integration as well as reduces loneliness.

Meetings and Coexistence

Encounters, exchanges and integration among people are components of health. In this sense it is believed that the strength of activities through singing are based on the playful experiences they provide, which are considered fundamental to living a full and happy life, whatever the state of a person's health. This does not mean the development of this dimension of life (the playfulness dimension) does not contribute to the strengthening of others (health, work, family), something that is difficult to measure objectively; however, it is possible to capture responses through the speech, facial expressions and gestures of those who participate in initiatives such the one presented in this work.

Initiatives such as the singing group create opportunities and spaces for different experiences, which in turn create conditions for the manifestation of the 'human of man' as described by Santin (2001), whether through art therapy, music or dance. In this research, the importance of this type of action was identified by the decrease of the social isolation of people, especially the elderly, due to the limitations of mobility and, consequently, autonomy. In this regard, the group's performances, which are circumscribed by home visits with singing activities, allow the elderly to be involved with the community, family members and people who are or have been part of their lives. This encounter, in turn, generates feelings of satisfaction, well-being and contentment, as evidenced in manifestations of laughter, concentration and occasionally even tears.

In this way, a situation occurred during a systematic observation of this research, when a visit was made to the home of Rudinei, a man who could not get out of bed. For this reason, when the singing group arrived at his home, he remained in bed. When the members of the group entered the room, they welcomed him and gathered around his bed. One of the volunteers of the group who played the tambourine knew that the man was very fond of this instrument, so he brought an extra tambourine for Rudinei. Rudinei held that tambourine until the end of the performance. He could not speak, but he hit the tambourine eagerly, looked at those around him with bright eyes and sometimes smiled. This demonstrates that the user can become effectively engaged with his or her community, family and friends, even for a few moments. In this process, affectivity gains prominence because it can contribute to the assimilation and improvement of people's state of health (Santos 1998).

Another example is the visit to the home of Josefa, a woman who had difficulty walking due to a serious problem in her knees. When the group arrived at her house, she was delayed opening the door; however, her steps could be heard outside. When she opened the door and saw the group, her eyes filled with tears. Everyone came in, greeted her and settled into her living room. She settled into a chair, and everyone began to sing. During some songs, she cried. On this day, Luiza was there. She is a very funny volunteer with a loud laugh. She made jokes about the songs and danced, which made Luiza smile at times. She had once been a volunteer of the group, so she had the opportunity to receive visits of the group, and during one of these visits, during a song, she said: "*You are still part of the heart of the group.*" (Field Journal, Sept. 1, 2015)

In this sense, it is shown that playfulness can produce reciprocity, interaction, dialogue, joy and solidarity. The act of singing or dancing appears to be able to modify the daily life of a person with an illness because it produces a unique reality of its own, allowing the user to overcome the barriers of pathology and limits of time and space (Mitre and Gomes 2004). In actions that are intended to be playful, human values such as sensitivity, creativity, solidarity, ethics, aesthetics, altruism and joy can be generated (Santin 2001).

The way the group was received in homes shows the mutual feeling between the users, volunteers and professionals, as was observed in the house of Beatriz, who said: "*You can't imagine the joy that it is to receive you here, it is a gift for me. I get a lot of love from you.*" On arrival of the group, Beatriz was in her living room waiting. She had juice, various cookies and popcorn on her dining room table. When the singing began, she was very happy and sang along with almost all of the songs. Her son and his daughter joined in the singing the whole time. At the end of the performance, she showed photos of the group's visit to her house from the previous year. Everyone was very happy to see the photos. Beatriz thanked the group for coming to her and gave a mini-rose to each member of the group. When asked what she liked best about the group, she replied: "*I like the singing, the people, the songs, which are old and I know them all.*" The family also thanked the group, and her son, Jonas, when questioned about his perception of the people who work in the group, said: "*They are very sweet and thoughtful people; my mom and I were very happy to receive them. They do good things for my mother.*" (Field Journal, Oct. 20, 2015)

Playful experiences such as those described above can create the possibility of living as one has at other times, engaging in other activities that the elderly body and disease no longer allow, but which can be experienced through remembering the past. Those memories were evident in the systematic observation of a visit to the home of Luís, a man who was in a wheelchair and who could not talk too well. Upon arriving at his house, the group gathered next to him and started to sing. Luís accompanied the songs and cried a lot when they played a love song, which was about a handkerchief that had been left by the beloved. Between one song and another, one of the volunteers, a friend of his, said: "*We've gone to carnival together; he played a lot in this life.*" The elderly man confirmed this with his eyes and subtle body movements (Field Diary, Oct. 13, 2015).

The above example emphasizes that playful enjoyment can result in innumerable benefits that are fundamental for the recovery of health in its broader aspects, not only individually but also collectively and on a human level (Federici 2015). In addition, it should be emphasized that users often only need the opportunity and/or stimulation to smile and have fun (Bezzerra and Sorpreso 2016; Prado 2016). According to Jurdi and Amiralian (2013, p. 276), "to produce health is to produce encounters that seek to connect people, not by pathologies or diagnoses, but by experimentation of art, work and leisure". In this sense, the singularity that permeates playful experiences can allow humanized practices to be built collectively by different actors who are involved in the process, generating benefits for users, their families and even the professionals.

Reciprocal 'Healing'

During the observations of the singing group, as well as through interviews, it was found that benefits are configured reciprocally, that is, there are benefits not only to the users (those who are bedridden and sick) but also to the professionals and volunteers who are involved in the singing and playing of musical instruments. The interfaces of this process may have resonance with the interaction and full enjoyment of the group, which in its dedication to the purpose of improving the lives of users, demonstrates a collective reflection of the benefits.

Regarding the group's eclectic configuration, Neuza explains that there is not a rigorous selection process to become a volunteer in this group because, according to her: "*From the moment that a person who likes to sing wants to be a part of the group, they just end up joining us.*" (Interview, Oct. 30, 2015) The participation of several professionals and volunteers corroborates the discussions presented by Isayama (2009) regarding multidisciplinarity as a guideline to action in the context of leisure, advocating for the involvement of professionals from several areas of knowledge. However, the singing group goes beyond this principle because, in addition to uniting different areas knowledge and offering a distinct form of health care, the aim of the group is to address the entirety of the human being, and thus it requires the involvement of the population, which is an important element of health promotion, as is explained above.

A relevant fact is that most of the people who work in the health centre were born or live in the neighbourhood in which the institution is located. In this way, they know many people from the neighbourhood, which makes it easier to recruit volunteers. An example is the case of Elias, who plays the tambourine. He is the father of one of the social workers. It should be noted that there are other realities of rapprochement with the group, such as Heitor, who plays the guitar and comes from another neighbourhood to provide this service to the community. Regardless of how far they live from the neighbourhood, when asked about their reasons for remaining in the group, these two volunteers answered: "*For me, it is almost a second family; we help those who cannot leave their homes.*" (Heitor—Interview, Oct. 20, 2015) and "*There are several reasons, but the main reason is that we bring music to families and people who are in need, and for us, it also a joy, a pleasure to be around, enjoying others, singing.*" (Elias—Interview, Oct. 20, 2015) This joy and willingness to participate were also evident on a day in which there were few people, and Neuza said: "*Today we are not so many people, but we're going anyway.*"

The observations and interviews that were carried out in this study confirm that in addition to the service that is provided by the leaders of this group, we find the people who participate in this group feel a constant healing process when they participate in the visits, as noted by Elias: "*We also go for us, because we also cure ourselves from many things by doing this work.*" (Field Diary, Sept. 8, 2015) According to Boff (2005), the word 'care' in Latin means 'cure', which is used in the context of human relationships of love and friendship, when the existence of the other has importance and thus becomes part of our lives. In this way, people are affectively involved, which suggests that their feelings are shared and that they can generate empathy and collective healing.

A (fortunately) common reaction of those who participate in this group is a feeling of gratitude for the work from both users and families, as perceived in every word, smile, hug and look as they sing and dance along with the music. In addition to the patients and their families, the volunteers report they also observe changes in their own general health by participating in this group: "*For me, it's healthy, everybody participates, others participate with us, so it is always a stimulus for health.*" (Elias— Interview, Oct. 20, 2015); "*I feel very good when I come and participate in the Group.*" (Adir—Interview, Oct. 20, 2015); "*Sometimes, I'm really sad and discouraged, but when I go to sing, I let it go, it's really good.*" (Neuza— Interview, Oct. 30, 2015)

It is clear that the involvement of the volunteers and health professionals as well as the community in this process makes the service more humanized, minimizing the suffering of users and empowering the individuals involved, improving job satisfaction. It should be noted that during these visits, no invasive measures were used, such as blood collection, blood pressure measurement or other daily practices of health professionals. This sort of visit is subjective medicine, working through a look, a touch or song; in effect, playfulness.

In this respect, similar results were found in the research of Côrte and Lodovici Neto (2009) when they assessed a group of elderly people with Parkinson's disease, who participated in music therapy (playing instruments, singing in a group, performing music-oriented exercises), as well as the professionals who were involved. The capacity for the elderly participants to live with their disease improved, they accepted their condition better, and they experienced greater optimism, hope and autonomy, as well as improvements in their social relationships with family and those around them. It is worth mentioning that this action was multidisciplinary, that is, it involved various professionals and was aimed at sharing experiences among the elderly.

With regard to the singing group, it was observed that the expected result of the performance reached and went beyond the users, as was evident in Neuza's statement:

> We have already had a lot of results. After we start to sing in the home of these people who are in bed, many of whom do not talk, began to talk; the ones who are discouraged are happier, and we also noticed that since we started to sing, very few elderly people have died, very few so far. People who were very depressed, very sick, became more stimulated. This is already a great thing for me, a victory. In addition, those of us who work in the group also feel better and happier. (Interview, Oct. 30, 2015)

This outcome can be attributed to the expressive interaction among users, family members, professionals and volunteers, considering that the group created a bond of friendship and sharing, whether through home visits, the songs that marked their lives or even the cookies and coffee that they received as a form of thanks. Neuza describes how this kind of playful, attentive and sensitive care in their day-to-day lives can be the source of pleasant and transformative moments:

It's so rewarding to see happy and joyful people, who don't seem like they're sick when we arrive at their houses. People even cry when they receive us, and we also cry because we feel joy to participate in that. That's like a great medicine. (Interview, Oct. 30, 2015)

It is evident that even with formal evaluation mechanisms, such as validated questionnaires or protocols, we would not obtain responses different than those which could be observed weekly, nor would the responses be more precise. This is confirmed by Neuza's response, when she was asked about how patients evaluated the group's work: "*We do not ask about it, because we see it. The person already talks to us that they like [it], that [it] is cool, until they invite us to perform again.*" (Interview, Oct. 30, 2015) In this way, the project is configured to be an effective means of a less traumatic treatment to improve physiological and biological aspects in a fun and playful way, to generate bonds, to involve family and to allow the free expression of feelings through music for all participants.

Final Considerations

Health care can be more leisurely when playfulness is incorporated, such as that afforded by singing and other therapy performed in the home and involving all. The difficulty experienced in travelling along with limitations caused by disease keep elderly individuals from attending outside social spaces and experiencing leisure activities other than those normally done in the home. The singing group generated a unique moment of joy for patients and all others who participated.

The singing group received recognition within the community and was awarded a prize for 'good practices' in 2015 for developing a program guided by a playful, coherent, professional and sensitive perspective, acknowledging the humanization process in the health arena. The award was granted by the Health Department of Santa Catarina State, which seeks to value innovative and effective ideas in health care.

We conclude that this type of experience, circumscribed by playful enjoyment, illustrates the importance of the reconfiguration of health practices, which can occur through awareness, appreciation, zeal, tenderness, warmth and delicacy, in physical or visual contact with the users of the service, as has been identified in the work of the singing group.

Therefore, we believe the current approach of human development (directly observing people, their opportunities and their abilities) runs contrary to focusing on economic growth that defined the well-being of a society solely based on its resources or generated income. The findings of this study are in line with an idea of human development that focuses on the human being.

Notes

1. The HDI in Brazil, according to the United Nations Development Program (2016), is 0.754, which is considered to be a high HDI in countries such as Mexico and Granada; however, it is lower than that of other countries in South America, such as Chile and Argentina.
2. Nahas (2005) writes from a biological perspective on health without focusing on cultural issues, which in turn reflects a restricted understanding of leisure, limiting it to a set of activities or opportunities in which it may occur. This interpretation is predominantly held by experts in the area (Marcellino 2002; Melo and Alves Junior 2003). Among leisure options, Nahas (2005) considers active leisure to be essential. By 'active leisure' he means "a lifestyle in which physical activity is valued and integrated into daily life, with an emphasis on leisure" (2005, p. 8). We should not overlook this possibility, although in this text, our understanding of leisure is extensive. We believe leisure options may be linked to those activities not necessarily or exclusively active. For example, contemplation and laziness can be considered leisure pastimes, as well. The individual who derives pleasure from this type of activity is after all the best judge of such experience, legitimizing a sociocultural phenomenon that is subjective and complex, corroborating the ideas defended by Pimentel (2012).
3. The National Council for Scientific and Technological Development (CNPq), an agency of the Ministry of Science, Technology, Innovations and Communications (MCTIC), has as a main goal the fostering of scientific and technological research and encouraging the training of Brazilian researchers. Created in 1951, it played a founding role in the formulation and implementation of policies for science, technology and

innovation. Its work contributes to the national development and recognition of Brazilian research institutions and Brazilian researchers by the international scientific community.

4. Principles: universality, equity and completeness. Guidelines: regionalization, decentralization, hierarchy and social participation.

5. This research was approved by the Committee of Ethics in Research with Human Beings (CEPSH) of the State University of Santa Catarina (UDESC) under the number of process 916.511/2012 (2012).

References

Albano, M. A. S., & Correa, I. (2011). Lectura de cuentos infantiles como estrategia de humanización en el cuidado del niño encamado en ambiente hospitalario. *Investigación y Educación en Enfermería, 29*(3), 370–380.

Azevedo, A. L. M., & Costa, A. M. (2010). A estreita porta de entrada do Sistema Único de Saúde (SUS): uma avaliação do acesso na estratégia de saúde da família. *Interface—Comunicação, Saúde, Educação, 14*(35), 797–810.

Bardin, L. (2010). *Análise de Conteúdo*. Edições 70, Lisboa.

Bergold, L. B., & Alvim, N. A. T. (2009). A música terapêutica como uma tecnologia aplicada ao cuidado e ao ensino de enfermagem. *Escola Anna Nery Revista de Enfermagem, 13*(3), 537–542.

Beuter, M., & Alvim, N. A. T. (2010). Expressões lúdicas no cuidado hospitalar sob a ótica enfermeiras. *Escola Anna Nery Revista de Enfermagem, 14*(3), 567–574.

Bezerra, I. M. P., & Sorpreso, I. C. E. (2016). Conceitos de saúde e movimentos de promoção da saúde em busca da reorientação de práticas. *Journal of Human Growth and Development, 26*(1), 11–16.

Boff, L. (2005). O cuidado essencial: princípio de um novo ethos. *Inclusão Social, 1*(1), 28–35.

Brasil. (1990). *ABC do SUS: doutrinas e princípios*. Brasília: Ministério da Saúde.

Brasil. (2000). *Portaria Nº 511, de 29 de dezembro de 2000*. Brasília: Ministério da Saúde.

Brasil. (2005). *O SUS de A a Z: Garantindo Saúde nos Municípios*. Brasília: Ministério da Saúde.

Brasil. (2006). *Política Nacional de Práticas Integrativas e Complementares no SUS*. Brasília: Ministério da Saúde.

Brasil. (2013). *Política Nacional de Humanização*. Brasília: Ministério da Saúde.

Canadian Index of Wellbeing. (2016). *How Are Canadians Really Doing?* (The 2016 CIW Report). Canadian Index of Wellbeing of University of Waterloo, Waterloo.

Casate, J. C., & Corrêa, A. K. (2005). Humanização do atendimento em saúde: conhecimento veiculado na literatura brasileira de enfermagem. *Revista Latinoamericana de Enfermagem, 13*(1), 105–111.

Conselho Nacional de Desenvolvimento Científico e Tecnológico (CNPq)— Ministério da Ciência, Tecnologia, Inovações e Comunicações (MCTIC). (2016). *Institucional.* Available at: www.cnpq.br/apresentacao_institucional. Accessed 22 Feb 2017.

Côrte, B., & Lodovici Neto, P. (2009). A musicoterapia na doença de Parkinson. *Ciência e Saúde Coletiva, 14*(6), 2295–2304.

Federici, C. (2015). Práticas corporais, alegria e saúde. In I. M. Gomes, A. B. Fraga, & Y. M. Carvalho (Eds.), *Práticas Corporais no Campo da Saúde: uma Política em Formação* (pp. 163–189). Porto Alegre: Rede UNIDA.

Ferland, F. (2006). O brincar e a criança. In F. Ferland (Ed.), *O Modelo Lúdico: O Brincar, a Criança com Deficiência Física e a Terapia Ocupacional* (3nd ed., pp. 1–18). São Paulo: Roca.

Galiassi, C. V., Ramos, D. F. H., Kinjo, J. Y., & Souto, B. G. A. (2014). Atenção domiciliar na atenção primária à saúde: uma síntese operacional. *Arquivos Brasileiros de Ciências da Saúde, 39*(3), 177–185.

Gil, A. C. (2002). *Como Elaborar Projetos de Pesquisa* (4nd ed.). São Paulo: Atlas.

Gomes, L., & Amaral, J. B. (2012). Os efeitos da utilização da música para os idosos: revisão sistemática. *Revista Enfermagem Contemporânea, 1*(1), 103–117.

Huizinga, J. (1971). *Homo Ludens: O Jogo como Elemento da Cultura.* São Paulo: Perspectiva.

Isayama, H. F. (2009). Atuação do profissional de educação física no âmbito do lazer: a perspectiva da animação cultural. *Motriz, 15*(2), 407–413.

Isayama, H. F., Siqueira, F. T. R., Araújo, N. S., Pinto, G. B., Souza, T. R., & Nunes, L. M. (2011). O lazer na humanização hospitalar: diálogos possíveis. *Licere, 14*(2), 1–26.

Jurdi, A. P. S., & Amiralian, M. L. T. M. (2013). Ética do cuidado: a brinquedoteca como espaço de atenção a crianças em situação de vulnerabilidade. *Interface—Comunicação, Saúde Educação, 17*(45), 275–285.

Kalichman, A. O., & Ayres, J. R. C. M. (2016). Integralidade e tecnologias de atenção à saúde: uma narrativa sobre contribuições conceituais à construção do princípio da integralidade no SUS. *Cadernos de Saúde Pública, 32*(8), 1–13.

Marcellino, N. C. (2002). *Estudos do Lazer: uma Introdução*. Campinas: Autores Associados.

Marinho, A. (2004). Repensando o lúdico na vida cotidiana: atividades na natureza. In G. M. Schwartz (Ed.), *Dinâmica Lúdica: Novos Olhares* (pp. 1–16). Barueri: Manole.

Marques, E. P., Garcia, T. M. B., Anders, J. C., Luz, J. H., Rocha, P. K., & Souza, S. (2016). Lúdico no cuidado à criança e ao adolescente com câncer: perspectivas da equipe de enfermagem. *Escola Anna Nery Revista de Enfermagem, 20*(3), 1–8.

Mello, C. O., Goulart, C. M. T., Ew, R. A., Moreira, A. M., & Sperb, T. M. (1999). Brincar no hospital: assunto para discutir e praticar. *Psicologia: Teoria e Pesquisa, 15*(1), 65–74.

Melo, V. A., & Alves Junior, E. D. (2003). *Introdução ao Lazer*. Barueri: Manole.

Mitre, R. M. A., & Gomes, R. (2004). A promoção do brincar no contexto da hospitalização infantil como ação de saúde. *Ciência e Saúde Coletiva, 9*(1), 147–154.

Moran, C. A. (2016). Use of Music During Physical Therapy Intervention in a Neonatal Intensive Care Unit: A Randomized Controlled Trial. *Journal of Human Growth and Development, 25*(2), 177–181.

Mota, A., Schraiber, L. B., & Ayres, J. R. C. M. (2017). The 'Paulista Way'; Building Collective Health in the State of Sao Paulo, Brazil. *Interface, 21*(60), 5–11.

Nahas, M. V. (2005). *Experiências de organizações sociais em programas de saúde e lazer por meio de atividades físicas e esportes*. Paper Presented at the Seminário Internacional Vida Ativa e Ação Comunitária, SESC, São Paulo.

Nahas, M. V. (2013). *Atividade Física, Saúde e Qualidade de Vida: Conceitos e Sugestões para um Estilo de Vida Ativo* (6nd ed.). Londrina: Midiograf.

Noordhoek, J., & Jokl, L. (2008). Efeito da música e de exercícios físicos num grupo de pessoas reumáticas: estudo piloto. *Acta fisiátrica, 15*(2), 127–129.

Oliveira, G. C., Lopes, V. R. S., Damasceno, M. J. C. F., & Silva, E. M. (2012). A contribuição da musicoterapia na saúde do idoso. *Cadernos UniFOA, 20*, 85–94.

Paim, J. S., & Teixeira, C. F. (2007). Configuração institucional e gestão do Sistema Único de Saúde: problemas e desafios. *Ciência & Saúde Coletiva, 12*, 1819–1829.

Pimentel, G. G. A. (2012). O passivo do lazer ativo. *Movimento, 18*(3), 299–316.

Prado, A. R. (2016). Travessia (perigosa…) pelo PET-Saúde: reflexões a partir de experiências na atenção primária. In F. Wachs, U. R. Almeida, & F. F. F. Brandão (Eds.), *Educação Física e Saúde Coletiva: Cenários, Experiências e Artefatos Culturais* (pp. 335–349). Porto Alegre: Rede UNIDA.

Ribeiro, J. P., Gomes, G. C., & Thofehrn, M. B. (2014). Health Facility Environment as Humanization Strategy Care in the Pediatric Unit: Systematic Review. *Revista da Escola de Enfermagem da USP, 48*(3), 530–539.

Santin, S. (2001). *Educação Física: da Alegria do Lúdico à Opressão do Rendimento* (3nd ed.). Porto Alegre: Edições EST/ESEF.

Santos, S. M. P. S. (1998). *O Lúdico na Formação do Educador* (2nd ed.). Petrópolis: Vozes.

Saura, S. C. (2013). O imaginário do lazer e do lúdico anunciado em práticas espontâneas do corpo brincante. *Revista Brasileira de Educação Física e Esporte, 28*(1), 163–175.

Silva, L. W. S., Francioni, F. F., Sena, E. L. S., Carraro, T. E., & Randunz, V. (2005). O cuidado na perspectiva de Leonardo Boff, uma personalidade a ser (re)descoberta na enfermagem. *Revista Brasileira de Enfermagem, 58*(4), 471–475.

Simon, H., & Kunz, E. (2014). O brincar como diálogo/pergunta e não como resposta à prática pedagógica. *Movimento, 20*(1), 375–394.

Souza, T. P. (2005). *'Música e idoso: uma proposta de intervenção do serviço social com arte', master's degree*. Rio de Janeiro: Pontifícia Universidade Católica.

Souza, B. L., & Mitre, M. A. (2009). O brincar na hospitalização de crianças com paralisia cerebral. *Psicologia: Teoria e Pesquisa, 25*(2), 195–201.

Thomas, J. R., & Nelson, J. K. (2012). *Métodos de Pesquisa em Atividade Física*. Porto Alegre: Artmed.

United Nations Development Programme. (2016). *Human Development Report 2016: Human Development for Everyone*. New York: United Nations Development Programme.

Universidade do Estado de Santa Catarina. (2012). *Comitê de Ética em Pesquisas com Seres Humanos*. Available at: www.udesc.br/comitedeeticaepesquisacomsereshumanos. Accessed 22 Feb 2017.

Velloso, M. P., Guimarães, M. B. L., Cruz, C. R. R., & Neves, T. C. C. (2016). Interdisciplinaridade e formação na área de saúde coletiva. *Trabalho, Educação e Saúde, 14*(1), 257–271.

4

Celebration of Ramadan: The Case of Turkey

Zuhal Yonca Odabas and Günnur Ertong Attar

Introduction

As a social institution, religion, especially monotheistic ones (Judaism, Roman Catholicism, the Protestant reform movement and Islam), regulate life in a transient world, and at the same time convey the rules of the infinite, eternal world. It can be accepted that religion sets out the rules of life in society and seeks to make it possible for people to believe in the future and sacrifice of themselves through various means. Thus, religion attempts to maintain social order. Among the most well-known examples of the social sciences in this regard are those of Weber (1930) regarding asceticism. According to Weber, the religious teaching of asceticism greatly influenced the birth of capitalism. The tenet of Calvinist belief

Z. Y. Odabas (✉)
Çankırı Karatekin Üniversitesi Edebiyat Fakültesi Sosyoloji Bölümü Fatih Mahallesi, Cankiri Karatekin University, Çankırı Merkez/Çankırı, Turkey

G. E. Attar
Mersin Üniversitesi Fen Edebiyat Fakültesi Sosyoloji Bölümü, Mersin University, Yenişehir/Mersin, Turkey

© The Author(s) 2018
A. Beniwal et al. (eds.), *Global Leisure and the Struggle for a Better World*, Leisure Studies in a Global Era, https://doi.org/10.1007/978-3-319-70975-8_4

concerning work and taking enjoyment only in God is an obstacle to excessive consumption of goods; rather, it encourages the accumulation of capital (money). Self-examination, self-discipline, hard work and asceticism in this example, where the enjoyment of work is taken as to be sacred, and it facilitated the accumulation of capital, a creed still held in a secular society.

In Islam, also, each person is regarded as an entity with limited free will, living in this world within the frame of religious rules. These rules are in a similar manner to asceticism, setting restraints to desires. One must consider these rules across all aspects of his or her life, including use of free time. Just as modern societies categorize the days of the week in terms of work and free days, the Islamic religion accepts Fridays and religious holidays (Eid al-Fitr (Ramadan) and Eid al-Adha) as 'vacations', but believers not free from their worship responsibilities on these days. They are regarded as free time, a way of getting away from this world's affairs. During these days, by fulfilling religious practices (such as religious duty, salaah), believers develop themselves in a spiritual sense. This phenomenon may be explained in deLisle's (2003: 85) argument that leisure is a theoretical construction and these free times are an essential condition for the fulfillment of religious practices and rituals. In addition to spiritual development, one's religion determines the content of leisure time in order to strengthen the community and family ties.

In this study, the month of Ramadan, and the fact that this time period has become more visible in Turkey over the last two decades, is considered within the concept of leisure time. Fasting in Ramadan is one of the five fundamental rituals of Islam. Ramadan month occurs in the ninth month of the lunar calendar, lasting 29 or 30 days. The lunar calendar does not correspond to the Gregorian calendar; therefore, every year Ramadan occurs nearly 11–12 days earlier than the year before. Ramadan is a holy month for Muslims from all around the world. It is accepted by Muslims that God (Allah) is more forgiving during this month than any other time of the year. There are many reasons for this belief; the Islamic holy book, the Quran, was revealed during this month, is one. During the month of Ramadan, people fast from sunrise to sunset, however Ramadan is much more than just abstaining from food and drink; it is a time to purify the soul, refocus attention on God, and practice self-discipline and sacrifice. It aims to teach one self-control and provides insight into the life of the poor. It is the month in which social bonds are strengthened and the hierarchy between people decreases. The idea that everyone is equal in the sight of God is one of the basic assumptions and beliefs of early Islam, and is certainly relevant in the month of Ramadan. Those who cannot fast during this time (children, sick people, pregnant women, travelers, etc.) either take up their fasting after Eid al-Fitr or give money to the poor. Ramadan is also the month of celebration. Because of its religious importance, Ramadan includes various social events, which tie Muslims each other in the name of Allah. It is a time of creating and re-creating the idea and the feeling of 'we' in both public and personal spheres.

In Turkey, the meaning of Ramadan has been transforming since the beginning of the millennium. During the time of AK Party's power, conservatism in both public and private spheres has become more visible. Religion—and all kinds of religious activities—are no longer 'the other'; a marked difference from the past, during times of secular political power. Then, religion was 'the other', not accepted as normal in the public sphere but appropriate for only the private sphere. This attitude applied also to Ramadan. Ramadan celebrations, part of both Turkish and Islamic traditions, are more permitted publically now than they were a decade and a half ago.

Theoretical and Conceptual Frame

When we look at the historical development of leisure time, it is evident that the way this free time is used reflects the rationale of modern industrial society. All activities taking place outside of work are within this context. These actions, leisure time activities, also provide most of the conditions necessary for a person to fully fulfill the roles required by his or her status. In this conceptualization, which reflects the logic of the functionalist point of view, it is possible to maintain the status quo through the re-creation of the person.

When choosing or practicing these activities, one perceives himself as independent from external factors. Individuals often regard these preferences as a reflection of their own free will. This fiction, which is based on volunteerism, does not consider external factors. In this case the individual prefers to live in a taken-for-granted world in order to stay away from an unfamiliar world. Thus, wellbeing and life satisfaction requirements are met, especially in psychological terms (Murphy 2003).

Stebbins (2007: 197) speaks of two elements common to leisure definitions: 'choice' and 'freely chosen activity'. According to him, within the discipline of sociology both defenders and critical appraisers exist with regard to the two dimensions of leisure: 'choosing' and 'freedom'. This is actually a clash between the views of Durkheim and of Marx: arguments based on balance and harmony on the one hand; while on the other side are debates trying to determine the ideological direction of these arguments.

These two camps, both taking a macro perspective and often regarded as competitors of each other, have come to the realize the limits of their approaches as opposed to micro-sociology, which focuses on the process of evaluating, perceiving, and interpreting events, situations and relationships in terms of the individual subject. More so than absolute and universal definitions and causality, micro-sociology prefers a narrative within context by taking into consideration the effects of multiple causalities. It is thus possible to make a comprehensive assessment of the content of an individual's leisure time and how these activities are perceived by the participants.

A proposition that might apply to all perspectives, whether macro or micro, comes from Turner (1974: 68), who argues that leisure is the product of industrialized, rationalized, bureaucratized, large-scale socio-economic systems with an arbitrary rather than natural delimitation of 'work' from 'free time' or 'time out.' Leisure is predominantly an urban phenomenon. When the concept of leisure begins to penetrate rural societies, it is because agricultural labor is tending toward an industrial, 'rationalized' mode of organization, and because rural life is becoming permeated by urban values of industrialization. This is relevant for the 'Third World' today, as well as for the rural hinterlands of long-established industrial societies.

Regarding the classification of leisure, which is a product of industrialized society, Stebbins (1992: 3) presents three types: 'serious', 'casual', and 'project-based' leisure. Serious leisure consists of activities the individual finds interesting, practiced in an amateur or a voluntary manner such that the person has the opportunity to use the knowledge and skills he or she possesses; it requires conscious involvement in one's leisure time activities. Casual leisure, in contrast, consists of immediately, intrinsically rewarding, relatively short-lived pleasurable activities requiring little or no special training to enjoy. As such, it is fundamentally hedonic: these activities are performed in order to receive pleasure and satisfaction. Project-based leisure is a short-term and moderately complicated creative undertaking, performed once or occasionally (though infrequently), carried out in one's free time and requiring considerable planning, effort, and sometimes skill or knowledge.

Rituals and festivals are examples of leisure activities. Touzani and Hirschman (2011) state that societies are ritualistic by nature, and it is possible to encounter such rituality in many areas of social life. For example, in birthdays, marriage ceremonies and graduation ceremonies, people perform predefined roles. For Maisonneuve (1995), rituals have three basic functions (cited in Touzani and Hirschman 2011). Firstly, they are about mediating with the divine through rituals. This is a matter of establishing a connection with the sacred through certain symbols. Secondly, rituals allow social values and social ties to be reproduced by establishing and strengthening social connections among community members. Finally, these rituals create a sense that the community and its members are safe from uncertainty and threatening situations. Through social solidarity and worship, people are provided with a feeling of trust.

Rituals in modern industrial societies also are considered leisure time activities. Turner (1974) claims that leisure time allows people to be freed from all personal, corporate, technological and bureaucratic organizational responsibilities, free to enter the symbolic worlds of entertainment, games and sports activities. Freedom from social structural limitations can potentially increase creativity at both an individual and community level. This creativity opens to way for critics to subvert or invert the status quo. In other words, it is possible to escape from the 'iron cage' (Weber 1930) or make visible the 'I' (Mead 1934) through leisure in the form of such rituals.

This chapter is placed at the intersection of several subfields of sociology such as sociology of religion, leisure and celebration. 'Symbolic interactionism' is the basic theoretical perspective, as it is well suited to helping us understand the fluid relationships between religions and social structures and between religions and cultural change, as well as the personal transformations experienced by individuals moving between religious systems of meaning. In addition to this theoretical perspective, the arguments and concepts of Victor Turner regarding 'festivals', 'liminality' and the 'liminoid' are used to understand the process of construction of identity at the personal level. In addition to these concepts, in this chapter Ramadan is accepted as 'a story telling narrative' since it helps connect to their past, specifically to their own childhood. But it is also noted that recent Ramadan celebrations in Turkey have an ideological aspect, as well. Through these Ramadan celebrations, and 'turning back to old times', the feelings of 'we' and of disconnection from one's 'roots' are created and recreated, mostly in the minds of individuals. These individual minds become a 'collective mind' again with the aid of leisure activities in the form of Ramadan celebrations.

Symbolic interactionism is one of the theoretical perspectives used in this study. The main focus of symbolic interactionism is the perceptions, understandings, and emotions of self-possessed individuals toward both themselves and the people and things around them. This perspective, which concentrates mainly on interpersonal interaction, is also concerned with the interactions between the societal structure and the individual, and in the processes of production, creation and re-creation of actions and meanings. Rather than a pre-determined social environment, there is a social environment that exists in the process of interpretation. Blumer (1969), one of the most important representatives of the approach, attempts to remove the distinction between structure and individual by examining the ways habits and structures are formed, beginning with human experience and meanings. Blumer argues that the actions of human beings toward other people and things around them are based on the meanings they ascribe to these things, which arise out of social interactions with these people, objects, or situations. These meanings have a dynamic quality and are produced, reproduced, and transformed through these relationships. The process of formation of social and leisure identities can be considered from this point of view.

These embodied meanings have a functional nature in the interaction process. In relation to these symbols, it is necessary to mention Turner's (1974) methodological and conceptual discussions about 'comparative symbology', another important concept in the social sciences. Along with his concepts of liminality and the liminoid, comparative symbology is another conceptual framework preferred in this chapter, focusing on the process of celebration in the Ramadan festivals of present-day Turkey. Turner (1974: 52–53) defines symbology as an attempt to interpret symbols, and emphasizes the need to analyze the meanings of symbols at both the individual and structural level. Accordingly, this chapter discusses the meaning of Ramadan practices in Turkey, both structurally and at the individual level, and the social processes that are effective in constructing these meanings.

Turner (1974: 53–55) describes comparative symbology as focusing on the relationship people create between symbols and concepts, feelings, values, and ideas. Thus, interpretations in the individual sense may be evaluated; beyond the boundaries of semiotics, which focuses only on the relationship between symbols and signs, comparative sociology instead insists that individual meanings must also be included in these interpretations. In comparative symbology, data can be collected from written works, verbal and non-verbal symbols, rituals, and dramas and stories. Symbols are social and cultural dynamic systems, constantly losing and gaining meaning. These meanings are constantly changing and being produced in relation to each other. In order to understand these meanings and the conditions of their change and renewal, it is necessary to examine this meaning-making process. In other words, comparative symbology can be expressed as an analysis of process. This is a highly effective method of looking at the meaning of symbols in complex societies, such as large-scale industrial societies.

Turner (1974: 56) uses the concept of 'rite of passage' conceptualized by Van Gennep while constructing the concept of comparative symbology. Thus he states that rituals are practiced in three stages: separation, transition, and incorporation. Separation from pre-ritual condition is followed by the transition process in which all identities melt away. This liminal and ambiguous step is concluded by getting a new and higher status than before. Liminality is a phase of uncertainties and possibilities;

during this phase a new type of social state occurs, known as 'communitas'. These processes are part of rituals and an example of social drama. Turner advocates comparative symbology as the research method to best understand the meaning of these dramas, on both an individual and community level. Symbols, as socially and culturally dynamic systems, shedding and gathering meaning over time and altering in form, on the one hand evoke the desires of the people; on the other hand, they also foster social cohesion and integration. In other words, the meanings of the symbols have both emotional or desirous and ideological or normative poles. In the most general sense, symbols are the basic unit of ritual. The most important of the stages in the ritual process is liminality: a state 'between and betwixt'. Festivals, one area where rituals are performed, are by nature liminal. Liminality occurs mostly in tribal communities where work and entertainment are regarded as a single phenomenon linked to a divine source. Advanced industrialized, rationalized, and secular societies, in which work and leisure are fostered as separate activities, have a liminoid quality. However, this does not mean that liminal situations cannot happen in modern societies. The liminoid involves temporarily suspending or reversing daily routines. In these types of leisure activities, such as festivals, customary rules and conventions of daily life are thrown away, suspended and temporarily turned over. This interim period expires with the return to daily life. As opposed to the liminal phase, there is no change of social status following a liminoid state

Participatory observation, an insider point-of-view, is the basis of the discussion in this chapter. The data obtained with these tools are interpreted in terms of Blumer's arguments about the meaning of action and Turner's liminality and liminoid concepts. How the meaning of Ramadan is constructed in people's minds and how people internalize these meanings are the basic questions addressed here.

Ramadan in the Ottoman Empire

There are a limited number of studies on the celebration of Ramadan in the Ottoman Empire, which has an organic connection with the Republic of Turkey, and these studies mostly focus on urban areas (Georgeon ve

Dumont 2008: 41–43). Ramadan celebrations in the Ottoman Empire during the 18th century had the characteristics of a festival in Western terms. During the day primarily religious rituals were performed, particularly fasting, salah and reading of the Quran, and after iftar (the evening break of fasting), Ramadan celebration events, which are collectively more secular, were held.

Iftar dinners can be seen as an example of the collective actions performed by believers during the month of Ramadan. These dinners often involved invitations into someone's home, where relatives and acquaintances gathered to prepare and enjoy the iftar. As with the state of communitas (Turner 1974), social class differences were not observed with these invitations. After iftar, mostly men went outside to be part of festivals in public spaces. In these venues, specially prepared for Ramadan festivities, religious facilities, as well as music concerts, exhibitions of traditional games and shopping facilities could be found. Shopping was mostly in the context of basic needs and attention was been paid to avoid excessive consumption. Almost all of the activities in the public arena were carried out in Istanbul due to its political, religious and cultural significance.

Georgeon and Dumont (2008: 43–45) discuss how seasonal differences changed the spatial distribution of activities in the public arena during Ramadan. Outdoor entertainments were preferred on summer evenings and closed spaces were preferred in winter. Despite seasonal differences, several formal changes always took place with the arrival of Ramadan. For instance, the appearance of the city changed strikingly as hanging, illuminated messages (mahya) and other lights (mostly candles and oil lamps) began burning as iftar commenced. These lights, particularly those hanging between the minarets of mosques, were seen as one of the most important symbols of Ramadan and are still relevant today. In addition, during Ramadan economic life was linked to the night. The shops were kept open until the time of the sahur, allowing the basic needs of the people to be met. These activities are intensely observed in areas close to the city centers, and a sense of festival was created in these areas. Traditional arts as entertainment activities, traditional theatre, shadow theatre, and public storytellers (meddah), were presented for the enjoyment of audiences.

This vitality experienced between iftar and sahur is reflected in another situation specific to Ramadan—still practiced in many Arab societies today—the reversal of day and night with respect to everyday activities, with the night spent working and the daytime resting. This tendency was also practiced in the Ottoman Empire began to be abandoned with the Tanzimat period (eighteenth and nineteenth century) and the Western style of division of the day in terms of work and leisure began to be accepted.

Another change to daily living unique to Ramadan was the concentration of religious practices—still relevant today in most parts of Turkey. Religious leaders' engagement with large segments of the population was greater than in the previous months. This tendency, visible until the declaration of the Republic, gradually withdrew from the public sphere to the private sphere through the revolution and legislation since 1923, when the Republic of Turkey was founded.

Turner (1974) states that liminality is heavily observed in tribal communities where there is no distinction between religion and leisure. The Ottoman Empire was a largely Muslim society, so the political structure mostly preferred to place religious fellowship and ummah at the forefront. This tendency was also present in everyday life, and the people regarded themselves as members of the ummah. Fasting can be regarded as a liminal stage in traditional Ottoman society.

There are two liminal phases in regard to Ramadan. The first is a transition period from sahur to iftar and the second is another transition phase from the beginning to the end of Ramadan month. In both transition periods, that is to say in the liminal period, the creation of a communitas through ummah perception is a matter of interest. In these processes there are no social classes, racial differences, gender differences; a communitas constructed on the equality of everyone in the face of worship—that is, the creative God Allah—is then scattered with the ending of fasting and Ramadan month. This symbolic identity created around the brotherhood of religion (ummah) is one of the basic features of Islamic religion, but it is experienced more intensely during the month of Ramadan in accordance with the holiday's sanctity to believers.

Ramadan in Today's Turkey

Celebrations of Ramadan, which are regarded as sacred and valuable throughout the Islamic world, are now marked with features born of both its own past and that of the secular world—including Turkey. As such, the emphasis of industrialized societies on efficiency, control and order in society is of great importance. Ideologically, the connection between work and religion has begun to fray, with standardization attempts that aim to allow competition with sophisticated industrialized societies both economically and politically. As Turner (1974) points out, leisure, a city-based phenomenon of Western societies, imposed these urban values on non-Western societies, leading to this standardization on a global scale.

Religious practices and identities visible in the public arena in Turkey till 1923 were relegated to the private arena by the constitution of the Republic and the influence of secular policies. Traditional and religious activities that have influenced the reproduction of religious identities have also lost their visibility in the public sphere. This restriction, which applies also to the social activities carried out during the month of Ramadan in the Ottoman period, has been weakened some through the power of the AK Party (Justice and Development Party), which has been a prominent force in Turkish political life for the last two decades. Ramadan festivals—the main focus of this chapter—began to be celebrated again in Turkey at the start of the millennium and gradually spread over time. At first held only in Istanbul, they were soon celebrated especially by local governments affiliated with the ruling party.

It is possible to consider these festivals practiced recently in Turkey as one of the pioneering attempts to answer the challenge of the tendency of globalization toward standardization. This may be seen as an example of globalization (Morley and Robins 1995) and in fact this process, although it seems opposed to the standardization of globalization, also creates another standardization of the political, economic, social, and cultural spheres of societies. In the next section of this chapter, the role of the Ramadan festivals celebrated in Turkey since the 2000s is discussed in context of the construction of individual and community identities, and the processes of commercialization and commodification of Ramadan which take place along with it.

Liminality and Liminoid: Construction of Individual and Community Identities

The current Ramadan festivals in Turkey, which started in Istanbul then spread to different cities, are structured according to the iftar and sahur clocks, as they were in the Ottoman period. In other words, the festivities begin shortly before iftar—the end of fasting—and continue through the night until the sahur, which begins the time of fasting. These activities consist mainly of cultural events and traditional arts, in addition to these shared meals.

Turner (1974: 68) deals with leisure in two dimensions within the framework of freedom: the freedom to participate in the worlds of different leisure activities—and even in the process of producing new meanings within those world; and freedom to pass, even temporarily, beyond social structural boundaries. This second type of freedom provides an opportunity for the individual to realize his or her own 'me' (Mead 1934), which is constrained by social life, via liminoid behaviors that occur during these Ramadan festivals. This freedom arouses varied feelings in different social groups participating in the festivals. Especially for middle-aged and older, conservative-oriented groups these activities provide the opportunity to return to a remembered past, particularly to their own childhood and/or own youth, or to an ideological past they long for but have never experienced. The reflection of past Ramadan spaces in festival areas is very influential in awakening of this feeling.

The physical areas in which the celebration events are organized are mainly spaces with historical and religious meaning—in other words, symbolic meaning. Georgeon and Dumont (2008: 45) state that in the Ottoman Empire during 18th and 19th century, Ramadan in Istanbul was celebrated in the place named as "İki Direk Arası" or "Feshane". Again today, the Istanbul Metropolitan Municipality and the district municipalities affiliated with the ruling party prefer to hold the festivities in these spaces. With the help of nostalgia, Ramadan festivals provide people the opportunity to return to their previous identities and to practice liminoid tendencies by experiencing different psychological and cultural norms from those in place throughout the rest of the year. This experience is mostly sought by the social group that aspires to return to and live in the period of the Ottoman Empire—the largest empire in the world at that time.

People's desire to return to a simpler, safer, more peaceful environment of the past—whether directly experienced or imagined and wished for—and escaping from today's complex, chaotic and uncertain world may be realized via Ramadan festivals, giving meaning to the expression of leisure. Stebbins (2007: 200–201) states that sociological studies interested in the meaning of leisure for people often focus on the concept of the 'leisure experience'. According to him, this experience is commonly studied by examining its quality, duration, intensity, and memorability. Examining leisure satisfaction constitutes another way of assessing the meaning of leisure for the individual. The quality of this experience has an effect on psychological wellbeing; studies (Sterchele and Saint-Blancat 2013) show a mostly positive relationship between leisure and psychological well-being. The feelings of satisfaction, connectedness, and happiness emerging during leisure are the basic elements of psychological wellbeing. Involvement in Ramadan activities with the desire to relive the past accelerates the development of psychological wellbeing.

There is also a more specific 'liminal' time period within Ramadan. This period, called 'itikaf', covers the last ten days of the month of Ramadan. According to Islam there is a hierarchy of specific nights of the lunar calendar when Allah is more forgiving than other times of year; the most important of these is the Night of Decree, or Night of Power (Laylat al-Qadr). One reason for this importance is this was the night Allah first revealed the Holy Book (Qur'an) to the prophet Muhammed. Although the exact date of the revelation is uncertain, it is believed to be one of the last ten nights of Ramadan. Because of this night's importance for Islam, the period of itikaf covers these last ten days of Ramadan. During these days, at least one person from each neighborhood should stay at the mosque and exclusively pray. She or he should remove herself or himself from all worldly affairs. Women, however, are permitted to practice itikaf at their home instead of at the mosque, for instance if they must care for young children at home.

In the month of Ramadan, one of the religious activities practiced particularly at the neighborhood level is the reading of the Qur'an in its entirety by those willing to do so. Prayers are offered with a special ceremony, requested from Allah to accept the worship, after the completion of the reading of the Holy Book. Participants in these specifically neighborhood-level events are mostly housewives and retirees. These activities frequently take place in the mosque, however male and female believers are obliged to perform these prayers either in separate sections of the mosque or at separate times.

Another activity frequently practiced during the month of Ramadan is tomb visitation. These tombs belong to people considered important in the Islamic religion, and visiting them to offer prayers there is a very common activity in Turkey, in both urban and in rural areas. These visits increase during the month of Ramadan. It is possible to evaluate these visits within the framework of heterodox Islam, defined as a kind of Islam where Islamic religion and local cultural elements are combined. Niyazi Berkes (1964, 2017) refers to Islamic practice in Turkey as heterodox Islam. A great many women make visits to the tombs, and women's social capital is realized very effectively in such group activities. Women living in the same neighborhood often make such visits within their social networks. During the month of Ramadan, local administrations also support the visits, especially in terms of transportation support.

When Blumer (1969) looks at the origins of an individual's actions, he finds that the meanings attributed to something is of great importance to the actions taken. For middle-aged people and others who participate in Ramadan festivals as a way to connect to the past this desire may constitute the content of this meaning. However, as opposed to the elders, these activities are new to children and young people. It seems that Ramadan activities are effective in generating new meanings for children and youth. Through these festivals it may be possible to establish link these social groups with the past. This situation actually has an ideological meaning; in other words, Ramadan may serve as a means of creating collective consciousness. This is similar to Sterchele and Saint-Blancat's (2013) arguments about the effects of leisure on psychological wellbeing. According to them, leisure activities foster a gradual harmonization of gestures leading to the transformation of individual feelings into collective ones, helping participants to feel they are part of a moral community. The objects invested with the common attention and emotions become sacred to the participants as symbols of their unity. Similarly, individual feelings merge in the symbols of Muslim identity or having a common past through Ramadan events, so that all the features of societal difference are left to one side and a unity is formed through these common interests. This temporal conjunction of intellectual meaning loses its intensity after Ramadan. In addition to these activities taking place in the public arena, the common beliefs, values, and rules of social life in effect within interpersonal interactions create synergy among members of the community. Religious people argue that these beliefs, which aim to increase social solidarity, should be fostered more deliberately through various media tools and within the mosques. These beliefs, which include reconciliation and protection of relatives and the poor, are transmitted to members of the community during socialization and are reproduced across generations. This religious rhetoric is expressed frequently throughout the month of Ramadan by many sources (e.g. the media, religious people). This community that emerges and continues during Ramadan can be accepted as an example of Turner (1974)'s existential or spontaneous communitas, the transient personal experience of togetherness.

Turner (1974) refers to the period after the liminal period in tribal rituals as a period of gaining a new identity. With the acquisition of social status, the person has the potential to gain a better position than afforded by his identity in the preliminary period. Fasting, one of the essential rituals of Ramadan, may be understood as a liminal period. In contrast to Turner's concept, however, the participant does not gain a new status with the end of fasting. Rather, during the liminal period of fasting people experience this higher status; the social rule and practice of giving and showing respect to people who are fasting is one illustration. People who have conservative tendencies try to make their children learn and practice these values through the socialization process. Taking care not to eat in common spaces during Ramadan is an example of this respect.

Turner (1974) claims that during liminal periods there is always a social group that controls all the rules of the ceremonies. Contrary to Turner's claim, then, the control mechanism during the fast is the divine, the creator Allah, rather than any human being. In other words, no matter the social and religious status, no human has the right to control the ritual process of others. It is possible to see the disciplinary power of Foucault (1979) in this process, also referred to as a 'surrender to Allah'. There are rituals that must be fulfilled even at the end of the fast.

It is a common tradition that—as the symbol of sacredness—palm, olive, water, raw vegetables, or fruit are used to terminate the fast after praying to Allah to accept the believer's worship. The hadiths concerning the end of fasting are the basic sources of this ritual. The fusion of the structuring and restraining roles of Ramadan in the individual and the social spheres produces varied arguments surrounding the purpose of this fusion and control. This is discussed in the following section.

Ramadan Christmasization

Turner (1974) states that during liminoid periods people are free to move away from present status and roles of their daily lives. According to him being free from these roles gives people to practice different behaviors of which they do not practice in their "routine or normal" daily lives. The activities organized during the month of Ramadan in Turkey—first by the Istanbul Metropolitan Municipality and later by the other local governments—may be considered liminoid states of leisure. By allowing them to be free from their current status and roles, these Ramadan activities give people the opportunity to return to their own past, in contrast to Turner's (1974) liminoid conception During Ramadan various tools are utilized to create nostalgia, a feeling related to a desire for the life of the past, exemplifying the role of Ramadan as an ideological tool, a commodity. The mehter team, the traditional performing arts (public storytelling/meddah, traditional theatre, shadow theatre), the centers providing traditional handicrafts, and the whirling dervishes (semazen) are among the most common of these vehicles. The Ottoman Empire used the mehter team (military band) to motivate its soldiers on the battlefields. This team, understood as a symbol of the victories of the Ottomans against the world, is a common sight in Ramadan festivals. From this point of view the mehter team may be seen as a symbol of the past, and an expression of the sentiments and longing of Ottomanism and nationalism.

It is clear that local governments prefer traditional elements to be present at the celebration activities; for instance, the drummer—one of the important symbols of Ramadan—is still an influential figure today, used in many advertising elements, such as promotional posters for Ramadan festivities organized by public institutions, private organizations, and civil initiatives.

This use of the drummer can be seen as an example of the effort to create nostalgia. The duty of Ramadan drummers was to awaken the population by playing their drums and singing, so they could eat something at sahur in preparation for fasting. Although the drummers belong to past ages, when the population was low and their role was necessary, worthwhile, and holy, they remain with symbolic meaning and continue their activities today.

The process of creation of nostalgia also leads to the emergence of different service sectors. Companies specializing in the organization of Ramadan events realize the increase of consumption through creation of a 'hyper reality' (Baudrillard 1994). This hyper reality is linked to an environment of past times. Another process emerges during Ramadan is the "commodification of religion". Giving religious books and the Qur'an as gifts by newspapers and arranging religious programs by using holy joes who are mostly known by the public and give advices and information about the rules of Islam are can be accepted as example of this commodification process and Adorno (1975)'s "popular culture" concept. This can be regarded as a commercialization of religious information. Touzani and Hirschman (2008) state that contemporary Ramadan celebration takes the form of a consumption festival. During this month the commercial and media landscapes are transformed and directed toward urging individuals toward worldly and profane experiences. Resisting this cultural pressure becomes difficult, household spending rises dramatically, and hedonic desires are felt more strongly than ever. This is the Christmasization of Ramadan (Armbrust 2002).

The provision of financial resources through sponsorship, especially by the local administrations of the Ramadan festivals, reveals a professional business mentality: Ramadan is now an economic affair—this religion-focused phenomenon has entered the trade and political spheres. Economic and political interests are now at work behind the scenes, as indicated by Goffman (1959)'s 'front regions, 'back regions', and 'impression management' concepts. Ramadan is also now a political issue. Humans are pragmatists and produce written, visual, or performance based discourses to accomplish their goals; the spread of Ramadan festivals in local governments under the ruling party may be an example of an attempt to achieve political and economic power now or in the future.

In areas where festivals are held, the presence of particular visual elements representing local government (i.e. the name of the municipality) and sponsors may be seen as concrete examples of this trend toward commercialization and politicization. This trend also extends Ramadan across national boundaries, as international and foreign-based companies without religious or cultural ties to Ramadan organize festivals. In the backdrop of the so-called localization—that actually means globalization and localization rather than only localization—the desire to expand the scope of the market is of great importance. The fusion of Ramadan as a local element with features of the global community, particularly those of Western societies, is an indicator of the commodification of Ramadan.

Another tool involved in the commercialization of Ramadan may the use of nostalgia-creating activities, including traditional handicrafts. In the festival areas, the production of various handicrafts is demonstrated (ebru, glass etc.) and the crafted products sold. The producers of these traditional handicrafts—the majority of which are handmade—are predominately women. Women sell these products for mostly decoration purposes. It can be asserted that these products, which are mostly produced by handcraft courses in the framework of women's empowerment, are also aimed at strengthening traditional gender roles in the background.

Ramadan festivities strengthen the sense of community on the one hand; while at the same time functioning through the realization of individual interests. This paradoxical aspect of leisure activities has been examined in this study. A critical evaluation suggests that both dimensions have a functional quality in the continuity of the status quo. In other words, tensions caused by increasing individuality and urban life are reduced through Ramadan activities. In addition, in the community dimension, feelings of solidarity and belonging are reconstructed through the fraternity of common past and religion, so social connections between individuals are created at a perceptual level. This prevents any disruption that could lead to a deterioration of the status quo.

Conclusion

Ramadan is a holy month for the Muslim community. The sacred book that forms the basis of Islamic religion, the Qur'an, was delivered by Allah through the Prophet during this month. According to belief, the values of prayer and worship for Allah are higher in this month than at other times. The Ramadan festivals have been celebrated more clearly in the public arena for the last two decades in Turkey are organically related to this belief. These activities enable individuals to feel good, feel a sense of belonging, feel themselves to be safe and secure; on the other hand, they are based also on political and economic interests structurally.

Project-based leisure (Stebbins 2007) is a type of leisure time requiring planning in a short time and at a certain level. It is a short-term, moderately complicated, event (e.g. arts festivals, sports events, religious holidays, individual birthdays, or national holidays). Ramadan activities organized by municipalities and various organizations can be accepted as project based leisure, and as a project, there must be economic and political interests in this leisure. Thus the question of the instrumentalization of Ramadan, both politically and economically, is raised. This instrumentalization is hidden by the discourse created through sacredness.

With the created simulacra (Baudrillard 1994), people are entered into a magical world, and the pressure of modern life on an individual is removed temporarily. At the end of the liminoid process, the person returns to his or her usual life. It is necessary to admit that even if temporary, this liminoid experience has the function of maintaining the daily lives of the people.

References

Adorno, T. (1975). Culture Industry Reconsidered. *New German Critique, 6,* 12–19.

Armbrust, W. (2002). The Riddle of Ramadan: Media, Consumer Culture, and the 'Christmasization' of a Muslim Holiday. In D. Bowen & E. Early (Eds.), *Everyday Life in the Middle East* (pp. 335–348). Bloomington: Indiana University Press.

Baudrillard, J. (1994). *Simulacra and Simulation.* Michigan: University of Michigan Press.

Berkes, N. (1964; 2017). *Türkiye'de Çağdaşlaşma.* İstanbul: Yapı Kredi.

Blumer, H. (1969). *Symbolic Interactionism: Perspective and Method*. Englewood Cliffs: Prentice Hall.

Davide Sterchele, D., & Saint-Blancat, C. (2013). Keeping It Liminal. The Mondiali Antirazzisti (Anti-racist World Cup) as a Multifocal Interaction Ritual. *Leisure Studies, 34*(2), 1–15.

deLisle, L. J. (2003). Keys to the Kingdom or Devil's Playground? The Impact of Institutionalised Religion on the Perception and Use of Leisure. *Annals of Leisure Research, 6*, 83.

Foucault, M. (1979). *Discipline and Punish: The Birth of the Prison*. New York: Vintage Books.

Georgeon, F., & Dumont, P. (2008). *Osmanlı imparatorluğu'nda Yaşamak*. İstanbul: İletişim.

Goffman, E. (1959). *The Presentation of Self in Everyday Life*. New York: Doubleday.

Mead, G. H. (1934). *Mind, Self and Society*. Chiago: Chiago University Press.

Morley, D., & Robins, K. (1995). *Spaces of Identity: Global Media, Electronic Landscapes and Cultural Boundaries*. New York: Taylor & Francis.

Murphy, H. (2003). Exploring Leisure and Physhological Health and Wellbeing: Some Problematic Issues in the Case of Nothern Ireland. *Leisure Studies, 22*, 37–50.

Stebbins, R. A. (1992). *Amateurs, Professionals, and Serious Leisure*. Montréal: McGill-Queen's University Press.

Stebbins, R. A. (2007). The Sociology of Leisure and Recreation. In C. D. Bryant & D. L. Peck (Eds.), *21st Century Sociology: A Reference Handbook* (pp. 197–204). London: Sage.

Touzani, M., & Hirschman, E. C. (2008). Cultural Syncretism and Ramadan Observance: Consumer Research Visits Islam. *Advances in Consumer Research, 35*, 374–380.

Touzani, M., & Hirschman, E. (2011). Minority Religious Rituals in the Post Colonial World: Ramadan in France, European. *Advances in Consumer Research, 9*, 116–122.

Turner, V. (1974). Liminal to Liminoid, in Play, Flow, and Ritual: An Essay in Comparative Symbology, Rice Institute Pamphlet—Rice University. *Studies, 60*(3), 53–92.

Weber, M. (1930). *The Protestant Ethic and the Spirit of Capitalism*. London: Allen & Unwin.

5

Youth Well-Being and Leisure Time: An International Perspective

Anju Beniwal

Introduction

The word 'well-being' connotes a condition that comes about by process in which individuals collaborate to forge a life worth living. It is rightly said that while children are the future of the country, youth are its present. The energy, enthusiasm, dynamism, innovative ideas and creative thinking they possess make the youth population an important asset for any country's accelerated development. Leisure is related to health and well-being; if it fulfills the individual then it is constructive leisure. Young people in most societies have the largest amount of free time for leisure as compared to older members, but largely because they lack community programs and facilities for group activities, they indulge in pastimes which are not conducive to good health and well-being. Those forms of leisure that are not accepted are called 'abnormal leisure'. This chapter argues that desirable leisure should enhance health and well-being.

A. Beniwal (✉)
Department of Sociology, Government Meera Girls College, Udaipur, India

© The Author(s) 2018
A. Beniwal et al. (eds.), *Global Leisure and the Struggle for a Better World*, Leisure
Studies in a Global Era, https://doi.org/10.1007/978-3-319-70975-8_5

Leisure and Youth

Those who decide to use leisure as a means of mental development, who love good music, good books, good pictures, good plays, good company, good conversation—what are they? They are the happiest people in the world.—William Lyon Phelps

With regard to youth resources, India has a distinct edge over the developed nations, most of which will be facing the burden of a fast ageing population in the coming decades. India is experiencing a youth bulge. The latest United Nations Population Fund's (UNFPA) State of the World's Population report shows that with 356 million 10–24 year-olds, India has the world's largest youth population, despite having a smaller population than China (November 19, 2014). China is second with 269 million young people, followed by Indonesia (67 million), the US (65 million), Pakistan (59 million), Nigeria with 57 million, Brazil with 51 million and Bangladesh with 48 million. By 2020, India will be the youngest country in the world, with a median age of 29 years, which will be more than 40 percent of its total population. India's youth number 460 million; 333 million are literate. In many contexts, young people are required to use their non-school time to contribute to the livelihood and economic sustenance of family and community. Half of the world's population are under 25, and between 14 and 21 percent of the population in each of the world's major regions are within the age group of 15–24 years (The Indian Express July 30, 2015).

Around the world, young people are proving that leisure represents a prime opportunity not only for individual development but also for contribution and change. Rates of voluntary participation in community building and development have increased dramatically among youth in many regions. Human service was once seen to be the essential function of modern government, with various agencies and organizations having dedicated human service functions. Delivery of human services was based on linkages between agencies, providing a broader base of services than any one agency could provide (Niepoth 1983). This is known as the 'community development approach'. If we wish to develop community we have to focus on youth development.

Young people are known to be unfazed by the pace of change and the technologies that give adults anxiety attacks, as they learn to thrive on chaos, uncertainty and insecurity in ways their parents never have (Rushkoff 1996). For some adults this might be true, but for others there is a different situation. Richard Eckersley (1997) portrays the three perspectives of 'youth-post-modern', 'conventional', and 'transformational'. In the post-modern perspective, young people are well informed, educated and technologically sophisticated. The conventional portrait suggests most young people successfully negotiate the transitions of adolescence to become well-adjusted adults. They enjoy their life and are confident about their future. The transformational perspective used to reveal young people who were deeply cynical, alienated, pessimistic and disengaged. People having this type of perspective are confused and angry and many times uncertain about their future and role in society. These types of youth present a problem for a society and a nation. The first type of youth is problem free but still lacks knowledge, abilities or skills to function as a mature adult; the other are fully prepared but may not be using their knowledge and capabilities most effectively or pointing it in the proper direction.

Increasingly, the areas of leisure and recreation have come to be recognized as an important context for child and adolescent development. Young people benefit from the opportunities for socialization and peer interaction that leisure activities offer and the psychological and physical health benefits they foster. Participation in organized leisure and recreation by young people also are known to offer positive benefits to society, reducing as it does the amount of time available for engagement in anti-social behavior (Caldwell and Darling 1999). Internationally, it is recognized that youth from low-income backgrounds are often disadvantaged with respect to their participation in organized or structured leisure and free-time activities, whether due to financial constraints or a lack of provision of such activities and amenities in their local communities (Zeijl et al. 2001). Young people living in marginalized areas may have high levels of exposure to the sale and use of illicit drugs, criminal activity and anti-social behaviour. In general these social environments provide little in the way of leisure and recreational amenities for children and young people. Nowadays, due to commercialization, playgrounds and playing areas are often minimal, inadequate or non-existent, and the preferred and often only option for young people is to 'hang around' on the street. Involvement in anti-social behaviour by young people is generic, specifically to those living in marginalized communities.

According to the National Crime Records Bureau of India, reported incidents of crime against women increased 6.4 percent during 2012; a criminal act victimizing a woman is committed every three minutes. Sexual harassment is one of the most common crimes against women in India. Incidents of rape increased 3 percent from 2011 to 2012 (National Crime Records Bureau 2013). One may conclude that youth have no proper direction and lack moral values. Increased attention in the media and awareness both inside and outside India brings to attention the issue of rape in India. This greater attention has seemed to empower women to report the crime. After international news reported the gang rape of a 23-year-old student on a moving bus that occurred in Delhi in December 2012, the city experienced a significant increase in reported rapes. The indication is that youth has been exhibiting deviant behavior. A study of leisure participation encountered in mid-life was undertaken by Dodd (2004). In a review of literature on middle-aged men, he found that physical changes were more pronounced in mid-life than any time since childhood and adolescence, and he posited that appearance and physical condition set limits on the kinds of work and leisure activities men do. Young people are often associated with new patterns of culture and while sometimes exposure to them is beneficial for the growth of a nation, sometimes it is dangerous.

Arguably, adolescent leisure activities may conflict with societal norms and values, excessive alcohol drinking and drug use, thus confirming the modern image of young people as a danger to society, as immoral, irresponsible and displaying criminal tendencies (Hendry and Kloep 2003). This negative image of contemporary youth, often generated by the mass media, concentrates on the negative behaviour of young people whilst ignoring the factors that may underlie involvement in such behaviour, including limited or non-existent free time and leisure amenities within the social environment. It also has far-reaching outcomes in terms of influencing and informing social policies in relation to young people. Many of the lifestyle habits formed during youth are carried into adulthood and therefore an understanding of young people's leisure pursuits is vital to counteract any detrimental effects due to leisure or lifestyle choices. By the time people reach the adolescent stage, it is next to impossible to change their lifestyle and the meaning of leisure for them.

Youth is now perceived as a time during which conflicts with parents, resistance to adult authority, mood disruptions and engagement in risky behaviour are more likely than at any other time of life, although such pathways are by no means inevitable. This span of life is critical to the development of the individual in all senses. As the teenager negotiates increased levels of independence and autonomy, his peer group gains importance as a source of influence and companionship. Out-of-school and leisure contexts offer a chance for experimentation with various social roles, the establishment of individual preferences and the development of close friendships. Alcohol consumption and tobacco smoking is very common nowadays in school and colleges. Socio-cultural and demographic studies of alcohol use and abuse patterns have been conducted in Asia, including China and Thailand. Recent research in Asia also includes studies that examine alcohol consumption among young people. Among these, a study in Japan reveals that the youth are beginning to drink at a younger age, and rates of drinking have been on the rise among 13- to 17-year-olds (Desapriya et al. 2002). Among South Korean young people, a fairly high rate of alcohol consumption has been demonstrated, with one study showing 43 percent of young people drinking regularly and that boys are more likely to drink than girls (Hans et al. 2001). In addition, among a sample of 1040 young people in grades 6, 8 and 10 in Beijing, China, approximately 70 percent have reported prior alcohol consumption. Again, males were significantly more likely to drink alcohol than females. Even so, 61 percent of females reported prior use of alcohol. Another study among senior high school students in China reported that 83.5 percent of boys and 54.9 percent of girls had consumed alcohol (Li et al. 1996). This study showed that among both girls and boys, many were drinking. The young people surveyed had started to drink very early. The OECD report noted alcohol consumption in India rose by 55 percent over a period of 20 years.

Of considerable concern is that the young are initiated to alcohol much earlier than in previous times (Times of India May 17, 2015). Alcohol consumption was also related to risk-taking, leisure activities and failure to access health care services. It is also recommended that alcohol harm-reduction policies be implemented and integrated into measures to reduce levels of other health problems such as HIV/AIDS and non-communicable diseases. Although alcohol is freely available in most parts of India, some states and Union Territories in the country have various forms of alcohol bans in force. Gujarat is one of the first states of India to have a no alcohol policy. The state bans the manufacture, storage, sale, and consumption of alcohol. Foreigners are allowed to obtain alcohol permits valid for a month. Alcohol consumption is prohibited on all the islands of Lakshadweep, except on Bangaram. Sale and consumption of alcohol has been prohibited in the state of Nagaland since 1989. Ideally, such policies should be evidence-based and evaluated.

Alcohol is harmful to health; it is the leading risk factor in developing countries with low mortality rates, and ranks third in developed countries (World Health Report 2002). If drinking and smoking are adopted by younger children this behavior appears to enhance risks of later alcohol and drug dependency, which is harmful to physical and mental health. It is the moral duty of the individual, the community and governments to protect every young person from the harmful effects of alcohol use.

It is important to understand the ways in which young people think about leisure, their beliefs about and attitudes toward leisure, what leisure means to them, and the forces that influence and shape their involvement in leisure activities (Hendry et al. 1993). Understanding how young people view leisure is important to the researcher. There is general consensus that youth choose their leisure activities freely and that they are 'non-obligatory' in nature. Leisure time excludes time spent at school and doing schoolwork after school, time spent on household chores and time spent in paid employment. However, when it comes to non-obligatory activities, categories such as sport, media-related activities (listening to music, watching a movie, playing, reading, etc.), performance activities (drama, dance and music) and community service activities have been used. These activities are sometimes further described in terms of whether they are shared or solitary, active or passive, or relaxed or constructive activities. A final important distinction relates to whether free-time activities are structured and organized or unstructured and informal, involving 'hanging out' and socializing (Caldwell and Darling 1999). Indeed, much adolescent leisure involves hanging around, being with friends and being alone, a time when self and group identities can be explored and defined.

It is imperative youth be given a wide range of opportunities for meaningful participation within the community. As noted, an important context for youth development in adolescence is leisure and recreation. Development occurs when youth have an opportunity to increase competence, discover one's identity, experience self-efficiency, develop positive beliefs about the future, experience self-determination, and to be recognized for one's accomplishments (Caldwell 2005). The development process increases from adolescence to young adulthood. Therefore, a government's youth policy should be constituted on the common human needs of basic health, education, employment and political participation. Indeed, these areas are the foundations of human resource development in general, reflecting a continuum of goals from protection to prevention to civic and economic participation. They are the domains of responsibility within the public systems principally charged with providing services and opportunities for youth. They represent the core indicators against which governments and advocates track progress. Lobo and Parker (1999) have shown that people, when materially and psychologically deprived, are devastated. The free time enforced can diminish freedom rather than increase it. When apathy and a collapse of the sense of time take over, the negative version of freedom is evident. It must be said that a minority of people are minimally affected and yet a small number enjoy their new found freedom from the stresses of the work environment.

In every culture, there are hours in the day when young people are not formally required to be in school or engaged in household or paid work, when they may choose various activities, often including public and private programs, organizations and individuals who support their participation. The hours and activities and often even these programs are viewed by adults as optional but not necessary or even particularly important for young people. The absence or disappearance of free hours, activities and programs might not necessarily be noticed by policy makers, but they would be very much felt by young people. Public recognition of the importance of these leisure hours is low, a fact reflected in the scarcity of relevant data. Equally important, these hours, activities and programs are what government planners—and frequently, the public—have few qualms about reducing. When crime rates go up, the quality and quantity of young people's discretionary hours are often diminished by strict curfews. When test scores drop or family incomes dip, opportunities to participate in voluntary activities are often restricted, as the hours required for work or study are increased.

'Leisure' denotes any activity undertaken freely for the enjoyment it yields (Glyptis 1989). For social development there should be balance between leisure and work. Many activities can be included in the leisure category, but sport and recreation are regarded as highly important among them. Many factors like age, income and unemployment affects individuals and their health and leisure in unpleasant ways. The effects of unemployment on the individual have been studied from different perspectives. Unemployment causes stigma, a deeply discrediting attribute (Goffman 1968) and causes the individuals who suffer it to see themselves as social inferiors (Kelvin and Jarrett 1985). Warr and Jackson (1984) reveal that between 20 and 30 percent of unemployed men reported deterioration since job loss. Employment contributes to emotional satisfaction and the sense of security in the future for youth. As money is an important factor for pursuing leisure activities, those youth who are employed, in comparison to unemployed youth, enjoy life more in so far as it the extra income lets them be involved in desired leisure activities. Mental health changes of those youth lacking employment were typically described in terms of increased anxiety, depression, insomnia, irritability, lack of confidence and general nervousness. In India, unemployment is a big problem for young people, one which directly and indirectly affects their health. Sometimes it results in impulsive and occasionally violent outbursts, abuse of alcohol, violence against women, cigarettes and insomnia. The UN World Employment and Social Outlook report says unemployment in India is projected to increase from 17.7 million last year to 17.8 million in 2017 and 18 million in 2018 (United Nations International Labour Organization 2017). Youth are more anxious and concerned about their future than the present. In a country like India, where problem of unemployment among the educated and uneducated is creates great anxiety, leisure is less important. Deprived of the opportunity to develop intellectually, many suffer from relative isolation. Haworth and Evans (1987) indicate that engagement in personal meaningful activity has a moderating effect on the negative psychological impact of employment. Leisure is regarded as a vital contributor to the quality of life. A lack of money significantly impacted entertainment habits, and in the absence of entertainment the quality of the social and leisure world of the individual diminished: Unemployment caused membership in various clubs and associations to fall off. Material deprivation not only caused a decrease in leisure time, but it affected individuals' overall quality of leisure, too (Lobo 2001). These are the important issues related to youth, and a search for solutions to these problems drives the research.

International Status

Leisure time plays an integral role in young people's individual development and the development of their communities. The amount of leisure time available to young people varies considerably according to age, gender and culture. Developmental progress made during leisure time is not solely that of the individual: how young people use free time has significant implications for the communities in which they live. The ways young people engage in leisure time is also linked to pressing threats to their well-being and to issues of globalization and interdependence. Given these interconnections, it is critical that leisure be discussed as a context for the development of young people and their participation in the development of community and society. Pulling together a vast array of studies on how young people across cultures spend their time, Larson and Verma (1999) compiled a relatively clear picture of leisure hours around the world. Larson argues that adolescence, including leisure during this period, should be defined and understood as a time of preparation for family life, employment, good citizenship, lifelong learning and personal fulfillment (Larson 2002). It also provides an opportunity for the development of communities and societies.

Prominent news magazines in the United States lead with headlines when they report on young people's use their leisure time (Youth Media Council 2002). Coverage of children's leisure in South America and other parts of the developing world, especially that which makes its way to global media outlets, takes the street child as its primary figure, painting none too positive a picture. The press is not alone in representing leisure as a time of risk rather than opportunity. Young people are sometimes confused over what is considered to be in normal and abnormal leisure. Much of the international research on leisure focuses on young people's problem behaviour as well. Boyden (1997) explains how two problem-focused images of children—as potential victims of 'pollution' by a dangerous adult world and as young delinquents who pose a danger to others—form the basis for public policy as well as public attitudes. Whether imported or homegrown, this mindset is not easy to change; in Brazil, it was not until a constitutional reform process and a major movement spotlighting street children swept the country that a decades-old child policy that criminalized youth in 'irregular circumstances' was overturned and the focus shifted almost entirely to youth problems such as delinquency and abandonment (CYD Journal 2001). Problem-focused policies go hand-in-hand with problem-focused media coverage.

Some years ago, research on young people in the United States on television and newspaper reporting revealed an increase in coverage of juvenile crime just as actual crime rates dropped to their lowest levels in decades (Youth Media Council 2001). Perhaps in part because of such media coverage, focus groups of American adults refuse to change negative perceptions of youth, even when confronted with statistical evidence or compelling stories of young people's positive potential (Bales

2000). International documents including "Programming for adolescent health and development: report of the WHO/UNFPA/UNICEF Study Group on Programming for Adolescent Health" and Adolescence: A Time That Matters, published by UNICEF, and country documents such as the New Zealand Ministry of Youth Affairs Youth Development Strategy Aeteatoa, published in 2002, present a set of common features of environments that support young people's development. These include adequate nutrition, security of life, gainful employment, among other areas. Research and synthesis by McLaughlin (2000), Connell et al. (2000), the Forum for Youth Investment (2001) and most recently the National Research Council (Eccles and Gootman 2002) confirms that there are core principles relevant to learning that are developed during leisure time.

This set of central principles—in reality, conditions for effective learning and engagement—includes, among other things, the presence of caring relationships, challenge and relevance, choice and voice, high expectations, physical and emotional safety, and experiences of 'mattering' and contribution. Dube (1988) provided a list of human needs and quality of life requirements: survival, societal, cultural and psychic, welfare, adaptive and progressive at the individual level. In this manner, quality of life essentially requires some creative leisure activities (Chaudhury 1993). As we know, negative leisure experiences decrease chances for the formation of a good human being. It is important that the individual find an enjoyable, uplifting activity. In post-industrial societies, gender differences were less apparent. Overall, the time both boys and girls spent in labour activities were noticeably lower than in previous times: typically less than one hour per day. Instead, they spent large amounts of time doing schoolwork and using media. There were differences between East Asian youth, who typically spent more time with or near family members and doing homework, and North American adolescents, who had more free time to spend with peers in leisure activities. European youth fell in between the two patterns and had relatively large amounts of free time, but with fairly heavy homework assignments. The differences reflect economic influences, but they also reflect parental attitudes and cultural values about such factors as work, education, the roles of females and play. Whereas media use is not even mentioned in the studies of Larson and Verma (1999) on developing country time-use, it is a dominant force in developed societies.

Young people in East Asia, Europe and North America appear to spend an average of about two hours daily in front of the television, with boys watching more than girls (Lobo 2001). In terms of active, unstructured leisure, the time younger children spend in play appears to be supplanted during adolescence by labour in developing and transitional populations, and by conversation among American and European young people, while children and youth in East Asia spend relatively little time in unstructured active leisure. According to the Australian Council for the Arts (2015), creative arts are important for many Australians. At least a third of Australians created art regularly in 2013. Activities included creative writing, playing music, singing, visual arts or crafts, and participating in theatre or dance. Australians believe that arts make for a meaningful life. As in Australia, art and crafts are more popular with young women than young men. They also state that much of their leisure time is spent less vigorously "relaxing and doing nothing", listening to music, and going to the pub. Favorite activities for young women are listening to music, watching TV/video, visiting friends, reading, walking, dining out and formal sport. In the book *World Leisure Participation: Free Time in the Global Village*, Cushman et al. (1996) noted similar participation patterns in Canada, France, Germany, Hong Kong, Israel, Poland, Spain and the United States, although survey methodologies differed in the various countries. This issue is well discussed at the international level, as youth are the part and heart of any nation and leisure time aids the qualitative contribution of youth in the growth of nation.

National Status

The combination of immense diversity (within and across cultures, nations, regions, socio-economic situations and genders) and a shortage of data and credible studies (particularly those relevant to developing country contexts) make any generalization on leisure among youth difficult and tentative. In India in many cases, leisure time is seen first and foremost as an opportunity for problem behaviour—as the time when young people get in trouble, roam the streets and watch too much television. Yet, leisure time is also an opportunity for play and recreation—for self-expression and relaxation, and for young people to exercise their emerging self-control. Finally, leisure time is the context in which young people flex their muscles as contributors and change-makers, as participants in the development of their communities and societies. Too often, though, risk rather than opportunity is the focus of programs and policies that affect young people's leisure, and leisure is not imagined as a critical time, which it genuinely is; how leisure is perceived makes all the difference. A shift from a negative view of leisure to a positive vision that emphasizes the value of leisure in its own right is a critical first step towards protecting young people's right to discretionary time and to quality leisure activities. This message is important for the developing and least developed countries, where economic pressures often propel young people into the labour force at an early age; it is equally important for highly industrialized countries concerned about improving academic performance.

Leisure time plays an integral role in young people's individual development and the development of their communities. The amount of leisure time available to young people varies considerably according to age, gender and culture. In all countries, though, this time provides space in which young people make important developmental headway. Youth show signs of strain and depression in countries in which leisure time dips below a certain threshold. The developmental progress made during leisure time is not solely individual: how young people use these hours has significant implications for the communities in which they live. The availability of a range of constructive, voluntary activities and opportunities in which to engage is critical to young people's development and their contributions to the community. Activities should vary to address the broad range of young people's interests and needs; they should adhere to what is known about supporting development; and they should strive to offer outlets and support that are often more difficult to provide in larger institutions. The choice of institution is as critical as the choice of activity. Leisure activities and opportunities should be offered and made available by multiple institutions and organizations within the community. The decentralized infrastructure characteristic of most informal education, leisure-time and community-based programs is a useful counterpoint to large public institutions that determine not only what kinds of activities are done but which persons are involved.

Distinguishing Between Leisure and Abnormal Leisure

Many leisure activities are highly personal and solitary; joint participation in leisure is in a more organized manner. The role of leisure is equally important for the individual as well as society. Leisure is a relatively self determined activity; it provides opportunities for recreation, personal growth and service to others. Leisure helps in renewing the self and improves one's performance in everyday activities. In contemporary society people need more exciting activities to ease the pressures of employment and of any work, and of study and family pressures, among others. To support a normal society, behavior should be according to social norms. However, leisure behavior may sometimes transgress acceptable behavior. When leisure behavior is not in conformity with accepted behavior, society veers from what is considered normal. Such behavior can be seen as a 'dark side of leisure' or 'eccentric'. The dark side of leisure can range from self-indulgence, such as personal use drugs, self-destruction by alcohol, as in binge drinking, and exploitation (Veal et al. 2012). Leisure can be defined as that which is intrinsically enjoyable, motivating, and which is chosen freely. In general all the activities which help relax the body, mind and soul are a kind of leisure. Thus, taking drugs might be seen as a kind of leisure for some people, but it seems to most people a dark side of leisure because for social growth leisure should be positive.

In 1999 Chris Rojek offered a different definition of abnormal leisure, explaining that leisure studies have in the main come to accept that "the subject of abnormal leisure is the responsibility of criminologists [and that] medical practitioners contributed to the legalization and medicalization of abnormal leisure" (p. 146). He argues that any branch of scholarly study worth its salt must take into account abnormal behavior, and he does just this by outlining the close ties between abnormal leisure practices and so called ordinary, normal leisure practice. Abnormal leisure is a significant concept of the contemporary world. Rojek (2000) defines three types of abnormal leisure: invasive, mephitic and wild.

Invasive leisure focuses on abnormal behavior associated with self-loathing and self-pity. In this type of behavior, individuals experience anomie and personal alienation from the rest of the society. It refers to forms of behavior situated in leisure time that involve self-harm. This type of leisure found mainly in youth. That is, the responsible recreational use of drugs is popular and widely accepted among youth groups. In contemporary society, some leisure activities like gambling and drugs challenge the order of the society at that time (Veal et al. 2012). Gambling a means of entertainment can also lead to harmful behavior in some people. It has been proved to be addictive. Gamblers tend to show mood swings and secretive behavior (Manali 2008). Finally, invasive leisure may be the cause of prostitution, bankruptcy, excessive debt burden, high suicide rate, family violence and broken families. An excess of any recreational activity is always harmful to an individual and society. The stress from gambling may lead to health issues like ulcers, stomach problems, muscle pains, headaches and problems with sleep. According to the New York University, people with alcohol use disorders have a chance of developing an addiction to gambling 23 times higher than those who do not have alcohol problems. Over time, it becomes a habit and eventually an obsession that can't be overcome. Always the addiction has negative effects on one's physical and mental health.

Mephitic leisure experiences involve the individual's self-absorbed desire for gratification at the expenses of others. In this type of leisure, the individual harms others through activities like sexual harassment, prostitution, verbal and emotional aggression, and so on. Wild leisure tends to be opportunistic in character. It includes deviant crowd behavior such as rioting, looting, illegal trading, hacking and violence. However, Rojek advised that we should be cautious of these kinds of leisure activities. In his view abnormal leisure may belong to the forbidden and the deadly. This type of leisure defined as 'deviant' or 'purple' leisure, including property damage as a sensation-seeking activity or an adventure (Rojek 1999a, b). So planning and implementation of leisure activities are needed in any meaningful engagement of youth to ensure leisure is not abnormal.

Policy Recommendations

Great biological changes are associated with puberty; adolescence is a time of major social changes associated with transitions between grade levels and changing roles and expectations, and major psychological changes linked to increasing social and cognitive maturity. With so many rapid changes comes a heightened potential for both positive and negative outcomes. Although most individuals pass through this developmental period without excessive problems, a substantial number experience difficulty (Institute of Medicine and National Research Council 2002). Understanding adolescent development and the factors contributing to the healthy development of all young people is critical to the design and implementation of community programs for youth. A priority of the committee's work was identifying what is necessary for adolescents to be happy, healthy and productive at the present time, as well as successful, contributing adults in the future.

The involvement of voluntary organizations in youth programs that promote the well-being of young people—in leisure and in communiyt development more broadly—is essential. Direct consultation with young people should become a priority when designing or planning any services or leisure facilities for young people. Consultation processes should be accessible, flexible and sensitive to their needs. Broad policy recommendations in relation to the free-time and leisure needs of young people living in disadvantaged areas should be followed.

Conclusion

Leisure has the potential to enrich one's life more and to make it more meaningful. Creative leisure helps promote well-being. Leisure represents broad aspects of human functioning including emotional, spiritual, social, cultural and physical elements of well-being. A nation's youth is an important for its accelerated development. The area of leisure and recreation has come to be recognized as an important context for youth's development or well-being. Current perspectives on youth development have evolved significantly since early conceptualizations of adolescence as a period of inherent turmoil and stress for almost all youth. Leisure is a state of mind, a mental or possibly even spiritual place where one escapes from the stresses of life. The dynamic role of leisure is to protect youth's energy and give the young proper direction along with good health.

It is important to understand how youth feel about leisure and make sure they are involved in meaningful leisure activities. This is the job of some policy makers and service providers. It is safe to assume that the success and effectiveness of any new youth policy initiative requires a meaningful communication between policy makers, service providers and young people. Bearing this in mind, policy makers should strive to avoid stereotypical assumptions about the requirements and needs of young people living in disadvantaged areas. Policy makers should have an in-depth understanding of the local circumstances and situations young people encounter and experience in their day-to-day lives. This issue is well discussed at the international level, as youth are the part and heart of any nation. It could be concluded that leisure time plays an integral role in young people's well-being and their qualitative contribution to the growth of a nation.

References

Australian Council for the Arts. (2015). *Arts Nation: An Overview of Australian Arts* (2015 Ed.). Sydney: Creative Commons.

Bales, S. (2000). Reframing Youth Issues for Public Consideration and Support. In S. Bales Ed., *Reframing Youth Issues* (Working Papers). Washington, DC: Frameworks Institute and Center for Communications and Community/ UCLA.

Boyden, J. (1997). *Childhood and the Policy Makers: A Comparative Perspective on the Globalization of Childhood.* London: Falmer Press.

Brazil's Current Child and Youth Policies, in Contrast, Were Heralded as "the Best Child Protection Legislation in the World" by Former UNICEF Director James Grant. For More Information, See Klees, S. J., & Rizzini, I. (2001, Fall). Children and Their Advocates: Making a New Constitution", in the Forum for Youth Investment's "Standing for Their Rights. *CYD Journal, 2*(4), 54–63.

Caldwell, L. L. (2005). Recreation and Youth Development. In P. A. Witt & L. L. Caldwell (Eds.), *Recreation and Youth Development* (pp. 169–189). State College: Venture Publishing Inc.

Caldwell, L. L., & Darling, N. (1999). Leisure Context, Parental Control, and Resistance to Peer Pressure as Predictors of Adolescent Partying and Substance Use: An Ecological Perspective. *Journal of Leisure Research, 31*(1), 57–78.

Chaudhury, S. K. (1993). *Myopic Development and Cultural Lens.* New Delhi: Inter-India.

Connell, J. P., Gambone, M. A., & Smith, T. J. (2000). *Youth Development in Community Settings: Challenges to Our Field and Our Approach.* Toms River: Community Action for Youth Project.

Cushman, G., Veal, A., & Zuzannek, K. (1996). *World Leisure Participation: Free Time in the Global Village.* London: CABI.

Desapriya, E. B., Iwase, N., & Shimizu, S. (2002). Adolescents Alcohol Related Traffic Accidents and Mortality in 1999–2000—Problem and Solutions [Japanese, Abstract]. *Nihon Arukoru Yakubutsu Igakkai Zasshi, 37*(3), 168–178.

Dodd, J. (2004). The Capacity of Leisure Participation to Alleviate Problems Encountered at Mid-Life. In F. H. Fu, D. Markus, & T. K. Tong (Eds.), *Negative Events in the Lifecycle: Leisure and Recreation as a Counteraction* (pp. 58–81). Hong Kong: Professional Publications Co.

Dube, S. C. (1988). *Modernization and Development: The Search for Alternative Paradigms*. New Delhi: Vistaar Publication.

Eccles, J., & Gootman, J. A. (Eds.). (2002). *Community Programs to Promote Youth Development*, Committee on Community-Level Programs for Youth, Board on Children, Youth, and Families, Division of Behavioral and Social Sciences and Education, National Research Council and Institute of Medicine. Washington, DC: National Academy Press.

Eckersley, R. (1997). Portraits of Youth: Understanding Young People's Relationship with the Future. *Futures, 29*(3), 243–249.

Glyptis, S. (1989). *Leisure and Unemployment*. Milton Keynes: Open University Press.

Goffman, E. (1968). *Stigma: Notes on the Management of Spoiled Identity*. Harmondsworth: Penguin.

Han, S., Choe, M. K., Lee, M. S., & Lee, S. H. (2001). Risk Taking Behavior Among High School Students in South Korea. *Journal of Adolescence, 24*(4), 571–574.

Haworth, J. T., & Evans, S. T. (1987). Meaningful Activity and Unemployment. In D. Fryer & P. Ullah (Eds.), *Unemployed People: Social and Psychological Perspectives* (pp. 241–267). Milton Keynes: Open University Press.

Hendry, L. B., & Kloep, M. (2003). Young People, Unprotected Time, and Overprotected Contexts: Resources, Challenges and Risks? In I. Colozzi & G. Giovannini (Eds.), *Young People in Europe: Risk, Autonomy and Responsibilities*. Milano: Franco Angeli s.r.l.

Hendry, L. B., Shucksmith, J., Love, J. G., & Glendinning, A. (1993). *Young People's Leisure and Lifestyles*. London: Routledge.

Institute of Medicine and National Research Council. (2002). *Community Programs to Promote Youth Development*. Washington, DC: The National Academies Press. https://doi.org/10.17226/10022.

Kelvin, P., & Jarrett, J. E. (1985). *Unemployment: Its Social Psychological Effects*. Cambridge: Cambridge University Press.

Larson, R. (2002). Globalization, Societal Change, and New Technologies: What They Mean for the Future of Adolescence. *Journal of Research on Adolescence, 12*(1), 1–30.

Larson, R., & Verma, S. (1999). How Children and Adolescents Spend Time Across the World: Work, Play and Developmental Opportunities. *Psychological Bulletin, 125*(6), 701–736.

Li, X., Fang, X., Stanton, B., Feigelman, S., & Dong, Q. (1996). The Rate and Pattern of Alcohol Consumption Among Chinese Adolescents. *Journal of Adolescent Health, 19*, 353–361.

Lobo, F. (2001). *Leisure, Family and Lifestyle: Unemployed Young People*. New Delhi: Rawat Publications.

Lobo, F., & Parker, S. (1999). *Late Career Unemployment: Impacts on Self, Family and Lifestyle*. Melbourne: Hepper Marriott.

Manali, O. (2008). *Negative Effects of Gambling*. Retrieved from http://www.buzzle.com/

McLaughlin, M. (2000). *Community Counts: How Youth Organizations Matter for Youth Development*. Washington, DC: Public Education Network [second printing].

National Crime Records Bureau. (2013).

Niepoth, W. F. (1983). *Leisure Leadership*. Englewood Cliffs: Prentice-Hall.

Rojek, C. (1999a). *Leisure Studies: Prospects for the Twenty First Century* (pp. 81–95). State College: Venture Publishing.

Rojek, C. (1999b). Deviant Leisure: The Dark Side of Free Time Activity. In E. L. Jackson & T. L. Burton (Eds.), *Leisure Studies for the XXI Century* (pp. 81–94). State College: Venture Publishing.

Rojek, C. (2000). *Leisure and Culture*. Basingstoke: Palgrave Macmillian.

Rushkoff, D. (1996). *Playing the Future: How Kids' Culture Can Teach Us to Thrive in an Age of Chaos*. London: Harper Collins.

The Indian Express. (2015, July 30). Retrieved November 7, 2016.

Times of India. (2015, May 17).

United Nations International Labour Organization. (2017).

United Nations Report. (2014, November 19).

Veal, A., Darcy, S., & Linch, R. (2012). *Australian Leisure*. Sydney: Pearson.

Warr, P. B., & Jackson, P. (1984). Men Without Jobs: Some Correlates of Age and Length of Employment. *Journal of Occupational Psychology, 57*, 77–85.

World Health Report. (2002).

Youth Media Council. (2001). *Speaking for Ourselves: A Youth Assessment of Local News Coverage…; and S. Alequin and Others, "In Between the Lines: How the New York Times Frames Youth"*. New York: New York City Youth Media Study.

Youth Media Council. (2002). *Speaking for Ourselves: A Youth Assessment of Local News Coverage*. San Francisco: We Interrupt This Message.

Zeijl, E., DuBois-Reymond, M., & Te Poel, Y. (2001). Young Adolescents' Leisure Patterns. *Society and Leisure, 2*, 379–402.

Section II

Virtual Leisure and Pop Culture

6

Japanese Idol Culture for 'Contents Tourism' and Regional Revitalization: A Case Study of Regional Idols

Yuki Tajima

Introduction

The popularity of idol culture in Japan is well represented by the Japanese media. In recent years, however, these idols have transformed themselves from superficial beings, accepted and adored by their fans alone, into symbolic social entities that are distinctly Japanese with a large following in countries around the globe. Indicating how widespread this cultural phenomenon is, break-up announcements made on January 13 and August 14, 2016, by SMAP—one of the most popular idol groups produced by Johnny & Associates[1]—were picked up by popular domestic sports journals as well as the public broadcasting corporation (NHK) and international media.[2] Although idols in the past tended to focus their activities mainly in Tokyo, more recent idols have become increasingly rooted in specific geographic areas. These modern idols differ from their predecessors in that they personify 'regional characteristics' and 'regional authenticity' in the modern context.

Y. Tajima (✉)
Doshisha University, Kyoto, Japan

© The Author(s) 2018
A. Beniwal et al. (eds.), *Global Leisure and the Struggle for a Better World*, Leisure Studies in a Global Era, https://doi.org/10.1007/978-3-319-70975-8_6

Illustrating this trend is the popularity of AKB48—a group of female idols that debuted in 2005, produced by Yasushi Akimoto.[3] AKB48 has owned its own exclusive theater in Akihabara, Tokyo, and it has several sister groups (referred to as AKB groups): SKE48 (in Sakae, Aichi, since 2008), NMB48 (in Namba, Osaka, since 2010), and HKT48 (in Hakata, Fukuoka, since 2011). In addition, they have their own theaters in their hometowns. Idols are featured on *Amachan* in 2013, which is part of NHK's wildly popular morning serial TV drama[4] (also known as 'asadora'). *Amachan* is a highly rated dramatic series. Analysis of media reports related to *Amachan* reveal that the filming location for this series, Kuji-shi, as well as Iwate Prefecture, has had economic benefits due to an increased number of tourists to the area.

This type of tourism—inspired as it is by media content such as dramatic series on TV—is known as 'contents tourism'. Research on contents tourism has been evolving in Japan since 2010. Idols are indeed contents, and tourism and regional revitalization based on idol culture are one focus area for important discussions in the field of contents tourism research.

Since the occurrence of the Great East Japan Earthquake (henceforth, the Earthquake) in 2011, the Japanese have been rethinking the significance of their local community and reexamining the importance of the bond among its members. The Earthquake brought to the forefront the issues that Japanese society had already been experiencing, including an aging population and depopulation in regions other than urban areas. Meanwhile, the increasing number of users of social media, such as video-sharing sites, blogs, Facebook and Twitter, changed the way people—especially the younger generation—use media to communicate, easing the excessive focus on Tokyo as the source of popular culture and information. In other words, when more channels for the idols to communicate with their fans were provided, it created an environment where one could enjoy the idol culture anywhere since access to information about idols occurs in places other than Tokyo.

Looking at today's Japanese idols in this context, we notice that, starting from around 2010, there have been many so-called regional idols including those featured on the asadora, *Amachan,* whose activities focus on a specific geographical area. Most of these regional idols are groups of young females in their teens or early 20s that focus their activities in the region where they were born and grew up. Their main activities include performing live at local venues,[5] participating in local festivals and other events, and collaborating with local government and corporations to support community efforts. It can be said that the new phenomenon we call 'regional idol boom' was born out of a combination of the success of AKB48, the Earthquake, the reexamination of our concept of community and the ideas symbolized in *Amachan*.

In recent years, local regions have taken advantage of this regional idol boom by promoting related goods and fan tourism, utilizing the phenomenon for the region's prosperity. At the same time, there have been calls for a state policy of 'local Abenomics' (the economic policies advocated by Shinzō Abe) or regional development, as we head towards hosting the Tokyo Olympics in 2020. Accordingly, it is crucial to avoid an overly Tokyo-centric thinking and development but rather to allow a variety of regions to show their rich individuality and obtain brand power to convey their appeal at the international level.[6]

Looking at previous academic research, not only are studies into overall idol culture insufficient in this context,[7] but the topic of regional idols remains a nascent field awaiting future, cross-disciplinary research. In addition, there is next to no research from the field of contents tourism that has studied the effects brought about by regional idols.

This chapter uses *Amachan* as a case study and examines the reception of the drama series mainly in its filming location—Kuji-shi, Iwate Prefecture, in the Tohoku region—as well as the activities of Ama Club, which is the regional idol group born in Kuji-shi coinciding with *Amachan*. At the same time, by understanding the characteristics of regional idols using specific case studies as examples, this article discusses the potential of Japanese idol culture for contributing to contents tourism and regional revitalization. Therefore, taking regional idols as a case study, this chapter investigates the usefulness of regional development based on idol culture by examining the results of field surveys of regional idol members and related persons conducted by the author. The article defines regional idols with reference to past research, and investigates the meaning of their activities for the regional idols themselves.

The chapter thus considers the function of regional idol activities in realizing community building driven by residents, as has often been advocated in previous discussions of regional development and revitalization (Nara Prefectural University Regional Development Research Group 2005; Sasaki 2008).

Idol Culture and 'Contents Tourism'

The Origin of the Idol Culture

It is said that idol culture in Japan was born in 1971, with an audition-style musical program for young singers called "A Star is Born!" (Nippon Television Network, 1971–1983), made possible by the introduction of colour television in ordinary households (Ogawa 1988; Inamasu 1989; Ota 2011). This program produced many idols that were not necessarily talented singers or dancers but, rather, young and relatable people. The 1970s were the dawn of the idol era, when typical popular magazines of post-war Japan such as *Heibon* (Heibonsha, founded in 1945) and *Myojo* (Shueisha, founded in 1952), boasting more than one-million readers consisting mainly of teenage boys and girls, published a wealth of information on idols (Sakamoto 2008; Tajima 2014a). According to Tajima (2014a), during the same period *Myojo* published many papers on the 'triumphant return home' of youngsters who left their homes to go to Tokyo with the dream of becoming an idol. In other words, we can identify representations of 'regional idols' that have bonds to a region from the 70s' *Myojo* just as we are seeing today.

Defining 'Regional Idols'

Existing research has indicated that variety is one characteristic of regional idols (Muraki 2013; Hashimoto 2014). Meanwhile, regional idol groups have come to be categorized and discussed according to how their members are classified (by gender, age and area of residence), their management, the area in which they are active, and so forth. Group categorization involves some difficulties, however, as members are frequently replaced and there may also be changes in management while the group is active—in such cases, the actual circumstances of the change are often not clear in the absence of direct inquiry. This research, therefore, fundamentally does not attempt to preemptively categorize regional idols; rather, it takes the position of showing what a regional idol is, based on the results of questionnaire surveys. Even in this case, however, there needs to be some conceptual organization and a defined research scope. Accordingly, this study draws on Muraki's comparatively inclusive definition: "engagement with these idols involves associations with a particular region" (Muraki 2013, p. 13). To be more specific, the term 'regional idols' is used to refer to 'idols' associated with a particular region through their group name, where group members are from, song lyrics, clothing, catchphrases, the location of their management and so forth.

In addition, this section will explain the reasons for uniformly using the term 'regional idols', ('*go-tōchi aidoru*', in Japanese) from amongst the many terms in use. The dictionary provides two original meanings for '*go-tōchi*': "(1) A word used to respectfully describe a place by visitors from another place;"(2) A word used to suggest elements which are special or unique to a given place or area."[8] Of these two definitions, *go-tōchi* may currently be widely used with the latter meaning, yet the original meaning of *go-tōchi* is the former. In other words, the essence of *go-tōchi* is an interrelated concept built on differentiation from and comparison with other regions, and if this is the case, there is an undeniable implication of, whilst indeed respecting each other, also competing with each other.[9] This is also closely related to current *go-tōchi aidoru* (i.e., 'regional idols'), which compete and ally with other idols in events such as the U.M.U. Award (held from 2010 to date),[10] the National Regional Idol Ranking Battle (*zenkoku go-tōchi aidoru rankingu batoru*, detailed previously), and the Tokyo Idol Festival (held from 2010 to date). In light of this characteristic, the present research chose the term '*go-tōchi*'.[11]

Next, due to the large numbers of active regional idols, it was necessary to narrow the scope of this research to a certain extent.

To examine those who could be estimated to have a degree of social influence, with information and news about them transmitted and shared via mass media, this paper selected regional idols with their own public website, who were confirmed to be continuously active at present, and who fulfilled one of the following criteria: (a) they had to be featured in a printed publication featuring regional idols—namely, "Local Idols: A Perfect Guide" (Ikaros Publications Ltd., 2013), "National Idol Map 2013–2014" (Enterbrain, 2013) or "Local Idol Mapple" (Shōbunsha Publications Inc., 2015); or (b) they had to appear as 'love regional [*koi-jimo*]' supporters in the NHK "Love Regional [*koi-suru jimoto*]" campaign. These publicity campaigns were developed in relation to the TV drama series *Amachan*.

What Is Amachan?

Amachan uses the same triumphant return narrative as idols in *Myojo* during the 1970s, which was broadcast on NHK for six months, from April to September in 2013, as the 88th asadora morning drama production. Out of the 26 weeks, the first half (weeks 1–12) takes place in Kitasanriku-shi, Iwate Prefecture (a fictional name given to Kuji-shi, Iwate Prefecture), to which the main character, an 11th grader named Aki Amano (played by Rena Nonen), and her mother, Haruko (Kyoko Koizumi) return from Tokyo. It is here, in her mother's hometown, where Aki grows up while living and interacting with local people including her grandmother, Natsu (Nobuko Miyamoto). The storyline in the second half (weeks 13–26) revolves around Aki's struggle and her eventual debut as an idol back in Tokyo. As the Tohoku region is one of the settings, it portrays the Earthquake during the final phase (week 23) and some characters of the story are seen caught in the midst of it. The storyline continues with Aki, who together with her classmate Yui (Ai Hashimoto), forms a regional idol group called Shiosaino Memories to help rally the community of Kitasanriku. This is an example of Japanese idols representing 'regional characteristics' and 'regional authenticity' at the dawn of the era during the 1970s.

Contents Tourism

This particular drama series earned an average household viewing rating of 20.6% (according to Video Research Kanto Region) far exceeding the rating of its predecessor (17.1%). It not only attracted a large audience, it also created a passionate fan base. Furthermore, the analysis of the media reports related to *Amachan* revealed that the filming location for this series, Kuji-shi, as well as Iwate Prefecture, benefited economically from an increased number of tourists visiting the area (Tajima 2014b.)

Research on this type of tourism we call 'contents tourism', inspired by media content such as in a TV drama series, has been evolving in Japan since 2010. Internationally (mainly in Europe and the US) tourism based on films and TV programs is often called 'film-induced tourism', 'movie-induced tourism' or 'media-related tourism'.

Up until now, in studies related to film-induced tourism, the context of discussions has been the above-described effect that films and TV dramas had on the region of the filming location. Regarding films and TV dramas, it is the latter that has more strongly evoked emotional bonds among viewers, probably because of the length of broadcasting periods, the serial format and the greater element of ordinary everyday life in the content. It is thought that increasing viewer involvement in media works raises the potential for tourism in the location where the work is filmed (Kim and Long 2012; Kim and Wang 2012). Kim and Long (2012) discuss the importance of focusing attention on the concept of the 'genre' because it has the role of shaping the modality of viewers.

On the other hand, looking at prior studies in Japan, TV dramas have become points of contestation. This is most evident in the genres of NHK's Taiga historical fiction TV drama and the asadora morning drama. Academic disciplines related to research focusing on the latter consist not only of the field of tourism studies but also on a multitude of subjects ranging from humanities and social sciences through economics.

Maruta et al. (2014) provide a thought-provoking critique of *Jun to Ai* comparing it with *Amachan*, which it preceded. They observe that although the broadcast of *Jun to Ai* brought about an increase in the number of tourists to the Miyako Islands, where it was filmed, the impact on tourism was not as dramatic as had been expected by tourism-related parties there before the series was broadcast. It was thought that the drama's depiction of the Miyako Islands and people was not well-received by the Miyako people themselves, and consequently it was not possible to capture their hearts.

The results of studies relating to previous contents tourism and the asadora morning drama have, in the way mentioned above, formed a basis for case research from the 2010s, as contents tourism research has also developed further. This research implies that although one can expect the media content of asadora morning drama to induce tourism and thereby provide a certain economic boost to the region of the filming location, it cannot guarantee an emotional bond between the drama and the local people on which the drama setting is composed, nor can it guarantee such an effect is sustained.

It is worth noting, however, that the concept of contents tourism involves a wider range of media content, such as manga, anime and video games. Tourism based on manga and anime, called 'pilgrimage' by some, is especially garnering much attention as a new kind of tourism that makes optimal use of the aforementioned advances in information technology (Okamoto 2011, 2013; Yamamura 2011). According to Yamamura (2011, p. 172), contents tourism refers to "the people's sensory experiences of the contents [narrative] using all of their five senses with the location or area serving as the media. It creates an emotional link among people [or people and other entities] through shared contents". Based on Yamamura's definition, idols are indeed contents, and tourism and regional revitalization based on the idol culture can be one focus area for important discussions in the field of contents tourism research. In fact, *Investigative Research of Cases of Regional Revitalization Efforts Bringing Economic Benefits to the Region* presented by the Regional Economic and Industrial Policy Group in fiscal year 2012 at METI included regional idols as one of its focus areas, which cemented idol cultures' status as part of the contents indispensable for regional revitalization efforts. Idols, however, have rarely been the subject of discussion in the field of contents tourism research, nor has there been research on the actual state of tourism based on *Amachan*.

Method

To close the above-mentioned gap in research, I selected *Amachan* as the media content for this research as it incorporates the narrative of regional idols. Specifically, I conducted continuous field research in Kuji-shi,

Iwate Prefecture, which is the filming location of the series, from 2014 to 2015, along with participant observation research and interviews of relevant personnel in the media contents tourism industry. According to Yamamura (2011), relevant personnel in the contents tourism industry can be categorized into three groups, namely, (1) producers, (2) fans (tourists) and (3) local residents. As this research's main interest is in the relationship between the media contents and the local residents as well as the activities of regional idols, the article will focus on the local residents.

The interviewees included personnel at Kuji City Hall, at the Kuji-shi Chamber of Commerce and Industry and at Kuji-shi Tourism Association as well as the production manager from the Fisheries Cooperative Association, members of Ama (women divers) Association in the Kosode district, female high school students in Kuji-shi who are members of Ama Club, owners of local shops, the owner of the restaurant on which the series is loosely based and, finally, fans of Ama Club. All of these people have, in one way or another, come in contact with the contents tourism industry including through the production of the series at the filming location or in dealing with tourists. The interviewer first explained the privacy policy and received consent for disclosure of research results from the interviewees before proceeding with the interview. This paper will concentrate on statements made by the members of Ama Club.

In addition to this, interview surveys were also distributed to several regional idols who were not members of Ama Club in order to understand the broader qualities of regional idols.

An investigation into regional idols following the research scope outlined in the first section of this chapter yielded a sample of 126 groups (908 people) as of September 1, 2016. The sample was composed of 5 single units (solo artists) and 121 multiple units (groups) (henceforth, both solo artist and group units will be referred to as 'groups'). Regarding the gender of the group members, 4 were males and 904 females. Classed by formation date, 16 groups were formed in 2009, 12 in 2010, 34 in 2011, 34 in 2012, 19 in 2013, and 11 in 2014 and 2015.

From the data above, it can be seen that most of the research subjects were female groups formed from 2010 onwards. Taking the representation of regional idols into consideration, this study therefore chose, as a cornerstone, to conduct questionnaire surveys with persons involved in the management of regional idols judged to be highly relevant to regional development. The chosen were amongst those formed from 2010 onwards, which were better-known and from regions with high numbers of 'regional idols'. Where possible, surveys were also undertaken with the members of these groups themselves (only where possible). The surveys were semi-structured interviews conducted in accordance with sets of questions prepared in advance; extra questions were added as necessary. Surveys of regional idols conducted up to the present (September 1, 2016) are listed in Table 6.1 below. Meanwhile, Table 6.2 summarizes the range of participants surveyed, as well as certain attributes (e.g., gender) of the subjects in greater detail. This reveals that while group members were almost entirely female, the majority of managers were male. As for age, there were sizable differences amongst all of the groups, with the youngest members being 11 years and oldest 29 years; nonetheless, group members were, at core, middle- and high-school students.

Table 6.1 List of regional idols (by the author)

Area of operation	Group name	Period of activity	The date of survey
Kuji City, Iwate Prefecture	Ama Club	2014–2015	2014. 12/14
Sendai City, Miyagi Prefecture	Michinoku Sendai Ori Princess Troupe [*Hime Tai*]	2011–	2016. 1/30
Niigata Prefecture	RYUTist	2011–	2015. 11/16
Toyama Prefecture	Vienolossi	2013–	2016. 2/14
Hokuriku	Thumb [*Oyayubi*] Princesses	2012–	2016. 2/14
Mito City, Ibaraki Prefecture	Mito Regional Idols (TBC)	2012–	2015. 8/24
Nagoya City, Aichi Prefecture (Ōsu Shopping District)	OS☆U	2010–	2015. 11/23
Inazawa City, Aichi Prefecture	LOVE♥INA30	2011–	2015. 11/22
Okazaki City, Aichi Prefecture	Sakura-HR	2011–	2015. 11/23
Fukuoka Prefecture	LinQ	2011–	2015. 12/22

Table 6.2 Summary of the surveys (by the author)

Group name	Member interview survey	Gender	Average age	Manager interview survey	Gender
Ama Club	O	Female	18.0	O	Male
Michinoku Sendai Ori Princess Troupe [*Hime Tai*]	O	Female	14.5	O	Male
RYUTist	×	Female	15.3	O	Male
Vienolossi	O	Female	15.8	O	Female
Thumb [*Oyayubi*] Princesses	O	Female	17.1	O	Male
Mito Regional Idols (TBC)	×	Female	18.2	O	Male
OS☆U	O	Female	18.8	O	Male
LOVE♥INA30	O	Female	17.6	O	Male
Sakura-HR	×	Female	18.7	O	Male
LinQ	O	Female	20.9	O	Male

Discussion

Preproduction Preparation at the Location

As there was no film commission in Kuji-shi, the city established the Promotional Committee for Supporting *Amachan*, consisting of 32 relevant organizations (for example, the Iwate Prefecture government office, chambers of commerce and tourism organizations) as well as five municipalities that agreed to serve as filming locations in July 2012 before the filming began. This committee provided support at the location, with the pre-production preparation, and for advertising to attract visitors. It also managed tours to promote tourism, prepared guidebooks, established facilities and secured venues for displaying stage props and costumes used at the locations, painted depictions related to the series on store shutters (or shutter art), and actively encouraged the creation of a town that made use of motifs based on the series. These activities helped convey the message both inside and outside the region: "Kuji-shi is the filming location used in *Amachan*".

Activities by Ama Club After the Series

Lingering at the back of the minds of the local organizations involved was the concern that the tourist boom would quickly lose its momentum following post-production activities. Their hope was and still is to use the series proactively as an opportunity to trigger further development of the region, inspire the city of Kuji and attract repeat tourists. Some of the activities are led by residents themselves rather than the municipality and its staff. One such activity worth noting is Ama Club consisting of five female 12th graders from Kuji-shi. The club was born when several high school students were inspired to help the community after witnessing the actual impact *Amachan* had on the number of tourists visiting Kuji-shi. Collaborating with the local tourism association, which also managed the group, the girls formed the group in April 2014 for only one year. The main purpose of the group was to give regular performances of their original songs and dance numbers, as well as those in *Amachan*, close to home to promote Kuji-shi. Ama Club performed to a roaring crowd in their farewell concert in March 2015 which was attended by approximately 350 fans from Kuji-shi and elsewhere and filled the Kuji-shi Cultural Center almost to capacity. When asked to look back on her activities, one member stated: "

> What really struck me was that I grew to love Kuji-shi more after I started with the club. Of course, I loved my city before joining the group, but the more I promoted my hometown to others, the more I really grew to appreciate it".

Similarly, other members also realized the value of Kuji-shi, their hometown. Another member added: "I really felt that this was where I belonged and felt inspired". Others expressed a similar sentiment: they felt that their own identity became more rooted within the community.

In this respect, what are the experiences of other regional idols?

Details of the Regional Idols Surveyed

This section clearly outlines the regional idols surveyed, starting with details such as their areas of operation, management, period of activity and the details of their formation (i.e., goals at the time of formation).

Firstly, regarding performance area, there are, of course, groups that operate on a scale broader than the prefectural level, for instance, those spanning Hokuriku (Thumb [*Oyayubi*] Princesses) and Kyūshū (LinQ); if we consider prefectures, however, in order of the greatest numbers of the regional idols targeted by this research, the core regions are Fukuoka (12 groups), Osaka (10 groups) and Aichi (9 groups)—all of which are large metropolitan areas, and also have their own AKB groups.

In Aichi in particular, as can be seen from two of the surveyed groups— Love.Ina30 from Inazawa (northwestern Aichi, population around 130,000) and Sakura-HR from Okazaki (central Aichi, population around 380,000)—there are regional idols with a degree of fame in terms of being featured in mass media in towns other than their prefectural capital, Nagoya (neither of the groups' hometown is an ordinance-designated city). Furthermore, Nagoya is rich in diversity; for example, OS.U is based in Ōsu Shopping District, located in Ōsu, Naka Ward; there is also idol training run by the owner of a sushi restaurant. Therefore, whilst this research thus far in principle focused only on one group per prefecture, Aichi was an exception and three groups—Love.Ina30, Sakura-HR, OS.U—were questioned.

Next, the 10 surveyed groups were sorted into the following three categories regarding management:

1. Public institution (local governments, incorporated associations, foundations, NPOs, etc.): Ama Club, Michinoku Sendai Ori Princess Troupe [*Hime Tai*], Thumb [*Oyayubi*] Princesses
2. Entertainment producers: RYUTist, Vienolossi, OS.U, LinQ
3. Individuals: Mito Regional Idols (TBC), Love.Ina30, Sakura-HR

Note, however, that the above are details from the point at which the surveys were conducted (or based on prior knowledge of future changes); there are cases in which active groups have changed management, such as Michinoku Sendai Ori Princess Troupe [*Hime Tai*], which started under management by a corporation and changed to an incorporated association in February 2016.

Additionally, to expand upon (3): 'individuals' here refers to cases where in reality it is an individual person with another occupation, such as a shopkeeper, who is involved in management as a job 'on the side', despite the management being officially designated (i.e., in mass media articles and on official websites) as '[Name] Executive Committee' or similar. For instance, Sakura-HR's parent organization is listed as '*Machidoru* Executive Committee', but the person who actually manages the group (the 'principal', Mr. I, is by day an employee at a public institution; he supports Sakura-HR mostly by himself, outside of his day job.

Lastly, regarding period of activity, it has already been stated that all of the groups were formed from 2010 onwards, and excluding Ama Club, all groups have been continuously performing regardless of the succession, retirement, and addition of members. Inquiring about the particulars of each group's formation revealed that, while objectives were initially aligned with the issues faced by each region, such as supporting disaster recovery (Michinoku Sendai Ori Princess Troupe [*Hime Tai*]), shopping district revitalization (OS.U) or energizing a summer festival (Love. Ina30), in terms of an overall desired direction, regional improvement forms the axis of each group's performances. Furthermore, as can be seen from the times at which the groups were formed, each was developed in a different context than that of the 'local Abenomics' regional development policy announced by the second Abe cabinet. Meanwhile, according to comments from those involved, it was not uncommon for groups to be concerned about freedom regarding the time and content of their activities, and even to distance themselves from public institutions.[12] Similarly, there are many groups which keep interaction with fans to a minimum to avoid excessive interference with management and the members.

The above observations reveal a common feature shared by the surveyed regional idols: they perform out of a consideration for regional improvement in the regions in which they are based.

Efficacy and Functions: Boosting Regional Affection

What are the effects on individual members arising from performing as a regional idol? First, members told us that their sentiment toward their home region changed throughout, which matches what was observed in the case of Ama Club. Below are quotes from several members (the underlined portions are comments on the quotes).[13]

One of the members of Love.Ina30, a group launched in July 2011 as a summer festival project aimed at revitalizing the local Inazawa Summer Festival, said:

> I grew up in Inazawa, so when I play with the local kids, I just think I want to be a representative of Inazawa. We are doing an enormous amount of events, and just being able to confidently say, this is how it is, instills a real sense of pride. That feeling that I really know Inazawa makes me happy. (Love.Ina30 member)

Then, one of the members of OS.U, which was formed in August 2010 with the aforementioned aim of promoting the revitalization of Ōsu Shopping District, or more specifically, bringing the 'otaku' (meaning 'geeks' but referring to both 'idol' fans and people with interests in subculture) into the shopping district, said the following about how she developed a greater interest in learning about the region after having the opportunity to reflect on her own ambivalence toward the area she grew up in while performing:

> It really made me think about how I didn't know anything about the town I grew up in. Given the opportunity to be an ambassador for the town and do those kinds of things, I gradually learned the good things about the town and its special points, and I grew to love my hometown much more. If I never had this opportunity, I don't think I would have ever learned about the place's history or anything else about it. But now I feel these things are really important. (OS.U member)

Promoting Local Participation and Intergenerational Social Interaction

Exemplary of the views of the members of OS.U, based in Ōsu Shopping District was this:

> Even when just hanging out around town, people in the shopping district greet us by saying, "Morning," or something else. It makes you feel like you're on real friendly terms with them. It makes me appreciate how wonderful the town is. You'd think it would be hard to be able to walk around and be so friendly with the people of the shopping district. It's like we've become family! (OS.U member)

In contrast to this, Inazawa-based Love.Ina30, although sharing the same Aichi Prefecture, has a strong affinity with the contemporary urban modality of their local region. As mentioned earlier, Love.Ina30 was formed with the aim of revitalizing the local summer festival. One of the venues where they regularly give stage performances is a shopping mall called Leaf Walk Inazawa.[14] Love.Ina30 have been appointed as the 'image girls' of Leaf Walk, and they hold regular performances several times a month on weekends and public holidays on a stage installed inside the shopping mall. As is typical of regional idols, the majority of their fans are men in their 30s to 40s. Although it differs among groups, many of these fans live in the areas surrounding their hometown. Love.Ina30 also attracts similar audiences at their regular concerts, but many of the people who stop to listen to their performance at Leaf Walk are general shoppers, and a particularly prevalent category of shoppers on weekends and public holidays are families with young children. On that topic, a member gave the following reply when asked about "what gives them joy while out performing":

> I remember not long after we started, I received a letter from this little girl. I get lots of letters from grownups [laughs], but the letters from younger kids really show how full of sweet innocence they are. Often I read that kind of letter from a child when I am feeling exhausted, and I get a bit teary-eyed. (Love.Ina30 member)

The 'grownups' mentioned here refer to the male fans in their 30s and 40s, but what stands out here is that the joy for members is not only the interaction with fans but also the opportunity for interaction with the local children. At the same time, it provides a glimpse of the next generation, which the members and managers may be looking to direct their performances toward in the future because the underlying suggestion in what the Love.Ina30 member says above is that she wants to be loved by children and to have a child fan base, and also for the group to be attractive to this audience.

From the perspective of local participation, the performances of Michinoku Sendai Ori Princess Troupe [*Hime Tai*] are insightful.

Hime Tai formed for the purpose of raising money and carrying out volunteer activities for disaster recovery in July 2011. While their base was the city of Sendai in Miyagi Prefecture, the members were mostly elementary and junior high school students from regions where the destruction of the Earthquake was extreme, such as the cities of Ishinomaki-shi, Shiogama-shi, Shichigahama-shi and Miyagino-ku in the city of Sendai, and members had firsthand experience of the disaster.[15] Consequently, *Hime Tai's* scope of activities included giving stage performances just like other regional idols, but in addition to that, the group was involved in support programs for disaster recovery (such as morale-boosting visits to disaster-stricken towns and temporary residential settlements, holding or participating in charity events for the affected regions, fundraising activities, sales of charity goods, and visits to places overseas that had given support for the disaster). Asked why she had become a regional idol, one of the members answered:

> I'm from Miyagi Prefecture and I have many relatives whose houses were washed away, so I was searching for something I could do to help. I was still only grade six at elementary school at the time, so I didn't really know much about anything. But as I really wanted to try to do something, they let me join. (Michinoku Sendai Ori Princess Troupe [*Hime Tai*] member)

The same member said the following when asked about changes she had witnessed through performing:

> Among the recovery support activities, I think there are various kinds of problems, but looking back over the five years that I have been doing this, at first we were visiting the temporary residential settlements and talking with the old men and women staying there. Now the activities are things like tree planting.[16] I guess my impression is that the practical activities aimed at building the future have been increasing over the five years. (Michinoku Sendai Ori Princess Troupe [*Hime Tai*] member)

From the above two remarks, it is apparent that during the initial period of confusion directly following the Earthquake, the *Hime Tai* member did not know how she could be of assistance, but through the interactions they had with various people in the affected areas through their performances over the years, the group's activities now relate to more practical issues and problems that their region faces. Although regional development activities greatly differ from the far more serious and urgent issues that need to be addressed during recovery efforts after disasters, by cooperating with local people across all generations, the members are fulfilling a role of local participation to 'make the region better', and we can expect to find common elements among the cases of other regional idols.

Improving Communication Skills

The performances of regional idols can have a great effect on how communication occurs between the members of idol groups:

> Originally, I was very shy and I hated doing things like performing in front of people. There was nothing that I felt I was particularly good at, and I was totally useless talking with people. I struggled with these communication obstacles, but I just started becoming amazingly proactive. I think it has given me the confidence to engage properly with people in ordinary life. (Vienolossi member)

One could easily assume that because these people are regional idol performers, they share a notable skill set for speaking and singing in front of people. However, as is evident by the above remark, the members disclosed that they are naturally shy and lack self-confidence. A surprisingly large number of members said that they became performers to overcome such characteristics. The member who made the above remark related that she was able to see herself differently through performance, and as a result, she found she was able to overcome important life challenges such as finding a job.

From the above, we see that performing helps members improve communication skills necessary for smooth interpersonal relations. At the same time, members of idol groups regulate their self-identity; in other words, being a performer gives adolescents the ability to establish autonomy.

Conclusion

Tourism inspired by *Amachan* and the activities of Ama Club not only established an image of the community as the filming location in *Amachan*, but also urged residents within the community of Kuji-shi to become more interested and attached to their own hometown, and created an opportunity for them to be more culturally aware. This case is different from that of the preceding production *Jun to Ai*. The residents of Kuji-shi favorably accepted the content, which led to the promotion of contents tourism. It can be said that at the same time it led to regional promotion activities utilizing *Amachan*. Consequently, the contents tourism driven by *Amachan* can be seen as a case in which there was an emotional bond between the drama and the local residents who composed the drama setting. Thus, the effects of contents tourism were sustained for a long time when compared with other asadora morning TV dramas.

Furthermore, these activities inspired the residents to identify more with their local community. The way the residents actively participated in the tourism effort also made a difference. Nevertheless, the activities of Ama Club were limited to a certain period of time due to the members' future plans after high school; however, the group succeeded in attracting fans to the region. In other words, the dramatic representation of regional idols in the asadora morning TV drama increased the effect of the related contents tourism. In addition, it showed the potential for contents tourism using regional idols. Contents tourism using regional idols was not only a promotion of tourism as simple entertainment, it also brought about the kinds of effects on members as summarized below.

The performance of regional idols broadly had the following three effects: (1) it increased love and attachment towards the group's base, i.e., the members' local area; (2) it encouraged local involvement—that is, thinking collaboratively about the region among local residents, irrespective of age, in order to address issues and problems faced by the area; and (3) it drove progress in resolving relevant issues and problems through communication with members and between members and management.

Lastly, whilst the regional idols surveyed in this paper were—with one exception—groups that gave performances on an ongoing basis, attention should also be paid to the fact that there are also groups with no choice but to perform for a limited period, such as Ama Club. It was decided at the time of the group's formation that Ama Club would disband after a year, a choice that was not unrelated to the fact that there is no university in Kuji for the group members in their final year of high school. Performances had to be stopped due to unavoidable circumstances faced particularly by young people, such as the pursuit of further studies and future directions. It is often true as well that several members of a group will face similar issues that do not result in disbanding.

Notes

1. Johnny & Associates is one of the leading entertainment production companies in Japan.
2. This news was broadcast on BBC in England, and France 24 in France, and it was reported in the UK newspaper, *The Guardian*.
3. Yasushi Akimoto is a Japanese lyricist, TV writer and producer known for having produced Onyanko Club, an idol group of amateur high school girls during the mid-80s.
4. Asadora is a morning serial drama, which has been broadcast on NHK since 1961. Judging from the series' storylines and the time slot, most of the viewers are thought to be housewives.
5. Some groups, such as AKB48, own their own exclusive theaters while others do not.
6. As shown by the involvement of AKB in the development of plans to construct a 'Cool Japan Mall' in the Philippine capital, Manila, to promote 'Japan appeal' in 2017, idols are being considered symbols for promoting Japan overseas.
7. Certainly, a number of general books have been published on idols, but research methods and theories of the majority of these are not clear, and they cannot definitively be included in the category of academic research.
8. JapanKnowledge, http://japanknowledge.com 2016(2016年2月11日)
9. According to Tamura (2014), attention paid to 'locality' is historically stronger in Japan than in other countries. The existence of various ranking tables in the Edo period may be given as evidence here.
10. This is an event held for the "Competition for Deciding the No. 1 Regional Idol [*Go-tōchi Aidoru No. 1 Kettei-sen*]", hosted every December

since 2010 by HoriPro, a major talent production company. Finalist candidates are selected from regional idol entries from across Japan, ten groups of which advance to the final round based on YouTube video views, web voting, screenings and so forth; the event determines the 'No. 1' from amongst these groups. 'U.M.U.' is an abbreviation of 'Under Major Unitidol'.

11. Although *rōkaru* and *go-tōchi* are conceptually interrelated, the antonym of *rōkaru* in Japanese is *gurōbaru* (global); accordingly, there is the worry that the term *rōkaru aidoru* carries the implication of 'idols representing Japan', with the object of comparison being overseas, which the study deemed inappropriate. Additionally, the use of *chihō* (regional, i.e., outside of the capital) was avoided as it implies a Tokyo-centric hierarchy.

12. The majority of participants indicated they had almost no involvement with public institutions for various reasons: Such involvement can lead to limits on the events that the group can participate in, extended working hours, impact on payment with regard to activities for which members may be paid, and so forth. In addition, participation in events hosted by public institutions and employment in roles such as educational characters fundamentally tend to be conducted in the form of competitions. However, it is sometimes the case that a group may be requested to participate in a national project, or may be funded by a local government; thus, it cannot necessarily be said that there are no ties involved. Meanwhile, there were also some comments that indicated doubts regarding the distance between the expectations of idol images and performances by public institutions and the actual performances given, even by groups with ties to public institutions.

13. Concerning the interview results (handling of individual testimonies), in order to protect personal information, the members were made anonymous through the use of a method that didn't specify their names.

14. Leaf Walk Inazawa is a shopping mall that opened in 2009 as part of a redevelopment project orchestrated by Inazawa City and an urban redevelopment organization.

15. The personal disaster experiences of members were reported by the mass media, such as by the Asahi Shimbun on January 1, 2016, in "Idols supporting recovery bring smiles" and by the Sankei News on February 6, 2016, in "Miyagi, Sendai—Michinoku Sendai Ori Princess Troupe [Hime Tai] have over 80 stylish costumes to brighten spirits of affected region."

16. Concerning the tree planting activities, an organizer described the activities as follows: "We are planting saplings that will serve as a defense for strong winds. We are donating to Sendai City's Green Fund. The saplings were grown outside the prefecture, in Tottori Prefecture, I think. These trees grow nice and tall, I think they grow in Fukushima. They will start to get big in about 30 years. We are doing this activity together with Sendai City."

References

Hashimoto, H. (2014). Visiting Locations for Regional Idols. In *An Introduction to Contents Tourism* (pp. 133–160). Tokyo: Kokon-Shoin.

Inamasu, T. (1989). *Idol Engineering*. Tokyo: Chikuma Shobō.

Kim, S., & Long, P. (2012). Touring TV Soap Operas: Genre in Film Tourism Research. *Tourist Studies, 12*(2), 1–13.

Kim, S., & Wang, H. (2012). From Television to the Film Set : Korean Drama Daejanggeum Drives Chinese, Taiwanese, Japanese and Thai Audiences to Screen-Tourism. *The International Communication Gazette, 74*(5), 423–442.

Maruta, K., Kanehama, S., & Tamayose, A. (2014). The Broadcast of the NHK Morning TV Serial Story "Jun and Ai", and the Reaction in MIYAKO Island. *Journal of the Faculty of Humanities and Social Sciences, 16*, 61–69.

Muraki, I. (2013). The Function of Local Idols for Regional Revitalization. *Collected Treatises on Contents Tourism, 4*, 6–71.

Nara Prefectural University Regional Development Research Group. (2005). *Invitation to Creative Region*. Koyoshobo.

Ogawa, H. (1988). *Society Where Music Lives*. Tokyo: Keiso Shobō.

Okamoto, K. (2011). *Research on Contents Tourism 1*, "An Introduction to Contents Tourism Research: Constructing a New Idea of Tourism and Its Research Concept in This Information Society" pp.1–10.

Okamoto, K. (2013). *n Dimension Tourism Creation: Anime Pilgrimage/Contents Tourism and Potential of Sociology of Tourism*. NPO Hokkaido Alternative Art and Publishing.

Ota, S. (2011). *Idols Evolution Theory*. Tokyo: Chikuma Shobō.

Sakamoto, H. (2008). *An Ordinary Era: The Youth and Popular Entertainment Magazines in the 1950s*. Kyoto: Showado.

Sasaki, K. (2008). *Tourism Promotion and Attractive Community Development: A Prospect of Regional Tourism*. Kyoto: Gakugei-Publishing.

Tajima, Y. (2014a). *The Magazine Myojo as Idol Cultural Apparatus During the 1970s* (Doctorate thesis for Doshisha University).

Tajima, Y. (2014b). The Relationship Between the Drama Series Amachan and the Locations Observed in Newspaper Reports. *Media Studies: Culture and Communication, 29*, 25–41.

Tamura, S. (2014). *'Go-tōchi-mono' and Japanese*. Tokyo: Shodensha.

Yamamura, T. (2011). *Local Development Through Anime/Manga: How to Develop Contents Tourism that Creates Fans*. Tokyo: Tokyo Horei Publishing.

7

Being There, Being Someone Else: Leisure and Identity in the Age of Virtual Reality

Jonathan Harth

Introduction

It is not the first time the emerging technology of virtual reality (VR) has raised questions about changes to leisure activities and its role in the management of identity for the modern person (Hobson and Williams 1997; Biocca 1997; Turkle 2005). But since last year these questions have become even more important: 2016 turned out to be the moment when, for the first time, advanced consumer VR hit the mass markets of Western societies.

In this context I would like to contribute to the (re)thinking of digital leisure and its role in the individual's identity management: "Living in a digital society cannot be understood without the recognition that computer software and hardware devices not only underpin [but] actively constitute selfhood, embodiment, social life, social relations and social institutions." (Silk et al. 2016) In this sense, leisure and identity in the digital age are tightly intertwined (Spracklen 2015). So, by adapting

J. Harth (✉)
Universität Witten/Herdecke, Witten, Germany

© The Author(s) 2018
A. Beniwal et al. (eds.), *Global Leisure and the Struggle for a Better World*, Leisure
Studies in a Global Era, https://doi.org/10.1007/978-3-319-70975-8_7

Turkle's perspective on the role of computers, I would like to shift my view from all the things virtual reality may do *for* us to what using it *does to* us as people (cf. Turkle 2005, p. 3). Therefore I would like to sketch out the thesis that advanced virtual reality poses significant new questions on the role of leisure activities for individual identity.[1] This potential lies within the possibilities of VR—as is to be shown—to be able to embody alternate bodies in alternate worlds. Many studies from the field of media psychology show that the potential of embodiment in virtual realities may have an (ever)changing impact on one's self-perspective. Thus, with a broader distribution of virtual reality, leisure will show even more its purpose in defining (and defending) individual identities.

In their book *Issues in Recreation and Leisure*, Macleod and Yoder (2005) try to foresee the possible future of advanced virtual reality for free time activities and virtual tourism, so to speak, and draw a vivid picture of potential leisure activities in the age of VR:

> The question is not when, it's what. Will we be able to visit an encampment of American Indians in the 1600s? Will we be able to travel to the most beautiful place on earth or beyond and savor a romantic interlude with the person of our dreams? Will we be able to watch and even interact with the rarest animals on the planet without disturbing them at all? Will the disabled experience everything—seeing, hearing, running—that the nondisabled experience? (Macleod and Yoder 2005, p. 171)

The authors clearly did not have in mind simple prototypes of home entertainment systems but rather technology that is becoming available nowadays. Even though VR may still seem to be in its infancy, its functionalities of visualization, interactivity and immersion provide and confront the user with similar experiences as those mentioned by Macleod and Yoder. To completely feel being present at another place in another time, and with all the corresponding issues—such as feeling tension, shock, or fright but without any actual danger: What a promise to make!

But what do these virtual experiences do to the users? What impact may it have to one's identity, when one immerses her-/himself in a foreign and maybe somewhat frightening environment, in a body of the opposite sex and talking to strangers, unsure if they are another person's avatar or only a bot. These questions may seem rather odd, but exactly this is possible today with the use of virtual reality.

> Prior to the current digital era, identity development used to be confined by the physical realities and constraints of the here and now, as well as by the need to build on the relatively limited collection of one's earlier experiences. (Nagy and Koles 2014, p. 279)

This leads me to the following thesis: The use of Virtual Reality offers alternative forms of embodiment, which not only sabotage the alleged "continuity of the body" (Bauman 1992) but may also lead to a changed self- and worldview. By being framed as leisure activities in the first place, these effects tend to push society's levels of reflexivity by introducing more contingencies, more reflexive stances, and more possible viewpoints from which one can determine the purposes of distinguishing between real and (only) virtual ontologies.

The following considerations serve as starting points for this thesis: Firstly, from a systems theory point of view, the body must always be regarded as an observed body. Consciousness does not simply rest in the body, which guarantees that there is only one consciousness, but we rather have to concede, that there is a polycontextural consciousness which creates a polycontextural body (Günther 1979; Fuchs 2012, pp. 67 f.).[2] Secondly, from a game studies' perspective, the virtual worlds of video games in general and the virtual environments of virtual reality in particular serve as contexts distinct from 'ordinary life' (Huizinga 1980; Caillois 2001), and are characterized by imperative rules and by the enabling of new experiences inside their 'magic circle'. Last but not least, from a point of view of philosophy of technology, the theoretical concept of 'virtuality' is a complex one that aims not only at an abstract possibility but is a real force, which even though it has no material representation is nevertheless real (Baudrillard 2008; Esposito 2011). Unlike a mere possibility, virtuality does not have to realize itself, because it is already real.

On the basis of these theoretical starting points, I will try to draw a picture of different—and maybe still unconnected—thoughts on the relationship between identity, body and society in the age of virtual reality. After a short introduction into current consumer oriented virtual reality I would like to discuss what makes VR so special. It is the possibility of being present in a virtual environment as well as in a virtual body? Both the experience of spatial presence as well as embodiment provided by VR lead to considerations about the utopian longing for human enhancement and/or liberation. After all, the technology of virtual reality seems to provide society with a new order of contingency which meets the requirements of a polycontextural society.

What Is It That Makes Virtual Reality so Special?

It was the successfully funded Kickstarter campaign for "Oculus VR" in 2013 that got keywords such as 'virtual reality', 'head mounted display' and 'metaverse' buzzing again. Shortly after, the so-called second generation of VR-goggles arrived. In 2016 a number of well-known brands (Oculus/Facebook, HTC/Valve, and Sony) launched their first advanced VR-devices. These VR-devices are characterized by the fact that for the first time virtual reality is made widely available (i.e. affordable) and with the target of mass market.[3] And these devices are no longer the kind of VR presented in the pioneering era of the 1980s and 90s, but advanced VR—as I would call it—that operates without any major technical restrictions concerning pixel density, tracking of head movements, etc. Even if 'virtual reality' may be currently hyped by the so-called early-adopters, the developers and the market are already betting on when VR-technology will establish itself as a new mainstream communication media. For more than four years major corporations like Facebook, HTC, Microsoft, Google, Apple, and Sony have signaled their interest in VR by shoveling multi-billion dollar investments into the VR ecosystem. This alone indicates there is something more to be expected. So although the final impact VR will have on society is far from clear, it is already driving the tech community as mad as the advent of World Wide Web. Therefore, it is not very surprising that in this pioneering climate we can find many voices arguing that VR will never again vanish (Stein 2015).

Why is it that VR claims to kill the video star? Promising nothing less than the 'ultimate display' (Sutherland 1965) by integrating all previous media technologies and merging reality with virtuality, the concept of virtual reality clearly inspired many imaginations. But what is it that makes VR so special? The magic of Virtual Reality lies in the ability to give the user the feeling of being present within the virtual environment. It has even been argued that the very definition of virtual reality involves presence: "A virtual reality is defined as a real or simulated environment in which a perceiver experiences telepresence" (Steuer 1992).

But how do we define presence and what is it about? Over the past years VR research has produced many definitions of the concept of presence (e.g., Heeter 1992; Steuer 1992; Lombard and Ditton 1997; Slater and Wilbur 1997; Witmer and Singer 1998). Early VR researchers Lombard and Ditton define the concept of presence as follows:

> Presence is defined as the perceptual illusion of non-mediation... an illusion of non-mediation occurs when a person fails to perceive or acknowledge the existence of a medium in his/her communication environment and responds as he/she would if the medium were not there. (Lombard and Ditton 1997, p. 9)[4]

In this chapter I would like to outline the ways we must assume that virtual reality does even more than introducing some new kind of alternative realities. Virtual reality is not only about immersing the user in some new surroundings, but is rather about the users themselves. Or, as Madary and Metzinger state: "VR is the representation of possible worlds and possible selves, with the aim of making them appear as real as possible – ideally, by creating a subjective sense of 'presence' in the user" (Madary and Metzinger 2016, p. 18).

The use of virtual reality and especially the concept of presence allow an alternative view of the existing world as well as on oneself. In comparison with cinema or video games, being involved in VR increases the level of immersion: the user does not only watch a predefined situation from a distance, he/she actually feels his-/herself to be in the scene. And with the help of the many modes of interaction within this environment (Vive's wand-controllers and 'Oculus Touch' controllers employ a level of interaction comparable to the real world) the user has the potential to get even more involved (see Steed et al. 2016). With state of the art VR we do approach the mode, which has been described for the first time by Martin Heidegger (1962): the mode of being-in-the-world.

Without presence, without the feeling—or rather: the perception—of being there, VR would be nothing more than another screen medium, from which one could alienate oneself easily (see Kilteni et al. 2012). Especially in the case of virtual reality, it becomes obvious that every perception is only momentary, immediate and compact. The perception of presence occurs only in the present tense. Or, as Maurice Merleau-Ponty (2005) points out: to a perception you can hardly say no.

The effect of spatial presence is even more enhanced by the effects of social presence. Per se, VR is no lonely media. Even if isolated from seeing and hearing the material world, the effects of being present in the virtual world are significantly enhanced if the user meets other users in this same place. The feeling of 'being with' someone else through the use of visual and auditory information relating to this second user (which may even be depicted in abstract, artistic, or minimalistic style) boosts the feeling of being present within VR (Lee 2004a, b).[5]

In VR the user is able to look in any direction within the virtual environment, but in particular "they can look towards their real body, and if the system has been so programmed they would see a life-sized virtual body visually substituting their own" (Bourdin et al. 2017, p. 2). If achieved, the more or less convincing impression of being present within another body can be quite startling. This effect is referred to as a full body ownership illusion.[6] When under this effect, most users attribute a feeling of ownership to these virtual limbs and do not disregard them as mere objects. These findings are well supported by many experiments and empirical research. With the use of virtual reality, it even has become possible to induce changes in the attribution of selfhood: "We found that during multisensory conflict, participants felt as if a virtual body seen in front of them was their own body and mislocalized themselves toward the virtual body, to a position outside their bodily borders" (Lenggenhager et al. 2007, p. 1096). The researchers "induced an illusion that makes it possible to quantify selfhood by manipulating attribution and localization of the entire body" (p. 1098). The experimental setups of Ehrsson

(2007) and Blanke and Metzinger (2009) confirm these findings.[7] Other experiments show that embodiment into an avatar of another gender (Slater et al. 2009) or age (Banakou et al. 2013), of another skin color (Peck et al. 2013) or through body-swapping (Petkova and Ehrsson 2008) may lead to similar phenomena. All these experiments have in common that they cast off the idea of being incarnated in just one body. Virtual reality holds the possibility to disconnect from direct physical experiences, and allows some kind of (temporal) 'disembodiment' from the material body (see Fuchs 2014). Therefore, we may conclude, observations in virtual reality seem to render the ontology of material reality to the disposition. And this leads us to some quite interesting and reflexive effects: In VR the users are able to observe how somebody else (who is themselves) could behave in different ways.[8] Thus, a change in virtual embodiment seems to come in hand with a change to one's common modus operandi. So, the question posed at the beginning of this chapter can be asked again: To what extent does virtual reality employ multi-perspectivity not only on reality in general, but on one's identity and corporeality in particular?[9]

It is interesting to note that almost every one of the studies mentioned above depends on exactly this connection: researchers design an alternate body, which then is made available for differing perceptions and observations of a changing self. It seems to be the permanent need for orientation from an 'egocentric space' (Briscoe 2014) that allows orientation in time and space in the first place.[10] The ability to perceive another body does seem to extend to perceiving within another body. Therefore, the results of these studies should be interpreted with regard to the specific form of perception.[11] It seems as if during these VR sessions the unit of distinction between the body and mind has to reconfigure itself on the basis of the alternate body. We have to assume that the form itself changes if one side of the distinction changes. If the body, which is fundamental for any perception, changes, the appropriate mind-set changes as well (see Varela et al. 1991). In a rather abstract sense, we then may conclude: Consciousness without perception, as well as identity without a body, is inconceivable. But to make it even worse, we have to consider a recursive process: Consciousness rides on perceptions, which are provided by a body, which in turn is only observable through consciousness and perception. Or in the words of system's theory: "The co-producers [consciousness and body; J.H.] are nothing without each other" (Fuchs 2012, p. 65).

But what does that mean for society when leisure practices of being present at another place and time, and maybe even embodied in another person's body, become common experiences?

Virtual Realities as Utopian Longing and Producers of Contingency

The advent of new technology and the corresponding advent of utopian longings tend to bound together.[12] At the same time, at least since the queer studies of the 20th century, we must assume that "the potential abilities of the body always exceed the actualities a culture can allow" (Angerer 1999, p. 178). Currently, this limitation seems to be negotiated mainly in the technical arena. Prosthetics, enhancements or augmentations are the key words of today. Already with Donna Haraway (2000) it became clear that the boundaries between subject and object are especially blurred through the use of modern technology. And so it seems legitimate to assume that the idea of a 'total self', as classic modernity had promised it, more and more will disappear again. The self and its identity management become increasingly fluid through its entanglements to the diverse possibilities of technology (Bauman 2000; Turkle 2005).[13]

According to Gehlen's (1988) theory of anthropology, human beings can be understood in terms of 'deficient beings', who since the very beginning of mankind have had to compensate for their relative deficiencies. The concept of 'deficient beings' refers to at least two levels: on the one hand, the level of subjective deficiencies, which are recognized by an individual and generate the desire to overcome these by oneself; on the other hand, the level of a more objective deficiency, which is subject to a physical limitation and/or failure and therefore implies a change of the (material) world in order to fix it. Presumably, both will always come together in one way or another. But both a fantasized and a factual deficiency will fuel a longing for change. In a sense, any media practice can be observed via this anthropological frame. It does not matter whether the digital utopian places are branded as some kind of escapism, demonized as a degeneration of the West, hailed as innovative practices of therapeutic settings, or used quite trivially as mere entertainment. Like every other technical invention, virtual reality offers a variety of possible uses and—of course—an even amount of possible misuses. Thus, the ideas of liberation connected to virtual reality are not too surprising.

On the more abstract level of society, we need to examine the changes to reflexivity and identity that come with the introduction of such a technology. Virtual worlds such as computer games are per se alternate spaces for the observation of reality: by 'duplicating reality' into a fictional reality of the game and a real reality of the non-game—as Luhmann (2002) points out—the texture of reality becomes more visible (see Žižek 1995; Angerer 1999, p. 165).[14] Therefore, the introduction of virtual reality has opened up new degrees of freedom for society, enabling users to observe reality in a new way. The digital worlds are in this sense no antagonist to 'ordinary' reality; they are rather an added alternative and can only be understood in the mode of homology. Virtual reality shifts the view on 'real' reality to another standing point, and reveals the limitations and inaccessibilities of common reality. Thus, acting and observing in virtual worlds is not intertwined with some kind of loss of reality, as one might expect, but rather with a gain of reality. The reality of the virtual and the reality of the real are juxtaposed, not fighting against each other. Accordingly, VR introduced to society new possibilities for observation and more degrees of reflexive freedom.

Being There, Being Someone Else: Living in Polycontexturality of the Next Society

With the help of Spencer Brown's form theory (1969) and Luhmann's theory of distinction (1995), the determination of virtuality as a producer of a new 'quality' of reality must be confronted. Virtual reality is no simulation of reality, nor is it a mere fiction that only exists as a possible alternative.[15] Virtual worlds are real in a sense that they provide real alternatives in the here and now. Just as the image of a mirror does not present a fictional (or alternative) reality but the real reality—just from a different angle—Virtual reality presents no *possible* reality. Although, I would like to emphasize the difference between fiction and virtuality, both share some similarities with reference to possible impacts on an observer's observations. The reality of virtuality as well as the reality of fiction both hold the potential to widen a user's experience: Through virtual reality as well as through fictional reality the contingencies of one's world and the reflexivity of observations become observable! And for Western society, which is increasingly exposed to the affordances of contingencies, the use of virtual reality would be a valuable exercise in reflexivity. In virtual Reality, new and unthought-of realities can be actively tested and experienced.

When discussing the impacts of VR on practices of leisure, we clearly have to expand on Spracklen's argument for digital leisure in general (2015, pp. 74ff.). Spracklen argues, that for "the users of the Net[16], digital leisure appears to be seamlessly communicative and liberating. Users are given the appearance of being liquid surfers, shifting their focus at the click of a mouse, share their ideas and cultural interests with people in the global networks" (2015, p. 7). If we expand on the concept of being a 'liquid surfer'[17] in digital leisure, we may recognize that in the new digital playground of VR the user is provided with new possibilities for liberation through changing embodiment, personhood and being present at some place. Click, click, and click: By surfing through the realities of VR the user becomes enabled to perceive the same situation from different points of view, from within bodies of different size, age, gender, etc. With virtual reality at hand, postmodern identity becomes even more fluid. But on the other hand, we always have to remember that the realms of virtual reality are artificially made environments—many of which are built for commercial purposes. We have to assume that being present in virtual environments and communicating with virtual friends is only liberating to the extent that the technology of VR does not become a (too narrow) "form of instrumental leisure" (Spracklen 2015, p. 8), serving as the ideal ground for external surveillance of one's personal leisure.[18] The ethical principles presented by Madary and Metzinger (2016) should be considered not only by consumers and researchers but also—so it seems— by the producers of immersive experiences as well.

It can be assumed that with the help of VR the fluid and blurring boundaries between not only the virtual and the real but also the social and technical will merge together even more. From its very beginning, the socio-technological 'cyberspaces' did appear to be the ideal place for hybrid entities (Turkle 2005). If technology and sociality can no longer be separated from each other, we have to assume an increasing hybridization of socio-technical reality. In cyberspace, human people tend to be equally easily digitally embodied as artificial non-human entities. Perhaps it is for this reason the basically unlimited realities of virtuality appear to be the next frontier of human adventure and conquest?

> VR technology will eventually change not only our general image of humanity but also our understanding of deeply entrenched notions, such as 'conscious experience', 'selfhood', 'authenticity', or 'realness'. In addition, it will transform the structure of our life-world, bringing about entirely novel forms of everyday social interactions and changing the very relationship we have to our own minds. (Madary and Metzinger 2016, pp. 1ff.)

Through digital avatars, the residents of virtual reality may construct their virtual identities according to their own very personal desires for liberation from the above mentioned 'deficiencies'. Being no longer restricted by material reality, the users of VR are directed to their individual longing for being someone (else). But the technology of virtual reality not only offers new possibilities for new identities but also the possibility to harden and enhance a well-established identity. Most users will find no need to constantly change identity; but the constant opportunity itself will change one's point of view on one's identity. The central question of "Who am I?" needs to be answered in VR as well, and it appears the need for an answer becomes more and more urgent while at the same time harder to fulfil.

The new hybrid agents wearing fluid identities and inhabiting the potentially ever-changing environments of virtual reality finally lead us to the 'Cyborg's Dilemma' that Frank Biocca was concerned about 20 years ago, in the very early days of VR:

The embodiment advanced in the form of virtual environment technology can be characterized as a form of cyborg coupling. This coupling underscores what I call the cyborg's dilemma, a kind of Faustian trade off: Choose technological embodiment to amplify the body, but beware that your body schema and identity may adapt to this cyborg form. (Biocca 1997, p. 24)

Leaving behind old schemes of bodily representation and perception, the use of virtual reality shatters the concept of the one and only body. Being able to embody other beings while at the same time change, trade or share different identities in various social contexts inhabited by human as well as non-human social agents, makes formerly known mechanisms of identity management obsolete.

Unfortunately, we cannot foresee what impact that may have on a societal level. Even nowadays, the massive use of computer-mediated communications has resulted in a social structure where people are 'alone together' (Turkle 2011); at what cost this has occurred has yet to be proven. But I would like to reiterate that with the use of virtual reality we are not confronted with a loss of reality, but quite the opposite: virtual reality grants an addition to the present reality! This is just the beginning for VR and there is still a long way to go. As one VR-developer noted recently: what we see today is only the 'PONG' version of virtual reality (see Stein 2015). Further, we should not forget that VR as part of leisure activity is not restricted to simulating material reality in an almost lossless copy. The true potential of VR unfolds by using it as a new foundation for imagination, fantasy, and art—by employing its differences from material reality. So this raises the question: Will the potentially limitless worlds of virtual reality therefore hold up to a limitless amount of potential identities and embodiments? Maybe we can answer this for the time being with the ground-breaking authors Biocca and Levy (1995), p. 17): "VR is not a technology; it's a destination." Nonetheless, as a new 'technology of the self' (Foucault 1988) the many possibilities of virtual reality are already open to us today; it remains exciting to see how society and individuals will deal with this new acquisition of realities.

Notes

1. To clarify, this article does not aim at an introduction of the role of the virtual within contemporary leisure practices such as playing video games or online social networking, but rather focuses exclusively on the relatively new phenomenon of embodiment in virtual realities with the help of head-mounted displays (and appropriate accessories). See especially Spracklen (2009, 2011, 2015) for a more thorough insight to the general aspects of meaning, purpose and role of leisure (in the digital age).

2. All quotations from works for which only the German reference has been given in the list of references have been translated into English by the author.

3. While complaining about the allegedly high price of the first generation of mass market devices, one should not forget that before these VR was only available to a small elite in military facilities or research labs.

4. A common confusion may surround the concept of immersion and the concept of presence, both indicating at some way of 'getting into' the virtual environments (VE): "One clear distinction between presence and immersion [...] is provided by Slater and Wilbur (1997). They suggest that presence in a VE is inherently a function of the user's psychology, representing the extent to which an individual experiences the virtual setting as the one in which they are consciously present. On the other hand, immersion can be regarded as a quality of the system's technology, an objective measure of the extent to which the system presents a vivid virtual environment while shutting out physical reality" (Cummings and Bailenson 2016, p. 275).

5. The concept of social presence seems even more important for constructing convincing virtual worlds due to its effect of forgetting the framing of virtuality. Following the research of Wirth et al. (2007), the concept of presence has to be considered as an oscillation: "Spatial Presence is a binary experience, during which perceived self-location and, in most cases, perceived action possibilities are connected to a mediated spatial environment, and mental capacities are bound by the mediated environment instead of reality." (Wirth et al. 2007, p. 497).

6. The idea of the (full) body ownership illusion is derived from the rubber hand illusion experiments by Botvinick and Cohen (1998). There, "a rubber hand is placed on a table in front of a person and seen to be

tapped and stroked synchronously with corresponding stimulation on their out-of-sight real hand" (Bourdin et al. 2017, p. 2).

7. For an up-to-date overview and first considerations on ethical concerns regarding the use and exploration of virtual realities see Madary and Metzinger (2016).

8. See for example the findings of Peck et al. (2013), in which virtual embodiment in a different skin color significantly reduces implicit racial bias.

9. Just to make sure, I would like to mention explicitly that for sociology it may on first glance seem rather trivial that a person generates multiple identities and multiple selves. Concepts such as roles, frames, and, at the very least, the theory of functional differentiation, have been drawing for a long time a telling picture of society's multiple selves. But in comparison with these concepts of social theory, I want to emphasize that with the use of VR these modes of multiplicity become voluntary, playful, and conscious acts of spare time activity. In the end, the question arises whether the conscious changing of multiple identities also leads to a reflexive mode of the body itself. How could the experience of temporarily being someone else employ an embodiment of reflexive and multiple selves?

10. With Briscoe (2014) it becomes clear that perception has to be considered as a multimodal affair: visual feedback is relatively useless unless considered against the proprioceptive orientation of the body in time and space.

11. Here, the notion of 'form' refers to Spencer Brown's "Laws of Form" (1969) which focuses on the unit of each distinction.

12. This holds true for VR history as well. The first 'stereoscopic' goggles, which were very popular in the late 19th century, can be understood as an early ancestor of today's head mounted displays. Even if its effect may seem far less impressive than current technology, the stereoscopes of the past triggered equally utopian fantasies, as Holmes states very vividly: "At least the shutting-out of surrounding objects, and the concentration of the whole attention, which is a consequence of this, produce dreamlike exaltation of the faculties, a kind of clairvoyance, in which we seem to leave the body behind us and sail away into one strange scene after another, like disembodied spirits" (Holmes 1861).

13. From the perspective of socio-technological hybridity (Latour 2005) we have never been modern, after all. Especially with the help of actor-network theory, the different phenomena of the fusion of real corporeality

and virtual bodies can be recognized as hybrid agents, who have always been living at the boundary of reality, virtuality and fiction.

14. Luhmann, at least in the fields of statistics, art, religion and play, (2002, p. 58) attempts to conceive the distinction between virtual reality and real reality with the notion of a 'duplicated reality'. The notion of duplication has tremendous effects on society: "To the world it has the consequence that the concept of reality gets a qualifying meaning. It is only by this that reality arises, which then can be indicated, that is, distinguished from something else. Then, the world contains something which is not real in a narrow sense, but which nevertheless serves as a position for potential observers and can be observed itself. Then, it is no longer simply all that is; real by being as it is, but a special, we could say, real reality is produced by the fact that there is something which differs from it... For an observer, reality only arises when there is something in the world from which it can be distinguished; only in this way reality can become hardened in comparison with a rather fluid world of imagination" (Luhmann 2002, p. 59).

15. In her essay (2011, p. 276), media sociologist Elena Esposito makes it clear that the virtual, in contrast to a simulation, which produces 'false real objects', produces 'true virtual objects' that follow the logic of the virtual. Therefore, virtuality does not appear as 'unreal' in comparison with the real, but should be considered more as a separate form of reflection of the world on itself.

16. Spracklen defines 'Net' as more than just the material web of circuits and cables, or just the hyperlinks connecting data and information. Spracklen's 'Net' is to be regarded as an actor-network in the sense of Latour (2005), integrating both human and non-human agents such as computers, cables, users, data storages, profiles, forums, communities, etc.

17. Spracklen is clearly referencing Baumann's (2000) concept of a fluid modernity.

18. And this may be true for virtual tourism as well, as Macleod and Yoder critically point out: "Some would argue that employing virtual tourism to see, feel, taste, smell, and hear other cultures is the final step in the commodification of all culture. When items become commodified, their *inherent* use value is reduced while their value as things that can be exchanged on the free market increases. Culture could be produced, reproduced, and sold like a computer or a car tune-up. We wouldn't have to worry about the comparisons between the real culture and the virtual culture because the original would have disappeared, leaving nothing to compare" (2005, p. 173).

References

Angerer, M.-L. (1999). Neue Technologien / Neue Grenzerfahrungen: Cyberbodies. In M. Faßler (Ed.), *Alle möglichen Welten. Virtuelle Realität—Wahrnehmung—Ethik der Kommunikation* (pp. 163–182). München: Fink Verlag.

Banakou, D., Groten, R., & Slater, M. (2013). Illusory Ownership of a Virtual Child Body Causes Overestimation of Object Sizes and Implicit Attitude Changes. *PNAS, 110*(31), 12846–12851.

Baudrillard, J. (2008) [1981]. *Simulacra and Simulation*. Ann Arbor: University of Michigan Press.

Bauman, Z. (1992). *Intimations of Postmodernity*. London/New York: Routledge.

Bauman, Z. (2000). *Liquid Modernity*. Cambridge: Polity.

Biocca, F. (1997). The Cyborg's Dilemma. Progressive Embodiment in Virtual Environments. *Journal of Computer-Mediated Communication, 3*(2). https://doi.org/10.1111/j.1083-6101.1997.tb00070.x.

Biocca, F., & Levy, M. (1995). Virtual Reality as a Communication System. In F. Biocca & M. Levy (Eds.), *Communication in the Age of Virtual Reality* (pp. 15–32). Hillsdale: Lawrence Erlbaum Associates.

Blanke, O., & Metzinger, T. (2009). Full-Body Illusions and Minimal Phenomenal Selfhood. *Trends in Cognitive Sciences, 13*(1), 7–13.

Botvinick, M., & Cohen, J. (1998). Rubber Hands 'Feel' Touch That Eyes See. *Nature, 391*, 756.

Bourdin, P., Barberia, I., Oliva, R., & Slater, M. (2017). A Virtual Out-of-Body Experience Reduces Fear of Death. *PLoS One, 12*(1), e0169343. https://doi.org/10.1371/journal.pone.0169343.

Briscoe, R. (2014). Spatial Content and Motoric Significance. *Avant, 5*(2), 199–218. https://doi.org/10.12849/50202014.0109.009.

Caillois, R. (2001). *Man, Play and Games*. Chicago: University of Illinois Press.

Cummings, J., & Bailenson, J. (2016). How Immersive Is Enough? A Meta-Analysis of the Effect of Immersive Technology on User Presence. *Media Psychology, 19*(2), 272-309. https://doi.org/10.1080/15213269.2015.1015740.

Ehrsson, H. H. (2007). The Experimental Induction of Out-of-Body Experiences. *Science, 317*, 1048.

Esposito, E. (2011). Die Realität des Virtuellen. In S. Knaller & H. Müller (Eds.), *Realitätskonzepte in der Moderne. Beiträge zu Literatur, Kunst, Philosophie und Wissenschaft* (pp. 265–283). München: Fink.

Foucault, M. (1988). Technologies of the Self. In L. Martin, H. Gutman, & P. Hutton (Eds.), *Technologies of the Self. A Seminar with Michel Foucault* (pp. 16–49). Amherst: University of Massachusetts Press.

Fuchs, P. (2012). Die Form des Körpers. In M. Schroer (Ed.), *Soziologie des Körpers* (pp. 48–72). Frankfurt: Suhrkamp.

Fuchs, T. (2014). The Virtual Other. Empathy in the Age of Virtuality. *Journal of Consciousness Studies, 21*(5–6), 152–173.

Gehlen, A. (1988). *Man. His Nature and Place in the World.* New York: Columbia University Press.

Günther, G. (1979). Life as Poly-Contexturality. In G. Günther (Ed.), *Beiträge zur Grundlegung einer operationsfähigen Dialektik* (Vol. 2, pp. 283–307). Hamburg: Felix Meiner Verlag.

Haraway, D. (2000). A Cyborg Manifesto. Science, Technology and Socialist-Feminism in the Late Twentieth Century. In D. Bell & B. M. Kennedy (Eds.), *The Cybercultures Reader* (pp. 291–324). London: Routledge.

Heeter, C. (1992). Being There: The Subjective Experience of Presence. *Presence Teleoperators & Virtual Environments, 1*(2), 262–271.

Heidegger, M. (1962). *Being and Time.* New York: Harper.

Hobson, J. S. P., & Williams, P. (1997). Virtual Reality: The Future of Leisure and Tourism? *World Leisure & Recreation, 39*(3), 34–40. https://doi.org/10.1080/10261133.1997.9674077.

Holmes, O. W. (1861). Sun-Painting and Sun-Sculpture; with a Stereoscopic Trip Across the Atlantic. *Atlantic Monthly, 8*(45), 13–29.

Huizinga, J. (1980). *Homo Ludens: A Study of the Play-Element in Culture.* London: Routledge & Kegan Paul.

Kilteni, K., Groten, R., & Slater, M. (2012). The Sense of Embodiment in Virtual Reality. *Presence: Teleoperators and Virtual Environments, 21*(4), 21–87.

Latour, B. (2005). *Reassembling the Social. An Introduction to Actor-Network-Theory.* Oxford: Oxford University Press.

Lee, K. M. (2004a). Why Presence Occurs: Evolutionary Psychology, Media Equation, and Presence. *Presence: Teleoperators and Virtual Environments, 13*(4), 494–505.

Lee, K. M. (2004b). Presence, Explicated. *Communication Theory, 14*(1), 27–50.

Lenggenhager, B., Tadi, T., Metzinger, T., & Blanke, O. (2007). Video Ergo Sum. Manipulating Bodily Self-Consciousness. *Science, 24*(317), 1096–1099.

Lombard, M., & Ditton, T. (1997). At the Heart of It All: The Concept of Presence. *Journal of Computer Mediated-Communication, 3*(2). https://doi.org/10.1111/j.1083-6101.1997.tb00072.x.

Luhmann, N. (1995). *Social Systems*. Stanford: Stanford University Press.

Luhmann, N. (2002). *Die Religion der Gesellschaft*. Frankfurt: Suhrkamp.

Madary, M., & Metzinger, T. (2016). Real Virtuality: A Code of Ethical Conduct. Recommendations for Good Scientific Practice and the Consumers of VR-Technology. *Frontiers in Robotics and AI, 3*(3). https://doi.org/10.3389/frobt.2016.00003.

Macleod, D., & Yoder, D. (2005). *Issues in Recreation and Leisure: Ethical Decision Making*. Champaign: Human Kinetics.

Merleau-Ponty, M. (2005). *Phenomenology of Perception*. New York: Taylor & Francis.

Nagy, P., & Koles, B. (2014). The Digital Transformation of Human Identity: Towards a Conceptual Model of Virtual Identity in Virtual Worlds. *Convergence: The International Journal of Research into New Media Technologies, 20*(3), 276–292. https://doi.org/10.1177/1354856514531532.

Peck, T., Seinfeld, S., Aglioti, S., & Slater, M. (2013). Putting Yourself in the Skin of a Black Avatar Reduces Implicit Racial Bias. *Consciousness and Cognition, 22*(3), 779–787.

Petkova, V., & Ehrsson, H. H. (2008). If I Were You: Perceptual Illusion of Body Swapping. *PLoS One, 3*(12), e3832.

Silk, M., Millington, B., Rich, E., & Bush, A. (2016). (Re-)thinking Digital Leisure. *Leisure Studies, 35*(6), 712–723. https://doi.org/10.1080/02614367.2016.1240223.

Slater, M., & Wilbur, S. (1997). A Framework for Immersive Virtual Environments (FIVE): Speculations on the Role of Presence in Virtual Environments. *Presence: Teleoperators and Virtual Environments, 6*(6), 603–616.

Slater, M., Perez-Marcos, D., Ehrsson, H. H., & Sanchez-Vives, M. V. (2009). Inducing Illusory Ownership of a Virtual Body. *Frontiers in Neuroscience, 3*(2), 214–220.

Spencer Brown, G. (1969). *Laws of Form*. London: Allen & Unwin.

Spracklen, K. (2009). *The Meaning and Purpose of Leisure. Habermas and Leisure at the End of Modernity*. London: Palgrave Macmillan.

Spracklen, K. (2011). *Constructing Leisure: Historical and Philosophical Debates*. London: Palgrave Macmillan.

Spracklen, K. (2015). *Digital Leisure, the Internet and Popular Culture. Communities and Identities in a Digital Age*. London: Palgrave Macmillan.

Steed, A., Pan, Y., Zisch, F., & Steptoe, W. (2016). The Impact of a Self-Avatar on Cognitive Load in Immersive Virtual Reality. *IEEE Virtual Reality (VR)*, 67–76. https://doi.org/10.1109/VR.2016.7504689.

Stein, J. (2015). The Surprising Joy of Virtual Reality. And Why It's About to Change the World. *TIME, 186*(6), 32–41.

Steuer, J. (1992). Defining Virtual Reality: Dimensions Determining Telepresence. *Journal of Communication, 42*(4), 73–93.

Sutherland, I. E. (1965). The Ultimate Display. *Proceedings of IFIP Congress,* 506–508.

Turkle, S. (2005). *The Second Self. Computers and the Human Spirit.* Cambridge/ London: MIT Press.

Turkle, S. (2011). *Alone Together. Why We Expect More from Technology and Less from Each Other.* New York: Basic Books.

Varela, F., Thompson, E., & Rosch, E. (1991). *The Embodied Mind: Cognitive Science and Human Experience.* Boston: MIT Press.

Wirth, W., Hartmann, T., Böcking, S., Vorderer, P., Klimmt, C., Schramm, H., Saari, T., Laarni, J., Ravaja, N., Gouveia, F., Biocca, F., Sacau, A., Jäncke, L., Baumgartner, T., & Jäncke, P. (2007). A Process Model of the Formation of Spatial Presence Experiences. *Media Psychology, 9*(3), 493–525.

Witmer, B. G., & Singer, M. J. (1998). Measuring Presence in Virtual Environments: A Presence Questionnaire. *Presence: Teleoperators and Virtual Environments, 7*(3), 225–240.

Žižek, S. (1995). *On Virtual Sex and Related Matters.* Welcome to the Wired World: ars electronica 95. http://90.146.8.18/en/archives/festival_archive/ festival_catalogs/festival_artikel.asp. Accessed 25 Jan 2018.

8

Video Games in the Family Context: How Do Digital Media Influence the Relationship Between Children and Their Parents?

M. A. Damian Gałuszka

Introduction

Video games have a relevant place in contemporary social space. They are "the supreme example of the technologies of simulation entering the sphere of popular culture" (Dovey and Kennedy 2006, p. 13) and a foundation for a prospective sector in the global market according to *The Global Games Market* report (de Heij et al. 2013). Prior reports on video games markets suggest that video gaming has become an important part of the daily routines of many people, both young (Lenhart et al. 2008) and adult (ESA 2016; ISFE 2012). Video games are a medium attracting a growing number of users. More than 50 years have passed since the first video game—Polish authors debate whether it was tick-tack-toe (Mańkowski 2010) or *Spacewar* (Filiciak 2010)—and video games have undergone an incredible transformation, not only in technological terms but also regarding cultural status and their role in the modern media sphere.

M. A. Damian Gałuszka (✉)
The Jagiellonian University Institute of Sociology, Kraków, Poland

© The Author(s) 2018
A. Beniwal et al. (eds.), *Global Leisure and the Struggle for a Better World*, Leisure Studies in a Global Era, https://doi.org/10.1007/978-3-319-70975-8_8

The changing role of video games, the increasing involvement in gaming seen among the general population, and my own experiences (as a child who played video games and as an adult gamer and researcher) have directed my research interests to the issue of the role of video games in a contemporary family. This chapter is based on data from my research project, which was divided into two main parts: quantitative (a questionnaire survey among young gamers) and qualitative (interviews with parents). The research was implemented in 2014 among Polish families, therefore the conclusions are presented in that context. This may be perceived as a significant limitation of the research, however this approach allows development of profound insight due to the qualitative method, focusing on personal histories and relationships between family members, and provides comprehension of the issue as experienced in Poland. Moreover, the research provides data concerning different layers of family life; issues of relationships related to video games, differences in attitudes among children and parents, communication, parental control and the role of social environment are all discussed.

The Concept of a Video Game

The term "video game", quite relevant to this research, should be examined first, but defining a video game is not simple due to the semantic complexity of the term. Dominika Urbańska-Galanciak, a Polish game researcher, notes that in the case of video games "we are dealing with an imprecise, unclear and extremely capacious concept, whose ambiguity arises from the abundance of contents and connotations associated with it"[1] (2009, p. 28). Moreover, the ludological definition of video games is complicated by the diversity and multiplicity of aspects constituting the basis of their description. Espen Aarseth, one of the most recognised game researchers, described the field of game research as "interdisciplinarily and empirically varied to the extreme" (2004, p. 1). The classical definition of a game was proposed in *Homo Ludens*, published in 1938 by Johan Huizinga. Huizinga noted that "genuine, pure play is one of the main bases of civilisation" (1980, p. 5). According to Huizinga, the entire social environment has ludic characteristics; play—he did not distinguish between the concepts of *play* and *game*, both of which are present in English and Polish—is primary to culture and pervades it from the beginning of civilisation (Huizinga 1980, p. 1). The author described 'play' as "a free activity...quite consciously outside 'ordinary' life, ...'not serious', but at the same time absorbing the player intensely and utterly...an activity connected with no material interest [and from which] no profit can be gained." ...[which] proceeds within its own proper boundaries of time and space according to fixed rules and in an orderly manner...[and] promotes the formation of social groupings which tend to surround themselves with secrecy" (Huizinga 1980, p. 13).

The above definition of play does not refer directly to contemporary video games, but was substantial to the constitution of ludology, its theory and methodology. Huizinga's definition was, among six other definitions of games, taken into consideration by Danish game researcher and designer Jesper Juul, who aimed to create a new definition of games based on previous ones, one "capable of explaining what relates computer games to other games and what happens on the borders of the field of games" (Juul 2003, no pages). Analysis, comparison and categorisation of previously published definitions have led Juul to a new concept based on six components describing every game: rules; variable and quantifiable outcome; values assigned to possible outcomes; gamer's effort; gamer's emotional attachment to outcome; and negotiable consequences (Juul 2003). A functional concept of games emphasising the relationship between a video game and a gamer was previously offered by Espen Aarseth, who proposed an original concept of games as "facilitators that structure player behaviour, and whose main purpose is enjoyment" (Aarseth 2007, p. 130).

Key Categories for the Analysis of Video Games

Video games, as a new digital medium, are characterized by certain features. Since the emergence of the concept of a *new medium* in the mid-1980s, the term has been considered an attempt to describe technology-based changes in the field of media (Szpunar 2012, pp. 59–61). Furthermore, Lev Manovich describes recognised characteristics of digital media based on five principles: numerical representation, modularity, automation, variability and cultural transcoding (2001, p. 44). How do these principles refer to video games? Video games are numerical representations as they are objects processed via digital devices and based on binary code produced by their authors, i.e. video game developers. The structure of video games can be considered modular as they are composed of multiple elements (like game engines, pictures, sounds or databases), which are designed and produced by developers or modified by gamers, using professional development tools or various game-modding tools. Video games are also developed in a partially automated process. Developers are able to improve the development process using various tools, such as *SpeedTree* vegetation modelling technology. The next quality of new media proposed by Manovich is variability, described as the existence of a media object not only in one, fixed version, but in "different, potentially infinite, versions" (2001, p. 56).

The category of variability seems worth expanding on. In the case of video games, there are a few domains where variability manifests. Gameplay may be variable as each subsequent launching of a video game may result in a different version of the contest. This occurs mainly in games that contain some elements of randomness, but also in games that allow the player to change some parameters (e.g. simulators, sandbox games). For instance, the sex or statistics of the main character, levels (maps), environmental conditions, etc., may be changed. Furthermore, video games are technologically variable as one title is often published on various hardware platforms (personal computers, stationary and portable consoles, tablets or smartphones). As a result, some differences in game design, control methods or settings are observed between different versions of the same video game.

Manovich's last digital media principle is cultural transcoding, which means that the new media consists of two layers: a "cultural" and "computer" layer (2001, p. 63). Culture-based elements—such as story, plot or point of view—belong to the cultural layer, while elements related to data transmitted through digital devices—such as sorting, compiling, compressing, functions and variables, data structures and technical specifications—compose the computer layer. Both layers interact with each other, hence the methods for production and distribution of the new media via digital devices might influence and alter the cultural layer. To summarise, video games can be perceived as a logical collection of files in a computer layer and a set of graphics, sounds and stories in a cultural layer. On one hand, video games are a binary code which is understandable to digital devices, on the other hand they are images, texts and meanings perceived and interpreted by players. In other words, video games consist of many layers, such as "rule-based space" and "mediated space" (see Nitsche 2008, pp. 15–16).

The concept of interactivity is also among the most important traits of video games. Interactivity is a feature widely associated with new media, including video games, while at the same time a widely criticised analytical conception. As Manovich stated, when "used in relation to computer-based media, the concept of interactivity is a tautology…Therefore, referring to computer media as interactive is pointless—it simply means stating the most basic fact about computers" (2001, p. 71). Therefore, I will not present a detailed explanation of this concept, but briefly explain interactivity as a type of relationship between a video game and a gamer that enables—through the interface of a particular application—not only passive reception of messages, but also sending the gamer's feedback reactions and messages to the game's programme. Espen Aarseth proposed a convincing term to describe the relationship between video games and gamers: ergodic, which derives from the Greek words *ergon* and *hodos*, meaning "work" and "path" (Aarseth 1997, p. 1). This concept relates to the phenomenon of hypertext literature and describes a type of relationship between the text and the reader in which the reader has to take some additional effort or actions, in addition to interpreting the meaning of the text. Aarseth pointed that reading an ergodic text differs from reading a lineal one because a ergodic text is that in "which a chain of events (a path, a sequence of actions, etc.) has been produced by the nontrivial efforts of one or more individuals or mechanisms" (1997, p. 94). The reader creates meanings using their own work and choices. In the ergodic medium there is no fixed course of narration, but various alternatives narrowed to a multidimensional event space that "unfolds through the negotiation of this space by text and user" (Aarseth 1997, p. 114).

Finally, the concept of immersion should be addressed. Immersion is usually considered a primary factor of the relationship between a video game and a gamer. Gordon Calleja suggests this phenomenon is a crucial part of gamers' experience, although he also notes that it is a "particularly awkward" concept as it can be applied to non-ergodic media (paintings, cinema), where it provides "forms of engagement that are qualitatively different from those of game environments" (2011, p. 18). Here I use the definition coined by Janet Murray, who refers to physical feelings to explain immersion:

> Immersion is a metaphorical term derived from the physical experience of being submerged in water. We seek the same feeling from a psychologically immersive experience that we do from a plunge in the ocean or swimming pool: the sensation of being surrounded by a completely other reality, as different as water is from air, that takes over all of our attention, our whole perceptual apparatus. (1997, pp. 98–99)

How is the effect of immersion created within the 3D reality? A detailed explanation was proposed by Alison McMahan, who argues that the sense of immersion results from a combination of three conditions:

1. the user's expectations of the game or environment must match the environment's conventions fairly closely;
2. the user's actions must have a non-trivial impact on the environment;
3. the conventions of the world must be consistent, even if they don't match those of 'meatspace' (McMahan 2003, pp. 68–69).

A Video Game in Relation to the User and the Family Context

Let's begin with the question "who is a gamer?" Espen Aarseth tries to answer this question by referring to the categories of potential player and actual player (2007, p. 130). Anyone may become a player, but only by adopting the structures and rules of the video game do they become actual players. Subjection to the regime of a game's system defines the player, who steps into this role by learning the structures and rules of a particular video game. Aarseth points to the fixed ontological status of a video game, because neither the rules nor structure change, regardless of whether anyone plays it. Thus, the scope of player activity—their subjectivity and freedom of decision-making—is limited by the nature of a video game, which seems to further a deterministic vision of player function. Aarseth proposes an additional model, however, of the implied player, which "can be seen as a role made for the player by the game, a set of expectations that the player must fulfil for the game to 'exercise its effect'" (2007, p. 132). These expectations are shaped by various elements of each video game, such as the user interface or representations of in-game avatars (in most video games avatars represent characters, but may also be vehicles or even more abstract things). The concept of the implied player encompasses the majority of potential gameplay experiences, because these experiences originate from a path designed by developers for players to follow. Therefore, it is a kind of controlled experience. Nevertheless, the so-called "secret area" exists, because games are "machines that sometimes allow their players to do unexpected things, often just because these actions are not explicitly forbidden...they are not part of the game's intended repertoire, and would in most cases have been rendered impossible if the game designers could have predicted them" (Aarseth 2007, p. 132) This allows for the possibility of transgressive play, which may be understood as the implied player's rebellion against "the tyranny of the game" (ibid.).

Now I would like to focus on a broader family context by addressing the concept of technicity, which refers to "the interconnectedness of identity and technological competence" (Dovey and Kennedy 2006, p. 64). The authors of this concept, Jon Dovey and Helen W. Kennedy, argue that technicity is of primary most importance for understanding contemporary cultural phenomena. Technicity is expressed in people's habits related to technologies (for instance smartphones, video games, computers, digital media, etc.) and, combined with their tastes, aptitudes and propensities, makes possible affiliations and connections with like-minded people (ibid.). Dovey and Kennedy believe that technicity can be "understood as a site of cultural hegemony in the twenty-first century" (ibid.). Moreover, they propose two specific technicities—represented by the characters of the hacker (recalling William Gibson's identities of people who are able to use technology in innovative and unexpected ways) and the cyborg (refers to Donna Haraway manifesto where the idea of new and intimate connection between humans and machines were presented)—from which the figure of digital media enthusiast emerges (ibid., pp. 65–67). These figures might be partially described in other words by the concept of digital natives, coined by Marc Prensky's (2001). We may assume that many Polish primary school students, who have grown up in the era of technicity hegemony, are digital natives, but what about their parents? For many Polish families it seems the demarcation line between the digital natives and the digital immigrants cuts across the parent-child relationship. The digital gap divides students and their parents, who are not prepared to cope with the challenges of the information age. In 2011, the Polish Chancellery of the Prime Minister published a report on the situation of young Poles, which highlighted problems of self-socialisation, among various issues. The report criticises relationships between parents and adolescents: "Parents focus on work and gainful activity has become an essential cause for which they devote less time to family life, leaving more space for young people" (Szafraniec 2011, p. 31). Among other aspects, the report mentions intensive engagement in the media environment observed among children and adolescents, based on individual decisions often beyond constant parental control (vide Arnett 1995). Krystyna Szafraniec illustrated this divide in the context of Polish adolescents by referring to Giroux's concept of the "abandoned generation" and Tenbruck's theory of self-socialisation (Szafraniec 2015, pp. 204–206). Moreover, some research suggests that parents are not particularly enthusiastic about playing video games with their children (Lenhart et al. 2008, pp. 37–38; ISFE 2012, p. 20). One Polish report concerning children's free time demonstrated that Polish parents seldom play video games with their children. Parents were asked about their preferences in terms of spending leisure time with their child as well as the most common activities shared with their child. For both categories playing video games was the least popular response (approx. 10%), far behind watching movies (approx. 30%) and even shopping (approx. 17%) (Squla.pl 2016, p. 18). Although difficult to fully explain, the limited engagement of parents with video games might be associated with generational differences (dissimilarity in socialisation resulting from different media environments: the mass media's era in the case of parents and the digital media's era in the case of children) and correlated to divergence in their technicities.

Some consequences of this divide are also observed in the educational context. Mariusz Przybyła argues that in the Polish education system, "the digital gap between technologically advanced youth and some teachers is a fact" and, due to its rigid structures, school is not able to effectively respond to dynamic changes in new technologies (2012, pp. 204–205). In turn, Marcin M. Drews refers to the distinction between two types of societies, i.e. the industrial society (the generation of parents and teachers) and the information society (the generation of students and pupils), and criticises the failure of the older generation to teach digital skills to the young members of the information society. As a result, young people have to develop their digital skills on their own—usually by satisfying morbid curiosity and seeking entertainment rather than via reliable and safe education (Drews 2008, pp. 59–60). These forms of entertainment are becoming increasingly virtualised, as Henry Jenkins described based on the example of his 16-year-old son, who spent more time playing in video game worlds than enjoying traditional playgrounds in the physical world (Jenkins 2006, pp. 330–333).

These considerations refer to the topic of cultural change. Margaret Mead developed the concept of culture as divided into three different types: postfigurative, in which children learn primarily from their forebears, cofigurative, in which both children and adults learn from their peers, and prefigurative, in which adults learn also from their children (Mead 1970, p. 1). My own long-term experiences as well as observations conducted among other families led me to conclude that for many children who play video games peers rather than parents are the most relevant reference group—which is typical of cofigurative culture. Mead argued that cofiguration is caused by a break in the postfigurative system, which can be due to ignorance of new technologies among mature and elderly people (Mead 1970, pp. 25–26). This explanation corresponds with my own observations and intuitions and has led me to William Ogburn's idea of cultural lag, according to which the development of material culture (technology) is always ahead of the progress in the aspects of intangible culture (art, play, science, education, norms and values) (Ogburn 1922, pp. 200–212). Rapid cultural changes embedded in technology bring not only technical novelties but also new forms of leisure (e.g. video games). While similar to traditional games in some respects, video games represent, as I have mentioned, novel qualities and require new cultural competencies that are gained with some effort. Unfortunately, not all parents are able to gain these (for various reasons). This generation gap concerning video game play can be reduced through a dialogue between children and their parents. However, according to Mead, its success depends on awareness of differences in language used by young people and adults. Only awareness of differences in meanings and experiences can allow for fruitful listening, understanding and questioning between the generations. At this point the prefigurative culture takes shape, in which it is "the child—and not the parent and grandparent—that represents what is to come". (Mead 1970, p. 68).

Research Issues and Methodology[2]

A review of literature suggests that some research involving children and family oriented analysis of video games has been conducted. However, some shortcomings in this area do exist. Examples include well-known reports like *Videogames in Europe: 2012 Consumer Study* (ISFE 2012) and *Essential Facts About the Computer and Video Game Industry* by ESA (Entertainment Software Association). Due to the quantitative nature of these reports, it is difficult in both cases to discuss an in-depth analysis of the phenomenon. The basic purpose of my research is to elicit deep knowledge about the function of video games in context of the family. I do this by analysing the family[3] context through the description of relations between a parent and a child, in reference to video games. I am also aware of the importance of the social environment that surrounds a family. However, a family is an institution that consists of many complex relations between different social actors (parents, children, grandparents, cousins and more) and serves multiple functions, including sexual regulations, reproduction, economic cooperation, socialisation, education and emotional support (Anastasiu 2012). Hence, the need to ask a number of specific research questions:

- How can young gamers living in the studied families be characterised?
- What is the level of parental knowledge about the medium of video games?

- How are video games present in verbal communication between the child and the parent?
- What is the role of video games in the life of a particular family?
- Does the issue of gaming among young people extend beyond the family context?

Satisfactory answers to these questions are not be possible without qualitative research, inscribed in the perspective of symbolic interactionism. There are a few reasons for this decision: the micro-social nature of the research area, a focus on the category of social interaction, an interest in the role of communication in human relationships (Babbie 2013, pp. 61–62). Selecting the perspective of symbolic interactionism entails the possibility of referring to useful concepts, such as a relational potential that is a "willingness to adopt certain behaviours at the time of interaction with other individual" and consists of ideas, a system of meanings, interpretive schemes and descriptions of roles which the interaction partner owns (Pawłowska 2006, pp. 8–9). My study was divided into two parts:

- Part I: exploratory in-depth interviews with parents,
- Part II: an anonymous survey, filled independently by the child of the interviewed parent.

Researchers often recommended combining quantitative and qualitative analysis in studies focused on the family (Tyszka 1997, p. 698); as such, this study takes advantage of methodological triangulation (Silverman and Marvasti 2008, pp. 156–157). According to Krzysztof Koniecki, the qualitative interviews "allow finding out about directly achieved interactional episodes, events, work processes, life experiences..." (Konecki 2000, p. 144). In my study I used in-depth interviews and sought information using a standardised list. I also prepared a questionnaire for children, which consisted of 20 open, semi-open and closed questions. The survey allowed for a comparative analysis of the declarations of children and their parents. This survey was ancillary and did not change the qualitative nature of the research project.

The study was conducted in the Sub-Carpathian region in a town known as Krosno and among several families living in a rural commune called Wojaszówka in the spring of 2014. I selected adults raising children who play video games, which in practice meant using a non-probability sampling technique called snowball sampling (Babbie 2013, pp. 129–130). During the field phase of the research, I performed 24 interviews of varying length (between 45 minutes to more than 90 minutes) with parents. I also conducted 31 (23 with boys and 8 with girls) surveys with their children. The average age of the surveyed children was 11 years, with the majority attending primary school. The choice of this age group was motivated by the desire to explore the interaction between children and their parents in the period of life when parental authority and the possibility of its enforcement are relatively large. The critical role of early childhood in the process of socialisation of an individual was an additional factor.

The elicited data were analysed based on the scheme proposed by Kathy Charmaz. In practice, recordings of the interviews were transcribed and then the textual data was coded and sorted to produce memos that led to more abstract constructs, such as categories or theoretical samplings (Charmaz 2006, p. 11). Both types of data—from the survey and interviews—were processed via computer software: Microsoft Excel and MaxQDA, which is a CAQDA (computer assisted qualitative data analysis software) programme designed to improve the process of qualitative analysis.

Ethical considerations are an important element of every study. They are even more significant when children are engaged in a research project. According to Bram Oppenheim, the "basic ethical principle governing data collections is that no harm should come to the respondents as a result of their participation in the research" (1992, p. 83). I followed this principle throughout the field research: participants received all necessary information about the study, I obtained written consent from parents to perform the survey with their children and also the rights of participants (anonymity, confidentiality, refusing to be interviewed, etc.) were respected.

Parents vs. Children in the Context of Video Games: A Brief Comparative Analysis

I would like to begin with a brief comparative analysis of the declarations of children and their parents participating in my research project. The surveyed children perceive computers as an inseparable element of their daily routine. They use them on a daily basis, with about 40% of respondents spending a few hours daily in front of a computer screen. Different proportions were observed among the surveyed parents. They generally avoid modern digital devices, except for work-related usage. Typical PCs or laptops are not the only digital devices children use to play video games. Mobile devices, such as smartphones and tablets, are becoming increasingly popular. Parents, however, often lack the necessary digital skills to use not only mobile devices and video game consoles, but even well-known PCs. Parental knowledge and authority are essentially limited to familiar appliances, like a TV. Moving on to video games, it should be noted that young gamers prefer sports and arcade games and avoid more demanding genres like simulators, educational, logic or role-playing games. Unfortunately, some video games played by children are only suitable for adult gamers. In their responses, kids reported playing adult themed games such as[4] *Grand Theft Auto, Call of Duty, Counter Strike, Saints Row, Contract Wars, Postal* and *Medal of Honor*. Although the research group was small, I observed some gender-related differences in the choice of video games. Girls were less likely to choose games abundant in violent or brutal images, as opposed to boys. However, parents who played video games preferred simple titles not requiring special manual skills or knowledge of the principles of the game, such as *Mario, Solitaire*, or mobile or social network games (*Farmville*, etc.). In a small group of respondents, the parent and the child tended to choose a similar or even the same game (e.g. a father and his son playing first person shooters like *Battlefield*). Unfortunately, joint play of video games is a very rare activity, usually initiated by the child if it occurs. Most parents are not interested in video games and resist engaging in this hobby. In turn, children over time abandon attempts to engage their parents in video game play. This may result from a closed attitude among parents, but also from the rapid development of gaming skills in young people who usually have a lot of time to accumulate their gaming capital (see Consalvo 2007, pp. 3–4) in single player games or multiplayer (or co-op) modes with peers. Therefore, parents usually do not become digital partners with their children, who instead share and inspire interests with peers. Negative consequences arising from this situation are not limited to missed opportunities to build relationships between the older (parents) and the younger (children) generation, but also include considerable concerns in the field of parental control. Nearly two-thirds of all games mentioned by the families were downloaded via the Internet (primarily among boys, the surveyed girls were less interested in downloading video games) or borrowed from peers, and so might be excluded from proper parental control. Interviews with parents showed that their ability to control online or mate-based sources of video games is very limited. Their frequent contact with violent and brutal images is alarming, though not surprising in the light of games played by the surveyed children. Nearly half of the surveyed children were exposed to this kind of content in video games. Less often young gamers felt fear during playing, and more than a quarter encountered vulgar expressions.

Relational Potential of Parents: Exploration

After presenting the general comparison, I would like to proceed to an in-depth analysis of the most important aspects of video games' presence in the studied families. I will begin with the level of parental knowledge and skills in this context. I will quote Interlocutor A (see code explanations at the end of the text; at the same time I would like to note that I will refer to direct quotations only to a minor extent, mainly providing my own interpretation of the raw data) to start with the most iconic example, who confessed: "I just don't know these games, I do not go into it at all…" The study revealed that such an attitude is not an exception but rather the norm among the parents interviewed, which has a multiplicity of implications for the relationship between the parent and the child. Therefore, we should consider the shortcomings of parental knowledge, primarily illustrated by serious difficulties recalling video game titles played by children or a vague and descriptive nature of knowledge of video games ("a kind of game in which the gamer builds Lego blocks" instead of providing the actual title of a specific video game, i.e. *Minecraft*). Young gamers, however, can easily provide the titles of games they play, including those in English—which seems problematic for adults (most adult respondents had significant difficulties with the foreign language). These shortcomings are probably related to the fact that the parents learn about video games primarily through accidental observations of children playing games or during occasional conversations with them. This has an impact on the nature of parental knowledge, which mainly consists of conjectures and unconfirmed (by the child or independently) facts. Superficial knowledge of video games is associated with lack of skills in other areas. Some parents openly admitted that their children had better developed digital skills. An inability to browse the content of digital devices (mainly computers) and search for installed video games is quite common among parents. These technical shortcomings relate to the parents' incomplete and descriptive knowledge about video games in that some parents would have difficulty not only searching through the device, but also assessing whether the installed application is a video game (difficulties in interpreting symbolic transmissions, such as game icons). On the other hand, most children are skilled enough to independently access video games. Even an 8-year-old (the youngest respondent) has no difficulty in downloading a game from the Internet, installing and then configuring it to their own preferences. Moreover, if multiple devices that can be used to play are available at home, children are likely to use this opportunity and freely switch from PCs to consoles or mobile appliances (smartphones, tablets). This raises questions about the effectiveness of socialisation of the children concerning media use; due to the described lack of skills, parents are sometimes unable to verify whether their child fulfilled their instructions. For example, discussing playing a banned video game, Interlocutor B mentioned:

> No, it was the second time. The first time I caught him I told him to delete the game completely and then he began with that racing game. And last week I went upstairs, he did not have time to turn off the game because he had the headphones on and did not hear me coming so I again caught him playing the same banned game.

Child-Parent Communication and Video Games

Video game-related communication between a parent and child is an important issue. In terms of daily communication, the surveyed parents mainly focus on problems with their children, such as long-term computer use, a delay in finishing a video game, requesting access to the device. Concerns of my interlocutors focused mainly on risk of the child's addiction to video games or the transfer of negative behaviours from games into the physical world. Concerns about the disappearance of direct relationships with peers or diminished importance of traditional (physical) play compared to video games were also expressed. Therefore, parents avoid, as defined by one of the interlocutors, positive stimulation of their children's gaming. If they speak about games, the context is rather negative. They warn their children against the risk of addiction, aggression and health consequences (headaches, visual deterioration). Overall, the intergenerational verbal communication between the surveyed parents and their children is rather situational, instrumental, limited to simple language codes. Children usually ask their parents for permission to play a game, turn on the device or buy a new game. They sometimes talk about events or objects in the game world or explain the rules of the game. Children also expand their language code by adopting some English words or specific video game terminology, which may be difficult for parents to interpret. On the other hand, parents are primarily focused on messages are related to their obligation to educate and control their children. Situational messages as a response to the gaming requests from children, as described above, are most frequent. Parents do not get involved in longer, in-depth conversations, but mainly limit themselves to short commands, except for those parents who share a passion for games with their children. During analysis of the research material, I noted a very important communication scheme, which I call a controlled information flow. A good illustration of this phenomenon is a fragment of a conversation with Interlocutor C:

> Where does my son get information about games? I know from my son only about this one game we have. My husband is not interested in it either, so he only knows about 'FIFA', and our son probably learns about games from his peers, probably some sports newspapers or from the Internet.

Thus, in the controlled flow of information, the parental "window" to the world of virtual entertainment is controlled by children to a large extent.

In turn, the child will derive unreliable and uncertain knowledge from the Internet and peers, and share some information with the parent, to a greater or lesser degree, at their own discretion.

Parental Control in the Surveyed Families

Care and education are some of the most important functions of family. Thus, I will focus mainly on the issue of controlling children's access to video games. Most of the interviewees reported setting limits on time their children spent in front of the screen. However, the results of the survey among children show that this control is ineffective in all families I visited. Computer time was at least two hours daily for nearly half of the surveyed children. In addition to time limitations, parents should pay attention to the content of video games used by their children. Unfortunately, this form of parental control is even more neglected. Analysis of the survey results showed that some children played games intended for adults only. I found during conversations with parents that although some of them are aware of this fact, they consciously allow their children to use such video games. The gaps in parental knowledge of video games, focusing only on the superficial (audio-visual) aspects of games, and depreciation of video games to the level of harmless entertainment might lead to situations where daily, several-hour gaming sessions are not perceived as signs of growing addiction. The same factors may be responsible for allowing children to play games with age and content ratings inappropriate for the age of the child. These are examples of parental role conflict. Although adults try to provide their children with conditions for proper development and entertainment, they often fail to control access to video games. This is seen in the methods used to limit and control this access. The majority of surveyed children claimed that their parents rely on a chance to peek into the room or peek over the shoulder to see the screen. Although this may seem relatively easy, it turns out to be highly inefficient. On seeing something disturbing in the game, parents may tell their children to uninstall the game, but these instructions are not always executed. A similar method involves overhearing a child who is playing a game. However, some children play in their own rooms, and with the use of headphones, which greatly limits parental control ability. These methods may delude a parent into a false sense of control. As discussed, one feature of video games are a variability in terms of technology and gameplay. In practice, this means that at one point the gameplay might resemble a racing game, which would not raise parental objections, whereas a few seconds later the game may involve brutal elimination of opponents. The vast majority of the surveyed parents avoided control methods requiring some technological competence. Securing a computer with a password, web browser history analysis, or using specialised parental control software are methods essentially absent in the investigated families.

The surveys showed that websites are the most important source of both information about video games and games themselves (downloading). Children visit these websites often, whereas their parents have virtually no knowledge of their content. Moreover, children acquire information and games mainly from their peers. For obvious reasons, adults are excluded from this type of intra-group communication, which is another factor limiting parental knowledge about their children's gaming activities.

Video Games and the Social Environment of the Family

The final issue I discuss is a limited attempt to pursue the analysis further, to the social environment of the family.

In the survey, most children declared that they also played video games outside their homes, mostly in their classmates' houses. Playing video games outside the home is associated with several problems; lack of parental control is one of them. Unfortunately, parents accept this situation without exchanging information about games played by their children. A voluntary confession by a child is usually the only source of information about their gaming activity outside their home. However, the quoted titles are usually unfamiliar to the parents. The interviews revealed that the long-term presence of television in family life has been the basis for parents to acquire certain educational competencies, including limitation of access to undesirable content (mainly sexual or pornographic), setting up parental lock on some TV channels, watching of movies and TV series together, checking information about TV programs watched (e.g. via teletext or electronic program guides). However, these parents generally seem to lack a similar initiative for computer games. Moreover, adults often interpret and assess video games in a way more appropriate to traditional media. They limit their assessment only to the visual aspects of games. The parents surveyed referred to the audio-visual fictitiousness of electronic games. According to some interviewed, death or killing people in games are not "real", meaning that they sometimes look realistic, but are not portrayed as dramatically as in films. However, parents are not aware that films do not require active involvement from players, as opposed to games. At this point I should mention one more issue often raised by parents: the lack of school support. The vast majority of parents reported that school does not deal with issues related to video games. Exceptions include situations associated with students' aggression, the use of mobile devices during lessons (this is not welcome in Poland) or meetings concerning Internet-related threats. More aware parents have specific expectations from institutions, e.g. as Interlocutor D said:

> I would like to learn more about, for example, advice for parents or all carers. About how to deal with children's access to games or computer, what is good and what is bad. I understand that no one will give me some golden definition, but a few rules or knowledge in this regard.

Summary

The analogy with Ogburn's and Mead's concepts cited above becomes obvious after presentation of the most important findings from the study. The lack of sustainable development in the areas of the material and immaterial culture is reflected in the daily practices of the surveyed families. Access to modern technology is not difficult, and popular devices such as smartphones, tablets and game consoles make it even easier. Those who are responsible for shaping the minds of young people, helping them gain computer skills and directing their curiosity to safe areas of the new media space also need guidance, as they were socialised in the environment of mass media, television in particular. The current situation in these families inscribes to the characteristics of Mead's cofigurative culture. Rapid changes in the media, particularly digital media, make parents fall behind children's interests and activities, with the key role played by peer groups. This situation produces many parental problems. Mead believed that dialogue can be a solution here. The analysis of the communication process between parents and children, however, shows that this dialogue does not occur. Why? It seems that both sides of this social interaction have different relational potentials and face disagreement in technicities. Their resources of social imagery are the origins of different conclusions about video games, which often lead to conflicts rather than mutual understanding. The surveyed parents rather support the asymmetric nature of their relationship with the child, in which caregivers have a superior position. Unfortunately, there seem to be no attempts to break such schemes, to try to play the role of another player, an opponent or a partner in the game. Therefore, it is difficult to expect a transition from the cofigurative to the prefigurative culture, in which the younger generation plays the key role.

It is also worth considering involving the school in the improvement of child-parent relationships in the context of video games. Sharing reliable knowledge, demystifying the image of video games, improving practical skills among parents—these are just some of the measures that can be undertaken by schools. These actions, supported by the authority of a teacher or other expert, might encourage parents to engage in their child's gaming hobby. Initiatives like these are also likely to have a positive impact on the quality and effectiveness of parental control in many families.

Referenced Interviews

A – a woman, age about 35 years, a 4-person family, very good financial situation, two sons in primary school age, her husband is a manager.

B – a mother of a 12-year-old boy, age about 40 years, 5-person family, average financial situation, children school age, she is a housewife and her husband is a labourer.

C – a mother of a 13-year-old video game player, age about 30 years, 4-person family, good financial situation, children school age, parents have higher education, mother is a primary school teacher.

D – a male, age about 45 years, 5-person family, very good financial situation, children school age, he is a financial director and his wife is a manager.

Notes

1. All quotes from Polish texts were translated by the author of this chapter due to the lack of English versions. Moreover, it should be noted that this chapter is a partially modified and expanded version of a previous work published in the Polish journal "Culture and Education" (Gałuszka 2016).
2. This study was conducted in the framework of my undergraduate work at the Faculty of Humanities of AGH University of Science and Technology.
3. A family typical for modern Polish society, which is a monogamous, patrilineal and to some extent (often still extended) nuclear family, and the impact of video games on its functioning.
4. All these titles are games made only for adults. They are classified for age category "+18"—according to PEGI (Pan European Game Information) video game content rating system.

References

Aarseth, E. (1997). *Cybertext: Perspectives on Ergodic Literature*. London: Johns Hopkins University Press.

Aarseth, E. (2004). *Playing Research: Methodological Approaches to Game Analysis*. Aalborg: Aalborg University.

Aarseth, E. (2007). *I Fought the Law: Transgressive Play and the Implied Player*. Available at: http://www.digra.org/wp-content/uploads/digital-library/07313. 03489.pdf. Accessed 15 Feb 2017.

Anastasiu, I. (2012). The Social Functions of the Family. *Euromentor Journal—Studies about Education, 2*, 133–139.

Arnett, J. J. (1995). Adolescents' Uses of Media for Self-Socialization. *Journal of Youth and Adolescence, 24*(5), 519–533.

Babbie, E. (2013). *The Practice of Social Research* (13th ed.). Belmont: Wadsworth Cengage Learning.

Calleja, G. (2011). *In-Game: From Immersion to Incorporation.* Cambridge/ London: The MIT Press.

Charmaz, K. (2006). *Constructing Grounded Theory.* London: SAGE.

Consalvo, M. (2007). *Cheating: Gaining Advantage in Video Games.* Cambridge: MIT Press.

de Heij, B., Bosman, S., Hagoort, T., & Warman, P. (2013). *The Global Games Market 2013. Key Facts & Insights on the Global Games Market 2012–2016.* Available at: https://newzoo.com/wp-content/uploads/2011/06/Newzoo_Free_Global_Trend_Report_2012_2016_V2.pdf. Accessed 15 Feb 2017.

Dovey, J., & Kennedy, H. (2006). *Game Cultures. Computer Games and New Media* (1st ed.). Maidenheard (u.a.): Open University Press.

Drews, M. M. (2008). Gry komputerowe a analfabetyzm funkcjonalny i informacyjny. *Homo Communicativus, 2*(4), 59–72.

ESA. (2016). *Essential Facts About the Computer and Video Game Industry 2016.* Available at: http://essentialfacts.theesa.com/Essential-Facts-2016.pdf. Accessed 15 Feb 2017.

Filiciak, M. (2010). *Światy z pikseli. Antologia studiów nad grami komputerowymi.* Warszawa: SWPS.

Gałuszka, D. (2016). Relacja dziecko–rodzic w perspektywie gry komputerowej . Wyniki badania nad obecnością gier wideo w rodzinie. *Kultura i Edukacja, 1*(111), 197–216.

Huizinga, J. (1980). *Homo Ludens. Study of the Play Element in Culture.* London: Routledge.

ISFE. (2012). *Videogames in Europe: 2012 Consumer Study.* Online: http://www.isfe.eu/sites/isfe.eu/files/attachments/euro_summary_-_isfe_consumer_study.pdf. Accessed 15 Feb 2017.

Jenkins, H. (2006). Complete Freedom of Movement: Video Games as Gendered Play Spaces. In K. S. Tekinbaş & E. Zimmerman (Eds.), *The Game Design Reader a Rules of Play Anthology.* London: The MIT Press.

Juul, J. (2003). *The Game, the Player, the World: Looking for a Heart of Gameness.* Available at: http://www.jesperjuul.net/text/gameplayerworld/. Accessed 15 Feb 2017.

Konecki, K. (2000). *Studia z metodologii badań jakościowych. Teoria ugruntowana.* Warsaw: PWN.

Lenhart, A., Kahnei, J., Middaugh, E., Macgill Rankin, A., Evans, C., & Vitak, J. (2008). *Teens, Video Games, and Civics.* Available at: http://www.pewinternet.org/files/old-media/Files/Reports/2008/PIP_Teens_Games_and_Civics_Report_FINAL.pdf.pdf. Accessed 15 Feb 2017.

Mańkowski, P. (2010). *Cyfrowe marzenia. Historia gier komputerowych i wideo.* Warszawa: Trio.

Manovich, L. (2001). *The Language of New Media.* Cambridge: The MIT Press.

McMahan, A. (2003). Immersion, Engagement, and Presence: A Method for Analyzing 3-D Video Games. In B. Perron & M. Wolf (Eds.), *Video Game Theory Reader* (pp. 67–86). New York: Routledge.

Mead, M. (1970). *Culture and Commitment: A Study of the Generation Gap.* New York: Natural History Press.

Murray, J. (1997). *Hamlet on the Holodeck: The Future of Narrative in Cyberspace.* Cambridge, MA: The MIT Press.

Nitsche, M. (2008). *Video Game Spaces. Image, Play, and Structure in 3D Game Worlds.* Cambridge, MA: The MIT Press.

Ogburn, W. (1922). *Social Change with Respect to Culture and Original Nature.* New York: Huebsch.

Oppenheim, A. (1992). *Questionnaire Design, Interviewing and Attitude Measurement.* London/New York: Continuum.

Pawłowska, A. (2006). Badanie relacji społecznych w organizacji z wykorzystaniem metod projekcyjnych. *Studia i Materiały, 1,* 7–17.

Prensky, M. (2001). *Digital Natives, Digital Immigrants.* Available at: http://www.marcprensky.com/writing/Prensky%20-%20Digital%20Natives,%20Digital%20Immigrants%20-%20Part1.pdf. Accessed 15 Feb 2017.

Przybyła, M. (2012). Digital Natives vs. Digital Immigrants. *Studia Edukacyjne, 23,* 203–216.

Silverman, D., & Marvasti, A. (2008). *Doing Qualitative Research: A Comprehensive Guide.* London: SAGE.

Squla.pl. (2016). *Dzieci po szkole—wolne czy zajęte.* Available at: http://www.edunews.pl/images/pdf/raport_dzieci_po_szkole.pdf. Accessed 15 Feb 2017.

Szafraniec, K. (2011). *Młodzi 2011.* Warsaw: Chancellery of the Prime Minister.

Szafraniec, K. (2015). Młodzież i nowe media: socjalizacja pod własnym nadzorem. In M. Federowicz & S. Ratajski (Eds.), *O potrzebie edukacji medialnej w Polsce* (pp. 181–208). Warsaw: Polski komitet ds. UNESCO i KRRiT.

Szpunar, M. (2012). *Nowe-stare medium Internet między tworzeniem nowych modeli komunikacyjnych a reprodukowaniem schematów komunikowania masowego.* Warsaw: IFiS PAN.

Tyszka, Z. (1997). Rodzina. In W. Pomykało (Ed.), *Encyklopedia pedagogiczna* (p. 698). Warsaw: Fundacja Innowacja.

Urbańska-Galanciak, D. (2009). *Homo Players. Strategie odbioru gier komputerowych.* Warszawa: WaiP.

9

Projecting Gender and Sexuality Through the Nigerian Music Industry

Aretha Oluwakemi Asakitikpi

Introduction

Mass media is a form of communication different from other forms namely because it involves the use of machines to aid in the projection of messages. The message in this context can be aural, visual or both. Mass communication is neither dependent on nor limited by human effort; the messages produced do not depend on how far the human voice can be heard or how far the human eye can see (Hiebert et al. 1979). Through technology that aids the communication process, the receiver does not have to be present or be near the sender of a message to receive the intended message. The message itself is based on 'symbols' that transfer its meaning from originator to receiver (Real 1980). Unlike other forms of communication, ones that usually involve an individual (as in face to face communication), a small group, or a larger group (public speaking), mass communication involves teams of people creating a message that is received by a variety of people in different places, sometimes even different

A. O. Asakitikpi (✉)
Southern Business School, Johannesburg, South Africa

© The Author(s) 2018
A. Beniwal et al. (eds.), *Global Leisure and the Struggle for a Better World*, Leisure Studies in a Global Era, https://doi.org/10.1007/978-3-319-70975-8_9

time zones. What brings these people together is their access to the means of reception.

The mass media comprise a variety of technologies that mass produce messages to be received or accessed by a number of recipients. The politics behind the selection and encoding of a mass-produced message often involves several elements, including the mass media personnel, members of the ruling government (in a democratic environment this also includes the opposition), opinion leaders of the society and economic power brokers (who may influence the economic status of a large percentage of the populace) (Vivian 2012). Through the mass media's messages, recipients are exposed to places and experiences they may never physically see or experience, meet people they may never be privileged to meet in person, be admitted to the advantages of the wealthy and powerful; as well as the troubles of the destitutes. With the introduction of reality programs, recipients of mass media messages can even get a hint of the emotional and everyday lives of their favourite entertainers.

Mass media producers continually struggle to ensure their programs fit a prescribed time and space, but the mass media message production process is often constrained by the complexity of reporting events and presenting issues, and; designing and producing drama, documentary and feature series for mass consumption (Shoemaker and Reese 1996). There are limits to the amount of information that can be mass produced at any particular time; likewise, there are limits to the amount of information a mass media consumer can receive, retain and remember within a given time frame. So, the mass media message producer must carefully select not only the content but also the source of information, the method of presentation, the target audience, and the time the message is relayed. This systematic process of selection produces a lens through which the public is informed and educated about activities, events, products, decisions and personalities (Meulemann and Hagenah 2009). By reporting on events (through news presentations) or creating fictional scenarios (through movies and series), media producers supply consumers with information that helps them understand the possible implications of actions and events upon their lives and situations presented. The audience is exposed to experiences and possible consequences without actually living out such encounters. Through this process the mass media creates scripts and narratives to inform its audience (Hout and Jacobs 2008).

The mass media, through the arrangement of photographs and other visuals, audio effects, and selected text, presents scenarios in a story format whereby characters and personalities are identified and subtly qualified. Events unfold and lessons are conveyed through the roles and interactions of characters. Studies have shown that a person's knowledge of the world, what anthropologists refer to as 'worldview', affects their basic processes of remembrance and interpretation of events (Rice 1980). As humans we depend on culturally constructed schemata that aid us in the processing, storing, recalling and organizing the information we receive daily. These schemata can be likened to an abstract pattern, guided by rules or strategies, of making meaning of or interpreting events and experiences as they occurred or occur.

In the communication process, cultural schemata play an important role not only in the decoding of information received but also in the creation of messages to be decoded. Research has shown that cultural schemata do not only aid in the comprehension and decoding of mass media narratives; they also serve as an important variable in the creation of stereotypes used for bringing to mind both the form and the content of narratives (Rice 1980: 154). This relationship between content and narrative has also been relevant in revealing how mass media messages are constructed and interpreted. A continuous presentation of a particular pattern of behaviour with an accompanied script and discourse for the description or relaying of an event has been known to reinforce existing stereotypes while creating new ones. Through a persistent depiction of a pattern of behaviour, media recipients deduce how they are to behave when confronted with such patterns. Their reactions often depend on whether the character depicted is good or bad, encouraged or discouraged, applauded or disgraced. The labelling of patterns of behaviour by the mass media is not confined solely to individuals; it also affects nations and races.

Nigerian Mass Media: The Evolution

In Nigeria, the foundation of mass media communication in the form we know today (many Nigerian cultures had other forms of mass communication, such as talking drums and other instruments that carried messages across vast distances) is the print media, which was introduced through the efforts of missionaries. Credit for the first printing press in Nigeria is given to the Presbyterian Mission in 1846; this was followed by the first Nigerian mass-printed newspaper (the first non-printed newspaper form in Nigeria was the Kano Chronicles). *Iwe Iroyin* was established by Reverend Henry Townsend of the Anglican Mission. The original aim of the newspaper, and indeed the printing press, was the dissemination of knowledge as a compliment to the missionary schools established at the time; access to this knowledge was dependent upon formal Western education—the ability to read and write. Even when the message was read out loud, listeners depended on those exposed to such education to interpret the message and its possible implications.

Nigerian mass media became a source of leisure with the spread of film, radio and television (Ambler 2002). Mass media between the 1920's and 1930's was a public experience, with crowds of people from the community gathering around an installed radio box for information and entertainment. This came in the form of programs transmitted from England to Nigeria to inform and educate the colonies about the activities and policies of the colonial government. After the transmission, listeners would remain to discuss the message in small groups. Short video documentaries developed by the colonial office to educate the colonies about hygiene and to show the efforts of the colonial administration at 'modernizing' a traditional and backward state were similarly viewed. The African audience was exposed to a variety of visual depictions, mostly foreign films, emphasizing a foreign culture and engaging audiences through action, drama and love. The owner of the mass media therefore, had the power to initiate leisure, facilitating the reception of mass media messages, but also facilitating conversations that followed.

Sex and Sexuality Through Nigerian Mass Media

In many contemporary studies of mass media representations of gender and sexuality in Nigeria, the female body represents a sexual commodity, controlled body and mind by the male members of her society, thus playing into an established Western capitalist structure. Such interpretations of how images of the female and her body can be ascribed meanings seem different when compared to more traditionally inspired images. An ancient perception of the female body can be gleaned from archaeological findings of pre-colonial Nigerian artworks. Eyo (1977), in his book *Two Thousand Years of Nigerian Arts*, presents explicit photographs of Nigerian artworks, including sculptural representations of the female body in varying degrees of nudity. Ojo (1966), in his analysis of the culture behind these sculptural images, notes that enlarged breasts are a common stylistic feature, which symbolized to members of the ancient Nigerian societies nourishment, continuity and fertility on the one hand, and innocence, virtue and strength on the other.

Fadipe (1970) identified the introduction of Western education as a major cause in societal perceptions of the Nigerian female body which he believes started around the late 1960's. He noted that Western education brought with it freedom from traditional taboos and a sense of adventure, as well as the desire for Western material luxuries. The print media has been identified by various Nigerian scholars as a foundational tool for the spread of these ideas. Scholars like Salawu (2011) and Aderinto (2015) in their research of female dominated columns in the Nigerian print media note the role newspapers played in redefining gender, sexuality, love and romance. Salawu (2006: 145), in his study of pornography in Nigerian soft sell media, describes the visual expression of the female body as one of "exquisitely provocative ladies, exposing in full, the breasts and buttocks of the models" with sexually suggestive titles such as *Better Lover, Nipples International, Tickles* and *Lagos Weekend*. The front pages had the characteristic display of sensual photographs of young Nigerian women with the obvious aim of attracting, retaining and inspiring potential (male) readers. Salawu (2011) in a later research (this time of newspapers printed in the Yoruba indigenous language) of columns written by women between 2002 and 2004 note the explicitness and boldness of the writers. The female columnists not only express their pleasure in sexual exploits but also boasted of their ability to dominate their men in the process. Salawu believes this phenomenon has cultural roots as indicated in traditional festivals. According to Salawu, the Yoruba people see sex as an expression of gender superiority and gender power not only for the male but also for the female. This study thus implies that the women of this ethnic group were not as sexually docile as many Nigerian literary and scholarly writers tried to imply.

The Nigerian print media during the colonial and independent eras served as an outlet for the expression of various emotions and this includes love and romance. Aderinto (2015) in his study of the pre-independence newspaper column titled 'Milady's Bower' printed in Nnamdi Azikwe's *West African Pilot* published between 1937 and the 1950's was characterized by a female columnist called 'Miss Silva' who advised both men and women about things pertaining to 'modern love'. The column allowed the reading audience to enjoy the contributions of other writers but also allowed anonymity to 'express their feelings about often controversial matters while escaping the societal sanctions such expressions might engender' (Aderinto 2015: 485). From his analysis, it can be gleaned that the Nigerian urban man was not as domineering as would have been expected but had to also negotiate and compromise in order to sustain a relationship. The study showed that a number of the urban Nigerian men of the time suffered from heartbreaks and being jilted; accusing their women of displaying 'counterfeit love'. Miss Silva in her advise often encouraged women to be educated, socially responsible, and financially independent and to find men who were ready to take financial and emotional responsibility; while the men were encouraged to stop their promiscuous acts and adopt acts of gentlemanliness in terms of dressing, actions and manners and to take up the responsibility of being a family breadwinner.

The presentation of gender roles and sexuality in the Nigerian urban setting via the broadcast media was drastically different. Borchers (2005) in his analysis of the power of the broadcast media using the television to make his point, notes that the narrative form of television dominates how the society thinks, communicates and perceives others. Through this narrative form, members of the society are exposed to scenes crafted to represent 'real life' and are indirectly taught how to behave, perceive, think about and react to societal concepts in their own lives as they observe the actions of the characters. This is unlike the print media where the only guide to visualization are the photographs that accompany texts and a writer's ability to use words to inspire imagination.

The introduction to Nigeria of the first foreign films and videos, and later Nigerian-based ones, aided in redefining the visual image of the 'modern' female body and ultimately contributed to its commercialization.

The redefinition of the female body as a commercial tool is continually reflected in Nigerian mass media. Scenes that 'teach' male viewers how to dominate and female viewers how to be sensually submissive are the prevailing depictions in today's film industry. In a society like Nigeria where patriarchy prevails, the redefinition of the female body as a commercial entity further encourages male dominance, despite a push for the education of girls and the economic empowerment of women in the society.

Mire (2001) believes that in the history of African social and political thought, the colonial experience in particular provided a symbolic space through which African men secured and contested power in and through the bodies of their women. Mire quotes Frantz Fanon, who symbolically compared the thirst for power by African nationalists to a lust for the female body. "[T]he look that the native turns on the settler's town is a look of lust, a look of envy; it expresses his dreams of possession—all manners of possession: to sit at the settler's table, to sleep in the settler's bed, with his wife if possible." (Fanon as cited in Mire 2001: 1).

Mire argues that the result of such symbolism is the entrance of African women into the nationalist literary and political imagination, not as subjects with political goals of their own but as mothers of the nation's children and as wives of the men, who are the real subjects. Thus, despite the fact that a number of African women contributed to the liberation of African culture and political emancipation, the focus was rather on the interests and aspirations of African men. As a result the contributions of African women were marginalized and at times even denied.

The mass media is known to be a powerful tool which can greatly influence the direction of cultural and social changes, especially when existing institutions of enculturation and socialization become dormant or irrelevant. A number of scholars have argued that the power of mass media images lies in the hands of men who are thus in control of the information formed as well as the frequency of the information disseminated through the media (Ross and Carter 2011). May (2011), in an analysis of Disney princess films, considers how gender roles are portrayed through female characters, arguing that the films play an important role in gender formation not only by themselves but also through the marketing of merchandise, with the ultimate aim of teaching young girls how to be women. More recent works cited by May show that women are still under-represented in Western films, despite the fact that they make up about 51% of the population. Characteristics given to the females depicted include being married, being a homemaker, being young and having a pink collar job, and often being Caucasian by race. Patricia Made (2000) echoes this observation. She specifically considers the plight of the African woman's representation in the media observing that they are either presented as victims or sex objects. She argues that many of the items presented to the public about women are chosen more for the entertainment value than as value for information that could empower the majority of the people.

Within the music industry the female body is also a subject of verbal and physical derogation. Armstrong (2001), in an analysis of gangster music, speaks of the possible effect of such songs on gender relations. Lyrics were gathered from 490 songs produced by 13 artists from 1987 to 1993; he noted three serious personal offenses directed at women: assault, forcible rape and murder. Some of the more current music videos depict male dominance over the female body through erotic sexual appeal. A predominant male over a number of female bodies at his beck and call is a strong message often sent by these music videos. A major feature includes fast, strong beats as well as provocatively dressed women who move body parts such as their waists, breasts and buttocks. Other music videos depict women in a more mature stance, focusing on the beauty and character of the female body.

The Nigerian broadcast industry is prevalent with a number of male dominated films, videos and drama series which suggest that the theories propounded in relation to females and their bodies are true within the Nigerian society. This was especially the case before the introduction of private broadcasting stations in the 90's. Nevertheless, with the introduction of the private media, the Nigerian broadcast industry has witnessed diversity and innovation in its production and themes. A few of these productions have pushed the envelope by presenting the Nigerian female not as objects of male sexual desires and domination as sometimes perceived. Although such narratives and images are literally choked by male dominated sterotypes, they nevertheless existed.

For this study, two of such representations within the Nigerian musical industry will be used as a case study to discuss issues of transformations as they relate to gender and sexuality in the Nigeria urban setting.

Methodology

This study uses discourse analysis methods to analyse the lyrics of the selected music videos. Discourse analysis is a qualitative method, which will enable this research to identify relationships between the variables of leisure and gender relations in the selected media forms. The research will also adopt a visual analysis of the selected music videos in relation to space, body movement and setting in an analysis of leisure and gender relations as projected by Nigerians through the music video industry.

In a consideration of visual imagery, a major factor to be considered is space; within this context, 'space' refers to the environment where gender relations are displayed in the selected musical videos. Within space, sexual identities can be negotiated and defined. These spaces are often depictions of leisure, and as Sweeney (2014) notes, they include parties and other social gathering spaces that enable the individuals to act out their understanding of gender, sexuality and power relations. The selected music videos present two major spaces through which gender and sexuality relations will be analysed: *Collabo* presents a space within the corporate world (formal space), and *JAMB Question* a space within a growing Nigerian town (informal space).

An Analysis of Lyrics and Representation of Gender Relations

Music Video 1: *Collabo* by P-Square and Don Jazzy

The video *Collabo* by P-Square, featuring Don Jazzy, was published on 23 February 2015 (https://www.youtube.com/watch?v=tUvF7yj531A&index=4&list=PLw20MWFzBdR0ZvK2_N_dIKLQWCZui3haP). The video received over 47 million views with over 124,000 likes within two years.

The lyrics offer a play on the word 'collaboration' as 'collabo' in the video. Collaboration within the denotative context refers to acts of teamwork, partnership, cooperation and alliance within a business setting. This word is given a connotative meaning, which in the video suggests a heterosexual and emotionally inspired relationship. The video enacts the discourse of men perpetually lusting after women and the concept of male competition to control women's sexuality through their own sexual prowess as variables that define masculinity (Sweeney 2014).

The words and feelings of the three singers describe what they assume to be the feelings of a female executive who wishes to partner with their business firm. This partnership is redefined by the men to mean she wants a sexual relationship with them. The use of phrases like 'she needs it badly' and a description of her emotions as a 'tornado' gives the impression that the woman is desperate for a sexually motivated relationship. It is also the recognition by the men that as a Nigerian woman she can be sensuous and sexually expressive (Salawu 2011). The lyrics speak to the male ego that assumes that men are the subject of this female desire. The use of the words 'it is sweet to her', suggests the female's inability to control the emotions the physical contact their masculinity brings out. This is described through words that imply the woman hollering and screaming in ecstasy. The sexual action is also implied with words like, 'as I fire her, I call her my 'molato'. (Here 'molato' refers to a fairer skinned woman whose beauty relies on her complexion). The singer says, 'I know you want the collaboration so let us start the collaboration'.

Each of the men fantasize that their ability to satisfy the woman's burning desire will satisfy her to the point that she will not regret her collaboration. The men convey their own emotions in the escapade, describing how they go 'insane' and it makes them 'blow'. The possibility of limitations financially is implied with the reassurance that they have an avenue through which they can borrow money (this is based on the stereotype that women are attracted to men based on their financial and material capabilities). All acts of resistance by the woman are interpreted as pretence, as the men are convinced that the woman needs the collaboration as defined by their terms. This is referred to in the phrase, "I get your password and you know say I don code" (implying they know just how to satisfy the woman's emotional and material needs).

Music Video 2: *JAMB Question* by Simi

Simi's *JAMB Question* video was published on *You Tube* on 22 June 2015 (https://www.youtube.com/watch?v=1mj7N_b1Bc4&list=PLw20M

WFzBdR0ZvK2_N_dIKLQWCZui3haP&index=1). Within two years it received over 2 million views and over 12,000 likes.

Simi a female and the central character, describes an incident which involves a young man who is apparently interested in her but does not know how to express his interest. So the man follows her to get her attention and then beckons to her saying, "Sister, sister please wait, I want to talk to you." The woman tries to be patient at this advance by asking politely what he wants; she does not want to appear proud or to lack good home training (within the Nigerian social context, these traits make a woman acceptable). She responds that she will listen when he reassures her that the conversation "will only take one second". To her surprise the young man begins to ask her what she terms as 'stupid questions'. Stupid questions within this context include: Have I met you before? Is your brother Paul? Did you go to my school, 'cause I recognize you. Do you live next door? Does your daddy play football?' He intends to start a conversation hoping to become more familiar with the young lady. Unfortunately for him, she is not fooled and her response is immediate and sharp. She tells him that she is not a 'dundee' neither is she a 'fool', telling him further, "Your style is just not cool." and she objects to being asked 'JAMB questions'. JAMB is a qualifying examination taken by senior secondary pupils in Nigeria to let them gain entrance into Nigerian universities. It is made up of many short questions with multiple choice answers, with only one correct option. She associates the array of questions presented by the gentleman to the design of such an examination, making it clear she will "pay you no attention" if he continues to ask such unrelated and obscure questions, which she sees as a display of his intellectual limitations.

Within the musical, Simi describes another scene where the same individual sees her at a movie with her boyfirend and begins to stare at her as if "he wan swallow me". The implication is that he can't control his physical attraction to her. For her, a man who publicly displays his inability to control his physical attraction to a woman is not a man. The gentleman observes Simi's disgust when she publicly ignores him and tries to correct this obvious limitation by telling her 'you look nice, don't be offended 'Omoge' (Omoge here refers to a young and beautiful woman). Again the gentleman begins to ask a series of JAMB questions like: 'What is the name of the movie? Is it a tragedy or a comedy? Is the guy going to die, or are they going to fight? Did you come here last week? I think I saw you with another chick. Will they catch the bad guy? Do movies make you cry?' At this stage the woman is obviously fed up and even though her boyfriend stands up in an attempt to physically deal with the meddling young man, Simi gestures to him to keep his peace as she is in control of the situation. She tells the gentleman, "You say you want to marry me, you say you like my quality, but you keep asking me stupid questions. Is that how your mates behave? You are not ashamed of yourself? You are not even afraid to ask me such stupid questions!"

Visual Analysis of Video 1

The music video *Collabo* has its setting within an office complex, indicating a formal setting. The three men who serve as the focal point of the video are presented as being in a middle career position in a successful company. Viewers know the company the men work for has initiated a collaboration with another company and the three men have been selected to brainstorm with the other company's representative, who turns out to be an attractive professional woman who maintains a professional physical space with her new colleagues. Despite her professional stance, her male colleagues believe she needs male companionship to make her complete. This may be attributed to the Nigerian perception that female executives/professionals find it difficult to attract a male companion as many males will be afraid of her success (Aderinto 2015). The men's fantasies are thus based on this assumption and their determination to prove that they are not afraid of the woman's success, believing they can meet her material and sexual needs.

The fantasies of the men are displays of masculinity, which suggests they are in total control of the woman's mind and body. The distance between their bodies in this fantasy is very close and intimate, in contrast to the reality whereby there is little to no physical body contact. Within the fantasy, it is suggested that a woman is always eager for physical as well as material leisure, and the men boast that they can provide both. At the end of the video, viewers get to see that the men have spent all their time fantasizing and doing little to no work. The woman's higher level of intelligence is shown as she plays along, asking each man individually to meet her in her private house. This indicates to the men that she had been pretending all along to be unimpressed. But rather than meeting a woman hungry for attention and affection, they meet a cool, calm, collected woman who dishes out the work they should have completed while she treats herself to a delicious dinner. A prominent message the music video conveys is the ability of the woman to be in control of her sexuality, emotions and situation. This is unlike the men in the video, who allow their emotions to control them. The video makes it clear such men will end up being mocked and losing respect in the eyes of the women around them.

Visual Analysis of Video 2

JAMB Question has a casual setting in a rising town in Nigeria. The young lady who is approached by the gentleman displays a control of the space and conversation. Her impatience for men who cannot control their emotions is made obvious in her sharp and almost rude responses to the young man's advances. Her irritation is shown in her lack of respect for him; she ultimately controls the physical space and emotional situation. This is especially depicted when the gentleman approaches while she is on a date. Despite the fact that she is with another man, the gentleman still makes advances to her. Her date makes an attempt to challenge him, but she tells him to step down and faces the meddling gentleman squarely herself telling him to keep away. Her boldness in this situation is quite different from any number of narratives on gender relations that depict women as dependent on men for emotional support.

Discussion

Music videos are a strong tool for shaping narratives mainly because they combine lyrics and visual action within a pop culture. The message the two selected videos convey in respect to male versus female domination within a relationship is quite different from a number of theories indicated in scholarly materials. In both cases, the women are determined to be in control and not to be used as tools of male promiscuity. The prominent discourse of male dominance is discouraged while the message of negotiations and responsibility in gender relations is encouraged. Just as Aderinto (2015) notes, such mass media messages (though few) are significant in helping members of the Nigerian society to understand and negotiate gender relations. Such messages if encouraged could serve as prerequisites for the development of gender related schemata which would further empower the Nigerian woman in terms of her gender roles and the expression of her sexuality.

The Nigerian mass media has not only seen a transformation in terms of the technical gadget of conveyance (evolving from the print to the broadcast media and more recently the social media) and ownership (from public to private), it has also changed in terms of its messages (Alao 2012). The music video industry in particular, because of its ability to promote both the music as well as drama, becomes an attractive medium through which new cultural schemata can be formed. It has a great potential in attracting and sustaining viewership. In the process, the messages the audience is exposed are more memorable and may be retained longer, thus making it possible for new stereotypes to be formed.

The selected videos demonstrate the attempt of the Nigerian music industry to empower women. Because this endeavour is made through entertainment, such messages have a greater appeal than would perhaps documentary or news items. The projection of youthfulness indicates that the target audience is made up of maturing members of the society who may need guidance in relation to how to develop heterosexual relationships. For example, being sexually aggressive is discouraged for men and being submissive to such advances by the women is likewise discouraged. This seems to be the Nigerian entertainment industry's way of reshaping the theoretical discourse which traditionally identified men as a dominant figure in gender relations

Conclusion

The Nigerian entertainment industry's determination to be visually reckoned with at the global level through Nollywood has encouraged other spheres such as Nigerian music and their accompanying musicals.

Through these avenues, factors which once promoted gender inequalities within relationships are modified and reshaped in order to create new stereotypes.

References

Aderinto, S. (2015). Modernizing Love: Gender, Romantic Passion and Youth Literary Culture in Colonial Nigeria. *Africa, 85*(03), 478–500.

Alao, A. (2012). Changing Technologies and the Nigerian Mass Media. *Kuwait Chapter of Arabian Journal of Business and Management Review, 2*(3), 94–101.

Ambler, C. (2002). Media and Leisure in Africa. *The International African Historical Studies, 35*(1), 119–136.

Armstrong, E. (2001). Gangsta Misogyny: A Content Analysis of the Portrayals of Violence Against Women in Rap Music, 1987–1993. *Journal of Criminal Justice and Popular Culture, 8*(2), 96–126.

Borchers, T. (2005). *Persuasion in the Media Age.* New York: McGraw-Hill Higher Education.

Eyo, E. (1977). *Two Thousand Years of Nigerian Art.* Lagos: Federal Department of Antiquities.

Fadipe, N. (1970). *The Sociology of the Yoruba.* Ibadan: Ibadan University Press.

Hiebert, R., Ungurait, D., & Bohn, T. (1979). *Mass Media: An Introduction to Modern Communication.* New York: Longman.

Hout, V., & Jacobs, G. (2008). News Production Theory and Practice: Fieldwork Notes on Power, Interaction and Agency. *Pragmatics, 18*(1), 59–85.

Made, P. (2000). Globalisation and Gender Training for the Media. In C. Sweetman (Ed.), *Gender in the Twenty-First Century* (pp. 29–34). Oxford: Oxfam.

May, B. (2011, December 15). *Beyond the Prince: Race and Gender Role Portrayal in Disney Princess Films.* Unpublished undergraduate article submitted to Saint Mary's College, Notre Dame.

Meulemann, H., & Hagenah, J. (2009). *Mass Media Research* (Working Paper). German Council for Social and Economic Data (RatSWD).

Mire, A. (2001). In/Through the Bodies of women: Rethinking Gender in African Politics. *Polis / R.C.S.P. / C.P.S.R., 8*, 1–19.

Ojo, A. (1966). *Yoruba Culture: A Geographical Analysis.* London: University of London Press.

Real, M. (1980). Theory: Contributions to an Understanding of American Mass Communications. *American Quarterly, 32*(3), 238–258.

Rice, E. (1980). On Cultural Schemata. *American Ethnologist, 7*(1), 152–171.

Ross, K., & Carter, C. (2011). Women and News: A Long and Winding Road. *Media, Culture & Society, 33*(8), 1148–1165.

Salawu, A. (2006). Sex in Yoruba Newspapers. In A. Salawu (Ed.), *Indigenous Language Media in Africa* (pp. 141–174). Lagos: CBAAC.

Salawu, A. (2011). Breaking the Culture of Mute Sensation: Female Expression of Power in Sexual Contest with Men in Yoruba Newspapers. *Journal of Social Science, 27*(1), 39–51.

Shoemaker, P., & Reese, D. (1996). *Mediating the Message: Theories of Influences on Mass Media Content* (2nd ed.). New York: Longman.

Sweeney, B. (2014). To Sexually Perform or Protect: Masculine Identity Construction and Perceptions of Women's Sexuality on a University Campus in the Midwestern USA. *Gender, Place and Culture, 2*(9), 1108–1124. https://doi.org/10.1080/0966369X.2013.817968.

Vivian, J. (2012). *The Media of Mass Communication* (11th ed.). New York: Pearson.

10

Doing Manga as Leisure and Its Meaning and Purpose: The Case of Japanese Female Manga Fans Called *Fujoshi*

Hiromi Tanaka and Saori Ishida

Manga: A Significant Leisure Form in Contemporary Japan

Tokyo International Convention Center is the largest convention center in Japan.[1] Known as Tokyo Big Sight, it has an area of 80,000 square kilometers. About 300 events are held every year. This exceeds other convention centers in the country. Since its opening in 1996, many events have been held, attracting many visitors. (The total number of visitors exceeded 100 million in 2007). For many, it is nothing special—just a convention center built and used for large-scale events such as motor shows and trade fairs. But for some it can be a special place for a very different reason. For people who love manga (Japanese comics) it is *the* place for Comic Market, the largest manga fair in the world.

H. Tanaka (✉)
School of Information and Communication, Meiji University, Tokyo, Japan

S. Ishida
Gender Center, School of Information and Communication, Meiji University, Tokyo, Japan

© The Author(s) 2018
A. Beniwal et al. (eds.), *Global Leisure and the Struggle for a Better World*, Leisure Studies in a Global Era, https://doi.org/10.1007/978-3-319-70975-8_10

Also known as 'Comiket' or 'Comike', this fair started in 1975 when a few fans organized an event, on a much smaller scale than now, to create a space for manga fans to show, sell or buy *dōjin* (*dō* = the same, *jin* = person), which are "self-financed, self-published works created by an individual or [by] collaboration between individuals" (Tamagawa 2012, p. 108). About 700 people attended this very first event. Since then, the number of attendees steadily increased, reaching 500,000 in August 2004 and 550,000 at the latest event held in December 2016.[2] As the event grew larger and larger, it was relocated at a larger venue, a convention center. Today attendees include newcomers and repeaters, individuals and groups called 'manga circles' or manga societies. Comic Market serves as a forum for exchange among manga fans. It is particularly important for those who produce their own works called *dōjin*[3]-*shi* (magazine or booklet by *dōjin*) because they are outside the formal channel for distribution, which is generally available only for professional artists and commercial publishers.[4]

The fact that such a large-scale event exists and has been held regularly for a significant period of time—ever since the 1970s—attests that manga is among the most popular and solid forms of leisure in contemporary Japanese society. It is known nowadays that media contents such as animation (anime), manga (comics, either works published as books or in, say, weekly or monthly magazines), games and idols (see Chap. 5 in this volume) are consumed by many people in Japan and abroad, and these people are often called *otaku*.[5] Among these, contents animation is particularly popular. Its product sales including films, videos, TV programs and online broadcasting were over 200 billion yen (1736 million USD) in 2015.[6] Sales of comics have not grown largely in the past years, probably due to the general decline of printed media and the rise of digital media. Still, they have been steady at around 500 billion yen (about 4340 million USD) in the 2000s and were about 445.4 billion yen (about 4016 million USD) in 2016 (Zenkoku shuppan kyōkai/Shuppan kagaku kenkyūjo 2017, pp. 4–11).[7] One reason for such solid popularity of manga is that its contents are often used for other types of media contents such as animation and games. Thus, many anime and game fans 'return' to original contents published as manga.

In short, manga is a cultural phenomenon in Japan that cannot be overlooked. . Researchers based in Japan and other parts of the world increasingly view its importance as a topic of academic discussion, as its fandom expands beyond national borders. This is owed in large part to the process of cultural globalization, driven by diffusion of new information and communication technologies.

Why are so many people attracted to manga and related cultural artifacts? What do these fans do and why? What happens when they enjoy manga? What does their practice mean socially and culturally? What role does it play in their individual lives, communities and wider society? This chapter explores the social and cultural meaning of this particular form of leisure—consuming manga and the various practices by those who enjoy manga as leisure, from buying and reading to more active involvement such as producing and selling fan works, communicating with others and building a community. This entails social processes such as the formation of identity and of a community of individuals involved in this leisure form.

Because manga fandom is quite large and diverse, we focus on one segment of manga fandom: female manga fans called *fujoshi* (腐女子), which literally means a 'rotten girl'. This word is a pun on another word, 婦女子, rather an old-fashioned word meaning 'women'. This word has one different Chinese character, the first one, but it is pronounced in the same way. 'Rotten girls' are seen, or even see themselves, self-derogatorily as being 'rotten' due to their 'deviant' form of leisure. They consume images of male homosexuality verbally and visually narrated in manga, and yet these manga are primarily produced by women for women, not gay men. A majority of these women have a heterosexual identity. Women are generally expected to enjoy heterosexual romance, which is in fact a major theme in *shōjo manga* (girls' comics) aimed at the young female audience. But, *fujoshi* do not follow this format. Rather, they adore male homosexual relationships in their manga reading and so develop fantasies surrounding male homosexuality. Also, *fujoshi* include both junior (say, early teens, even some primary schoolgirls) and senior women. Though some stop being *fujoshi* at some point in their life (they call this *sotsugyō*, graduation), many others continue.

Fujoshi constitute an important part of today's Japanese popular culture, a large portion of which is dominated by manga and related media contents. They may be a minority among all the manga readers including passive or occasional readers, but in the world of *dōjin*, in which passionate manga fans gather, as described above with the example of the Comic Market, *fujoshi* represent a major actor that cannot be ignored.[8] In this chapter we illuminate this particular female manga fandom and explore the socio-cultural meaning of their leisure practices and processes. To do so, we draw on our interview data[9] as well as existing research about *yaoi*, BL (meaning 'boys love') and *fujoshi*. Attention to *fujoshi* is important also because the dominant public discourse about manga fans has been primarily about men.[10]

In the following sections, we first explain terminological and historical backgrounds against which *fujoshi* emerged. We then examine *fujoshi* with a focus on two major dimensions of this leisure phenomenon: manga reading and community formation. We examine their relation to manga as a media text both as audience and producer of works such as *dōjin-shi* and the ways they develop individual and collective identities and build their own communities. To do so we deploy a critical sociological and feminist perspective to discuss the possibility of social change and social differentiation in this phenomenon. We believe this chapter can contribute to a better understanding of a subcultural dimension of contemporary leisure, one which we argue entails both opportunity and risk for individuals doing leisure, ultimately for their quality of life.

The Rise of *Yaoi*, *BL* and *Fujoshi*

The term *fujoshi* is rather a recent invention, but male homosexuality has been a theme in Japanese *shōjo manga* since at least the early 1970s. The origin of *fujoshi* is usually traced back to then, but a social and cultural phenomenon of *fujoshi* entails a new quality which the precursors lack.

In the 1970s a genre called *yaoi* emerged. *Yaoi* refers to "a way of expression by which a non-sexual relationship between male characters is replaced by a sexual romantic relationship" (Fujimoto 2007, p. 63). It is "also a general term for tales (mainly novels and manga) which use such expression as a motif" (Fujimoto 2007, p. 63). Today, a majority of *yaoi* are manga. At that time, several artists produced works depicting male homosexuality, initially for a female readership of girls' comics. For example, now legendary artists such as Moto Hagio and Keiko Takemiya published *Tōma no shinzō* (The Heart of Thomas, 1974) and *Kaze to ki no uta* (The Poem of the Wind and the Trees, 1976–1984), respectively. These works depicted interpersonal and sexual relationships between boys attending German gymnasiums. Having literary quality, they are admired as classics. These works were published in a weekly magazine, *Shūkan Shōjo Komikku* (Weekly Girls' Comics), a major manga magazine for girls' comics. Hence, manga with the theme of male homosexuality first found a place in girls' comics. Soon, however, a new magazine appeared, specifically dedicated to such manga. This magazine, entitled *comic JUN*, was published in 1978. It was later renamed *JUNE* and existed until 2013 as a commercial manga magazine.[11] The magazine originally contained both novels and manga, many of which were aesthetic (*tanbi*) in their style. Some other magazines such as *GUST* (1990) and *b-boy* (1991) followed in the 1990s, but *JUNE* importantly contained manga by amateur artists as well, a sign of *dōjin* culture in which less significance is attached to the barrier between professional and amateur artists.

In fact, when these commercial magazines were published, *dōjin* culture became quite active. The publication and subsequent popularity of two works in particular from *shōnen manga* are important in this context. These are *Captain Tsubasa* (1981–1988) and *SLAM DUNK* (1996). The first is a story about soccer, the latter about basketball. Both were originally published in a popular boys' manga magazines, *Weekly shōnen Jump* (*Shūkan shōnen janpu*). Quite a few homoerotic parodies of these two works were published in the 1980s and the 1990s, respectively. This is because both works are narratives of the male athlete homosocial world characterized by their strong bonds. There are a few female characters, but they are highly marginalized, outside the strong companionship between the male characters. Also, heterosexuality is presumed to be a norm. Though non-sports manga inspired fujoshi,[12] *Captain Tsubasa* and *SLAM DUNK* strongly influenced the rise of *fujoshi* fandom.

While parody production developed in the 1980s and the 1990s, the commercialization of male homoerotic manga for female audiences followed. Many manga of this kind were produced by commercial publishers. A new word for this genre showed up in the 1990s: 'boys love' or 'BL'. This term more directly refers to male homosexual themes, but some terminological difference is implied by *yaoi* and BL. The latter generally refers to works produced by professional artists and commercial publishers, whereas the former implies self-production or *dōjin* by amateur artists mainly of parodies based on already published works of professional artists (Shīna 2007). Importantly, '*fujoshi*' contains both these aspects. This means that broadly speaking, *fujoshi* include readers of BL, but they also succeed *yaoi*'s tradition of self-production, mainly parodies. This, however, does not mean *fujoshi* is just a new term and nothing else. It is important to note that the current *fujoshi* fandom emerged in a socio-cultural context different from that of the 1970s and the following two decades, during which *yaoi* and later BL developed. Namely, the rise of contemporary *fujoshi* fandom is strongly related to and was promoted by the introduction and the expansion of new digital media from the late 1990s to the late 2000s and traditional mass media's reaction to this new situation.

In Japan, Internet users increased when broadband services were introduced and expanded. Yahoo! Japan was launched in 1996 and 2channel, one of the most popular online forums, in 1999. Social network services called 'mixi' started to operate in 2004, offering a new, easy-to-use platform for communication to individuals. Two new services were added in the second half of the 2000s: Twitter (since 2006) and pixiv (since 2007). Both services are convenient for communicating and exchanging illustrations. Of particular importance is pixiv. It was created specifically for exchanging manga. In the past, amateur artists created their own homepages to upload and share their illustrations and/or manga. On the contrary, pixiv offers a ready-made platform to its users for this purpose, greatly appreciated by amateur artists who otherwise might not have had any channel for distributing their works. In addition, pixiv allows its users to communicate with each other in an easy format. Twitter and pixiv expanded dramatically in the late 2000s due to the introduction of smartphones such as iPhone (2008 in Japan). Smartphones enabled easy access to the Internet and promoted online communication significantly. *Fujoshi* made and still make much use of these new services and devices.

All these new technological developments contributed to the emergence of contemporary *fujoshi* fandom, which consists of both virtual and real communities, with the former as an indispensable part of their everyday leisure practices.

Though this virtual element is a key to understanding *fujoshi*, the role played by conventional media should not be forgotten. As mentioned above, the term '*fujoshi*' was originally used only in online communities. However, it became visible in conventional mass media in the 2000s. In the mid-2000s, general media began to cover or mention *fujoshi*. *AERA*, a weekly magazine published by The Asahi Shimbun, one of the major newspaper companies in Japan, featured *fujoshi* in 2005 and 2007. The literary magazine *Eureka* (2007) published an issue dedicated to *fujoshi* in 2007. This issue included a number of essays written by critics and academics and helped activate an intellectual discussion about *yaoi*, BL and *fujoshi*, from the identity of *fujoshi* to the possibilities and outlook of *yaoi*. Also interesting was that many authors came out as *fujoshi*. Besides printed media, TV also began to form a discourse about *fujoshi*. For example, a popular drama for junior high school students, titled *Chūgakusei Nikki* (Junior High School Student Diary) took up *fujoshi* in one of the drama's episodes in 2007.[13] This was surprising for many, because the broadcaster was NHK, the only public broadcaster in Japan. Coverage by the various media formed the public discourse on *fujoshi*, and this conversation not only made visible in society female manga fans who loved manga about male homosexuality, it also gave a new language to those fans, particularly those who mainly read but did not produce their own. They would come to identify themselves as *fujoshi*.

Reading Manga as a Media Text

Stuart Hall (1980) once proposed a typology of audience reading of a media text. He rejects a notion that audiences are passive beings, basically receiving media messages without critical interpretation, and instead argues that the reception of media audiences are not unitary, but that they can actively engage in their interaction with media texts.

Hall differentiates three types of reading in terms of audience reception of media messages encoded in the text: dominant, hegemonic or preferred reading; negotiated reading; and oppositional reading (Hall 1980). This typology can be useful for articulating different ways audiences react to media texts. Hall posits that in dominant reading the reader accepts a hegemonic meaning encoded in the text, with no reflection on the society's dominant ideology. In negotiated reading, an audience accepts a hegemonic meaning, yet with some reflection on their own social position or experience. So, there is some kind of intervention in the discursive space created by media. In oppositional reading, an audience rejects the dominant meaning. This is the most radical response an audience can take.

Fujoshi read manga in the sense of negotiated reading, negotiate the homosociality depicted in original manga and use it to produce parody. As homosociality is characterized by homophobia and misogyny (Sedgwick 1985), *fujoshi* thus confront the dominant ideology of gender and sexuality encoded in media texts. *Fujoshi's* manga reading involves a practice called '*yomikae*' (replacement reading) or '*mōsō*' (delusion). "A male friendship can be smoothly transformed [replaced] in a romantic one" (Informant G) in *fujoshi's* reading. For this 'homosexualization', *fujoshi* typically pick *shōnen manga* produced for a young male audience typically by male artists who narrate the homosocial world of men. In these original manga, explicitly sexual illustrations are rare, probably because this genre is primarily for boys including young children.[14] However, like many other genres, its worldview is based on heterosexism, even if unmentioned, and homosexuality is implicitly considered taboo. Homosexual characters are quite rare, and if they are depicted, they tend to be trivialized.[15] Replacement reading is a radical way of reading because it puts such taboo homosexuality at the foreground.

Replacement reading entails two other effects related to gender and sexuality. First, it allows *fujoshi* to create a space in which they are free from unequal gender relations with men, and the subordination that inequality produces. This structure exists in the society and penetrates manga, as several researchers discuss (Nakajima 1991; Fujimoto 1998). Women are not central characters in the newly created world of parodies; they are sometimes even invisible. Thus, women continue to be marginalized and subordinated as in the original manga. Female audiences can stay away from such a gendered pattern of sexuality in the new world, albeit in their delusion. Heterosexism and unequal gender relations in the parodies, however temporal and fictive, do not bother these female readers.

Second, replacement reading allows women to develop sexual subjectivities. In Japan as in other places, there is a sexual double standard. Women are expected to be pure and innocent and sexually passive (prostitutes and other 'types' of women are the exception). In manga, *fujoshi* found a new voice for talking about sexuality freely. Another aspect related to the subjective engagement of manga is the rejection of the male gaze (Mulvey 1975), which persistently exists in media. Women have long been positioned socially and culturally as an object of male sexual or sexist gaze. It is a daily reality for women, but as gender and media scholars point out, it is seen particularly in media. Women are often sexually objectified in various media content such as advertisements, TV commercials, movies, televisions, popular music, games and videos. It is no wonder women feel sexually anxious or even threatened (Nakajima 1991; Ueno 1998). In this context, *fujoshi*'s replacement reading uniquely creates a new space in which women are neither objectified nor sexualized. Some critics such as Fujimoto (2001) and Ueno (1998) contend that this is one reason *fujoshi* enjoy male homosexuality.[16]

Fujoshi therefore are active readers of manga and negotiate existing gender and sexuality norms, which are hegemonic in Japanese society. They radically transform homosociality, in which women and sexual minorities are marginalized, into male homosexuality, in which women are free from dominance by men, allowing both to partake in the social relations of gender and sexual minorities. Male homosexuals in particular are at the center of the stage. Considering that media are still not sufficiently democratic in terms of representation of women and minorities, *fujoshi*'s manga reading (through which a new medial and discursive space emerged) is innovative. However, this innovation has some limits.

First, *fujoshi* accept gendered representation of women in original works, usually without any critical engagement. For them, a heroin in an original *shōnen manga* is "a beautiful flower among guys" (Informant C), a flower so fragile it has to be taken care of. This means *fujoshi* generally accept a heroin as she is. They do not necessarily reject its gendered representation, even if they sometimes feel uneasy about portrayals of women as in the emphasis on femininity (e.g., dependent, passive) and portraying an idealized physical feminine beauty (e.g., slim waist, extremely large eyes and breasts). Such a heroin can be turned into a different type of character through replacement reading, but this does not happen. *Fujoshi's* main interest is male characters and their coupling. They do not pay much attention to other aspects such as the portrayals of women or the original stories. Second, they enjoy coupling male characters in their replacement reading who are clearly not sexually related in the original works; male homosexual relations *fujoshi* create often seem to be another version of gendered heterosexuality. For example, new couples created by *fujoshi* are often one man who typically plays an aggressor's role (*seme* or top) and the other man who plays a passive role (*uke* or bottom).[17] These limitations mean *fujoshi's* manga reading, despite its negotiation of certain aspects of existing gender order constructed in media texts, leaves other parts of the structure unproblematized. These unchallenged aspects are rather sustained, even reproduced, through *fujoshi's* parody making.

Enjoyment and Its Constraints in *Fujoshi's* Community

However limited for social change *fujoshi's* manga reading may be, most *fujoshi* probably do not care what kind of potentials their leisure practices have for the society. What is important for them is rather a fact that they enjoy this form of leisure. Csikszentmihalyi (2008) calls the state of an individual who is absorbed in and amused by a certain activity 'flow'. According to him, both pleasure and enjoyment are important elements of one's quality of life, but they are not enough; pleasure "helps to maintain order but by itself does not create a new order" (Csikszentmihalyi 2008, p. 46). Pleasure is the state in which expectations based on biological needs or social environment are met. This includes, for example, good food, good sex and good travel experiences. These things, which he defines as factors in pleasure, can meet one's expectations. Enjoyment, on the other hand, gives more meaning and complexity to life. It is experienced beyond one's expectation, such as getting a new perspective in doing sports, reading a book, or working hard on something.

Csikszentmihalyi (2008) stresses the importance of enjoyment in an individual's life if 'flow' is to exist. According to him, enjoyment promotes one's growth, while pleasure does not have this quality. For enjoyment individuals need to use their expressive skills, which enable them to express subjective experiences. Examples of this include a runner's high and loss of fatigue. Only expressive skills can make their activities meaningful and bring about enjoyment. In addition, these skills are often crucial in forging friendship and companionship in the leisure process.

For *fujoshi*, at least three factors promote enjoyment. First, replacement reading, as discussed in the previous section, offers a new way of reading manga, a way of developing fantasy and creativity. Second, those who produce their own manga challenge themselves in a positive way. It is not easy to produce good writing and art, and fujoshi make tremendous efforts to produce good manga. They experience a sense of accomplishment when their efforts turn out well. Their engagement is thus a flow. The experience of flow requires individuals to hold onto the original motivation. The impetus for pursuing enjoyable activities (for *fujoshi*, producing their own manga) must arise internally, without any external impetus (Csikszentmihalyi 2008). As one informant (G) put it well, *fujoshi* produce their own works for self-containment and nothing else. Third, they "have fun" (Informant G) in making friends with and communicating with them. Such an exchange can also promote self-development, because they "learn different perspectives" (Informant C) from each other. Csikszentmihalyi (2008) explains that shared objectives and activities in friendships bring about enjoyment. *Fujoshi* experience this, too, but it is even truer for them because it is not always easy for them to get to know other *fujoshi* due to their stealth identity in the public.

These factors play a positive role in enhancing *fujoshi*'s well-being, and they promote the formation of community among them. At the same time, however, several other factors need to be recognized because they can affect *fujoshi*'s enjoyment on both an individual and a community level. Of particular relevance in this context is external and internal differentiation between *fujoshi* and others and among *fujoshi*.

Fujoshi's community is united, partly because they emphasize differences between *fujoshi* and non-*fujoshi*, whom they call 'ordinary people' (*ippan-jin*). In other words, *fujoshi* are known only to other fujoshi because of their stealth identity. *Fujoshi* in Japan[18] think, "basically, they should not come out" (Informant C). Some even do not like their works to be distributed to the public. In fact, many *fujoshi* hide their identity from friends and family, disguising themselves as being merely manga fans. Such external differentiation can be observed in their own discourses about non-*fujoshi* people. One of our informants (Informant E), for example, compares herself with other non-*fujoshi* women who do things women are expected to do, such as "investing money in improving their appearance, going to a beauty salon, and saving money for future marriage". This informant clearly downplays herself for not behaving in accordance with social norms referring to expected femininities and instead is engaged in something she cannot openly talk about. In short, *fujoshi*'s enjoyment may coexist with stigmatization.[19]

Fujoshi's community is united, but this unity has also some cracks. *Fujoshi*'s community is originally thought to be a non-hierarchical, communicative space for mutual exchange and understanding. It has been said to be gap bridging rather than dividing. One sign of gap bridging is the attempt to lower the barrier between amateur artists and professional artists. However, their community is not completely free from tensions among its members. First, their tastes for works, characters and coupling as well as their interpretations of original manga vary, and sub-groups are formed easily. These sub-groups can clash. This "aggravates relations" (Informant B) between members and can cause distress in some occasions. Differences in the amount of resources possessed by community members can bring about tensions, too. Kaneda (2007) names three factors as important elements that lead to stratification within *fujoshi* community: drawing skills, interpretative skills and a commitment or 'attachment' to works without requiring anything in return. Our informants also emphasize the importance of drawing skills, which frustrates some who "cannot express [themselves] as [they] want" as artists (Informant F), while others appear to be good, and even quite talented.

Some even use their drawing skills to achieve commercial success, i.e., commercial publication of self-produced manga. Originally, *fujoshi*'s self-production was supposed to be something that involved a challenge for artistic self-expression and love for manga. Those who are aware of this objective cannot help but criticize those who seemingly have forgotten it and aim to make money or to fulfil a desire for recognition. If so, the original objective of producing personal manga may recede while the pursuit of success takes over. This can affect flow and enjoyment in the *fujoshi* community.

Epilogue: Complex Leisure Practices and Processes by *Fujoshi*

So far, we have focused on unique female manga fandom called *fujoshi* (rotten girls) and examined practices and processes of this leisure phenomenon. In closing, we argue the following three points on the basis of our analyses presented in this chapter.

First, these female manga fans have created their own media spaces in an androcentric heteronormative society. Replacement reading is a radical practice because it transforms men's manga media into a completely different type of media for female audiences about male homosexuality. Women called *fujoshi* create homoerotic narrations for themselves and enjoy these narrations. An alternative media practice can be seen in this way of enjoying manga, because the practitioners manage to develop ways to ward off some of the sense of subordination to men they feel as well as their distaste in being objectified by men.

This practice is, however, ambivalent and its agency for social change is severely constrained. This is the second point. *Fujoshi*'s manga reading partially challenges hegemonic ideology of gender and sexuality such as homophobia and misogyny. At the same time, they accept other gendered aspects embedded in textual worlds of manga. Heterosexual, unequal gender relations are incorporated in male homosexual relationships they newly create. They also avoid standing in direct opposition to the problematic gender representation in original manga. In principle, they show respect for the manga they parody. This means their enjoyment, despite some possibility for change, is not critical enough to bring about changes in manga and, more broadly, in the society as a whole.

Finally, a leisure phenomenon of *fujoshi* presents another ambivalence. *Fujoshi* enjoy themselves through reading and producing manga and exchanging it among them, but this enjoyment can be eroded if differences with non-*fujoshi* or differences among *fujoshi* themselves are emphasized. Regarding differences with non-*fujoshi* women, the key is how they negotiate dominant gender norms that stigmatize their identity as 'deviant' female manga fans. Regarding internal differences, whether *fujoshi* can retain the original democratic quality of their community is an important question. Drawing on Habermasian theory of communicative action, Spracklen (2009) argues that leisure has the potential to promote democratic, horizontal exchange based on communicative rationality rather than instrumental rationality. At least internally, a quest for horizontal communication, bridging differences and connecting with one another through a commonality has been strong among *fujoshi*. Even the hierarchy between professional artists and amateur artists is not absolute among them. Potential or actual existence of tensions needs to be controlled or at least balanced in their community so they can maintain the original democratic nature of their community and ultimately preserve the quality of enjoyment in this leisure activity.

The existence of *fujoshi* describes a complex leisure phenomenon, and it is evolving. New phenomena include a lowering trend in the age of *fujoshi*, their popularization and the possibility of destigmatization, the emergence of *fudanshi* (rotten boys; see Yoshimoto 2007) and transnational expansion of *fujoshi* fandom. What do these changes mean for leisure and society now and in the future? It is the task of future research to find some answers to this question.

Notes

1. Tokyo Big Sight, n.d., *History*, viewed March 4, 2017. http://www.bigsight.jp/topics/history.pdf
2. The Official Comic Market Site n.d., *Chronology of Comic Market, Comiket*, viewed March 4, 2017, http://www.comiket.co.jp/archives/Chronology.html

3. *Dōjin* is often spelled as *doujin* in English language materials.
4. In Japan, books and magazines are typically sold by publishers via distributors to bookstores. This is still the only formal way of selling printed media, though the emergence of Internet bookstores such as Amazon affects this established distribution system and the relative power of distributors.
5. In 2004, the Nomura Research Institute revealed major findings of their research about an *otaku* market in Japan, explaining the market has 2.8 million consumers and worth 2900billion yen. See Nomura Research Institute (2004).
6. It was 202.5 billion yen in 2015, which is about 1.75 billion USD. See Media Development Research Institute, Inc. (MDRI)'s Press Release on the animation market of 2015, published December 16, 2016, http://www.mdri.co.jp/review/data/2015anime.pdf (accessed November 3, 2017)
7. According to a monthly report published by Zenkoku shuppan kyōkai/Shuppan kagaku kenkyūjo (2017), digital comics accounted for 32.8 percent, digital comics magazines 0.7 percent, printed comics 43.7 percent, printed comics magazines 22.8 percent. Digitalization of media makes difficult the increase of sales of printed media, including comics, but manga as printed media appears to remain important, at least so far.
8. According to Kaneda (2007, p. 165), some 50,000 to 60,000 *dōjin*, or amateur artists, exist, and about 70 percent of them are women. Most of these women can be regarded as *fujoshi*.
9. We conducted semi-structured interviews with seven *fujoshi* in November 2013 and February 2014 in Tokyo and conducted a qualitative content analysis of the interview data. Our informants were seven heterosexual women aged from 20 to 32, who resided in the Tokyo metropolitan area. We approached them either directly or through mutual acquaintances, and they agreed to cooperate with our study. We made their names anonymous in this article. Regarding *fujoshi*'s sexual orientation, it is important to note that not all *fujoshi* are heterosexual women. However, little academic research exists elaborating sexual differences among *fujoshi*. Though not a systematic, empirical analysis, Mizoguchi (2015) briefly discusses a lesbian way of enjoying Boys Love, drawing on her personal experience.
10. As Hori (2009, p. 118) states, a majority of participants at Comic Market, both sellers and buyers, are women, yet, media reports usually cover male fans. According to Murase (2003, pp. 138–139), one reason

for this is that female *otaku* (manga and anime nerds) were so despised that they were pushed away from media discourses. This has been exacerbated by the stealth identify shared by most *fujoshi* in Japan.

11. Today, *JUNE* is published as a DVD manga magazine by JUNET. Its official homepage is at http://www.june-net.com.

12. For example, Saint Seiya (1986–1996) was also popular for parody production, but this was a manga about action or combat, not men's sports.

13. This episode, broadcast on May 19, 2007, was titled 'Datte suki nandamon! *Fujoshi* datte koi wo suruだって好きなんだもん!~"腐女子"だって恋をする~'. It featured female junior high school students who are *fujoshi* as main characters. One of these girls worries about losing her love because of her *fujoshi* identity.

14. Though *shōnen manga* are produced for young male audience, their audiences include young and adults, both male and female. Also, recently, an increasing number of female artists publish their works in *shōnen manga* magazines. In contrast, not many men read girls manga. See Ishii et al. (2009).

15. For example, *ONE PIECE*, one of today's most popular *shōnen manga*, includes a male homosexual character. He is highly trivialized as being passive, cowardly, weak, not good looking. He even despises himself as a 'faggot' (*okama*). See Sawada et al. (2017).

16. Some even see this reading as a kind of women's 'revenge' against men. See Nimiya (1995).

17. More recently, some *fujoshi* enjoy role switching, which they call '*riva*' (reverse or reversible). This is, however, rather a new trend.

18. As far as the authors are informed, stealth identity may not be not so important for *fujoshi* in other countries.

19. More recently, it has been observed that some *fujoshi* even in Japan do not share such stigmatization. This needs to be examined in future research.

References

Csikszentmihalyi, M. (2008). *Flow: The Psychology of Optimal Experience* (Paperback). New York: Harper Perennial.

Eureka ユリイカ. (2007). 'Fujoshi manga taikei' 腐女子マンガ体系 [*Fujoshi's* Comic Scheme], *39*(7). Tokyo: Seido-sha 青土社.

Fujimoto, Y. 藤本由香里. (1998). *Watashi no ibasho ha doko ni aruno?: shōjo manga ga utsusu kokoro no katachi* 私の居場所はどこにあるの?: 少女マンガが映す心のかたち [Where Is My Place?: The Shape of the Heart Reflected in Girls' Comics]. Gakuyō Shobō学陽書房.

Fujimoto, S. 藤本純子. (2001). 'Josei no "sei" wo meguru manazashi no yukue: shōjo manga toshite no "dansei dōseiai sakuhin" no hen-yō wo tegakari ni' 女性の「性」をめぐる眼差しの行方: 少女マンガとしての"男性同性愛作品"の変容を手掛かりに [The Whereabouts of the Look on "Sexuality" in Women: Tracing the Change of "the Male Homosexuality Work" as Girls Comics]. *Nihon gakuhō* 日本学報, *20*, 133–152.

Fujimoto, S. 藤本純子. (2007). 'onna ga otoko kakeru otoko wo aisurutoki: yaoiteki yokubō-ron shiron' 女が男×男を愛するとき やおい的欲望論・試論 [When Women Love a Man x Man: An Essay about yaoi's Desire Theory]. *Eureka* ユリイカ, *39*(7), 63–68.

Hall, S. (1980). Encoding/Decoding. In S. Hall, D. Hobson, A. Lowe, & P. Willis (Eds.), *Culture, Media, Language* (pp. 128–138). London: Hutchinson.

Hori, A. 堀あきこ. (2009). *Yokubō no kōdo: Manga ni miru sekushuariti no danjo sa* 欲望のコード: マンガに見るセクシュアリティの男女差 [Code of Desire: Gender Differences in Sexuality in Manga]. Kyoto: Rinsen shoten.

Ishii, T., Kawabe, s., Konno, H., Matsumoto, Y., Meguro, K., Tachibana, K., & Mochizuki, K. (2009). 'Gendā kara mita manga: akidaisei no shiten kara' ジェンダーからみたマンガ: 秋大生の視点から [Gender in Manga Culture Among the Students in Akita University]. *Akita daigaku kyōyō kisokyōiku kenkyū nenpō* 秋田大学教養基礎教育研究年報, *13*, 1–12.

Kaneda, J. 金田淳子. (2007). 'Manga dōjin-shi: kaishaku kyōdōtai no poritikusu' マンガ・同人誌:解釈共同体のポリティクス [Manga dōjin-shi: Politics of Interpretative Communities]. In K. Sato & S. Yoshimi 佐藤健二&吉見俊哉 (Eds.), *Bunka no shakaigaku* 文化の社会学 [The Sociology of Culture], (pp. 173–190). Tokyo: Yūhikaku 有斐閣.

Mizoguchi, A. 溝口彰子. (2015). *BL shinka-ron* BL進化論 [Theorizing BL as a Transformative Genre]. Tokyo: Ōta shuppan 太田出版.

Murase, H. 村瀬ひとみ. (2003). Otaku to iu ōdiensu. In N. Kobayashi & Y. Mōri (Eds.), *Terebi ha dō miraretekitaka: Terebi・Ōdiensu no iru fūkei,* テレビはどう見られてきたか: テレビ・オーディエンスのいる風景 [How Television Is Watched: A Scene with Television Audience], (pp. 133–152) Tokyo: Serika shobō せりか書房.

Murvey, L. (1975). Visual Pleasure and Narrative Cinema. *Screen, 16*(3), 6–18.

Nakajima A. 中島梓. (1991). *Kommunikēshon fuzen shōkōgun* コミュニケーション不全症候群 [The Dis-Communication Syndrome]. Tokyo: Chikuma shobō 筑摩書房.

Nimiya, K. 荷宮和子. (1995). *Otaku shōjo no keizai-gaku: Komikku māketto ni muragaru shōjo-tachi* [The Economics of *otaku* Girls: The Girls Who Crowd about "Comic Market"]. Tokyo: Kōsaidō shuppan 廣済堂出版.

Nomura Research Institute 野村総合研究所. (2004). *Mania shohisha-sō wa anime komikku nado shuyō 5 bunya de 2,900 okuen shijō: 'otaku-sō' no shijōkibo suikei to jittai ni kansuru chōsa* マニア消費者層はアニメ・コミックなど主要5分野で2,900億円市場 ~「オタク層」の市場規模推計と実態に関する調査~ [Maniac Consumers' Market Worth 2900億円 in Main Five Areas Such as Anime and Comics: A Study of Otaku Market]. News Release, 24 August 2004, viewed 11 March, 2017. http://www.nri.com/jp/news/2004/040824.html

Sawada, S., Suzuki, Y., & Miyata, K. 澤田駿, 鈴木康大, 宮田光八. (2017). 'Manga "ONE PIECE" ni miru gendā hyōshō' 漫画「ONE PIECE」にみるジェンダー表象 [Gender Representation in a Comic 'ONE PIECE']. *Jōkomi jānaru* 情コミ・ジャーナル, *10*, 80–91.

Sedgwick, E. K. (1985). *Between Men: English Literature and Male Homosocial Desire*. New York: Columbia University Press.

Shīna, Y. 椎名ゆかり. (2007). 'Amerika deno BL manga ninki' アメリカでのBLマンガ人気 [Popularity with BL Comics in America]. *Eureka* ユリイカ, *39*(12), 180–189.

Spracklen, K. (2009). *The Meaning and Purpose of Leisure: Habermas and Leisure at the End of Modernity*. London: Palgrave Macmillan.

Tamagawa, H. (2012). Comic Market as Space for Self-Expression in Otaku Culture. In M. Ito, D. Okabe, & I. Tsuji (Eds.), *Fandom Unbound: Otaku Culture in a Connected World* (pp. 107–132). New Haven: Yale University Press.

Ueno, C. 上野千鶴子. (1998). *Hatsujō sōchi: Erosu no shinario* 発情装置: エロスのシナリオ [Apparatus of Arousal: Scenarios of Eros]. Tokyo: Chikuma shobō 筑摩書房.

Yoshimoto, T. 吉本たいまつ. (2007). 'Otoko mo sunaru bōizu rabu' 男もすなるボーイズラブ [Boys Love Men as Well Are Said to Read]. *Eureka* ユリイカ, *39*(7), 106–112.

Zenkoku shuppan kyōkai / Shuppan kagaku kenkyū-jo 全国出版協会 出版科学研究所. (2017, February 24). *Shuppan geppō* 出版月報 [Monthly Publishing Report]. pp. 4–11.

Section III

Global Leisure and Responses

11

The Globalization of Comic-Con and the Sacralization of Popular Culture

Michael A. Elliott

Introduction

In 1970, the Golden State Comic-Con was held in San Diego, California, with about 300 people in attendance. At the time, it was a small convention of writers, artists and enthusiasts of comic books as well as science fiction and fantasy. Hence, the word 'comic-con' is an abbreviation for 'comic convention'. A comic, of course, is a story told through a sequence of drawings in boxes and tends to appear in newspapers (i.e., a comic strip) or in comic books (New Oxford American Dictionary 2017). While the precise origins of comics are the subject of ongoing debate, in the United States they are strongly linked to short story and pulp fiction narratives that were popularized in American magazines in the early twentieth century, though other countries such as Japan, France and Belgium have unique traditions as well (Bramlett et al. 2017; Duncan et al. 2015, Chap. 5). Newspaper or comic 'strips' are shorter, graphical

M. A. Elliott (✉)
Department of Sociology, Anthropology and Criminal Justice, Towson University, Towson, Maryland, USA

© The Author(s) 2018
A. Beniwal et al. (eds.), *Global Leisure and the Struggle for a Better World*, Leisure Studies in a Global Era, https://doi.org/10.1007/978-3-319-70975-8_11

narratives that also became popular around the same time and appeared as color supplements once a week (usually on Sundays) or as daily, black-and-white strips (or single tiers) (Lefevre 2017). In the late 1930s and early '40s, illustrated comic books in the United States began to feature 'superhero' characters such as Superman, Batman and Wonder Woman; the genre was an instant success. It is this form of illustration—superhero-based comic books—that the word 'comic' tends to be associated with today. And while 'conventions' exist for all types of occupations and special interests, those that feature elements of popular culture, such as comic books, have become immensely popular expressions of leisure interest and fan devotion.

Today, the San Diego Comic-Con (SDCC) is attended by over 130,000 people every July and is widely known as *the* premiere convention for fans celebrating comic-related art forms. Indeed, the comic-con 'model' popularized in San Diego has become a global cultural phenomenon, spawning similar events across America and around the world. These events and their associated activities have generated an intensely devoted following (Spurlock 2012). This chapter seeks to explore why comic-cons have become such popular events, particularly for fans, and why they have globalized in recent years. To this end, I begin by tracing the history and expansion of San Diego Comic-Con, as well as the development of particular activities that constitute the comic-con model. Second, I describe how this model has spread around the world, leading to the creation of new comic-cons in Europe, North Africa, the Arabian Peninsula, Asia, Australia and South America. Third, I consider several prominent theories related to the globalization of popular culture—cultural imperialism, neo-Marxism and functionalism/contagion—as potential explanations for this phenomenon. Finally, after briefly critiquing these theories, I offer a different explanation that borrows from the sociology of religion to argue (a) that comic-cons have successfully globalized because key aspects of comic culture (e.g., superhero stories) embody mythical archetypes that transcend national boundaries, and (b) that comic-cons are important rituals for devoted fans that embody elements of the sacred.

The Phenomenon of Comic-Con

Though it is neither the first nor the largest comic convention, the San Diego Comic-Con is arguably the most famous and has become a model for how to organize similar events around the world. For the record, other 'fan' conventions existed before the original SDCC in 1970. Science fiction fan conventions, for example, began in the late 1930s and one of the largest—the World Science Fiction Convention, or 'Worldcon'—dates back to 1939 (Comic-Con International 2009, p. 40). In addition, the one-day New York Comicon was held in the city in 1964, and the Detroit Triple Fan Fair, which featured fantasy literature, films and comic art, was organized in 1965. Nonetheless, the San Diego convention was the first on the West Coast of the United States and is now "the longest-running, continuously held comic convention" (Comic-Con International 2009, p. 41).[1]

Interestingly, the original SDCC was never exclusively about comics. Billed as "San Diego's Golden State Comic-Con" in 1970, it was a relatively small event that took place in the basement of the U.S. Grant Hotel in downtown San Diego. The inaugural event charged an admission fee of $5 (5 USD)at the door (or $3.50 in advance) and was attended by roughly 300 fans and professionals who wanted to express their appreciation for and bring greater attention to comic books and comic art, as well as animation, science fiction and fantasy literature and related films (Comic-Con International 2009, p. 20; Comic-Con International n.d.). Thus, from the beginning, this convention was both a fan-based and a professional gathering that revolved around a particular range of interests including, but not limited to, comics.[2]

This was reflected in the activities that took place at the inaugural SDCC, which have now become standard attractions at this event and others like it. In 1970 these included: a dealers' room with comic books and memorabilia for sale, program rooms featuring discussion panels and celebrity guests, an art show with cartoon and comic art, a promotional booth for the official Marvel fan club (Marvelmania) and several fan-favorite film screenings (Comic-Con International 2009, p. 20). In the coming decades, other notable attractions would follow, further expanding the comic-con 'model' and contributing to the increasing popularity of this convention. During the 1970s, SDCC added a masquerade (i.e., a costume and theatrical contest featuring life-like costumes and a short theatrical portrayal of particular characters), an award recognizing the professional achievements of special guests, Japanese animation ('anime') screenings, and advanced promotion for upcoming films, such as the original *Star Wars* (Comic-Con International 2009, pp. 23–24).

In the 1980s, other notable attractions were added, such as 'Artists' Alley', where comic book artists could sign autographs and sell their works, a dedicated room for games and gaming, and additional professional awards. Japanese anime and comic (or manga) artists began to consistently attend SDCC during this decade as well (Comic-Con International 2009, pp. 60–63). During the 1990s, the practice of 'cosplay' (short for 'costumed play') became a more widespread and routinized activity, following the lead of manga fans who would faithfully recreate and wear their favorite characters' costumes. Hollywood movies and television shows also developed a more consistent presence during this decade, sending famous actors, directors, and studio executives (Comic-Con International 2009, pp. 96–100). SDCC even became a hub for finding jobs, with official portfolio review sessions for aspiring comic artists as well as those seeking employment in movies and animation, or video- and role-playing games (Comic-Con International 2009, p. 46; see also, Spurlock 2012).

By the end of the 2000s, the size and scope of SDCC began to reach the physical limits of its permanent home at the San Diego Convention Center. Today, the Exhibit Hall (formerly the dealer's room) takes up nearly 43,000 square meters and includes comic and art book publishers, manga and anime producers, toy companies, video game and role-playing game dealers, movie and television studios, movie memorabilia and jewelry and apparel retailers (Comic-Con International 2009, p. 45). Hollywood also has a massive presence at SDCC, especially for comic-, sci-fi- and fantasy-oriented movies and television shows. Fans wait in line all day to get into the famous Hall H, which hosts the most popular Hollywood panels and promotional events, and seats 6500 people (see Spurlock 2012). Gaming companies also have a major presence. Indeed, some attendees come to SDCC solely for this aspect, where they can play electronic games, board games, trading card games, and miniatures games, as well as participate in associated gaming tournaments and live-action role-playing (LARP) (Comic-Con International 2009, p. 45). Not surprisingly, media coverage in mainstream U.S. newspapers, magazines, and television has followed suit (Comic-Con International 2009, pp. 152–56). Over the decades, increases in attendance also highlight the skyrocketing popularity of this event. The first convention in 1970 drew 300 people; in 1989, it drew 11,000 people; in 1999, it drew 48,000 people; and by 2008 the entire four-day event sold out weeks in advance and drew over 125,000 people (Comic-Con International 2009).

Though SDCC has grown and expanded beyond the world of comic books per se, they are still a foundational component of this event. This is reinforced by the organization's mission statement, which reads: "San Diego Comic-Con International is a nonprofit educational corporation dedicated to creating awareness of, and appreciation for, comics and related popular art forms, primarily through the presentation of conventions and events that celebrate the historic and ongoing contribution of comics to art and culture" (Comic-Con International n.d.). As such, this remains a central theme as comic-cons have spread worldwide.

The Globalization of Comic-Con

To some degree, SDCC has always had a global presence. From the beginning, international artists and writers came to participate in this event—Filipino artists in the 1970s, Japanese anime and manga creators in the 1980s, European artists and writers (especially British) in the 1980s and 1990s, as well as press representatives from around the world who come to San Diego every July (Comic-Con International 2009, pp. 106–107). But the original comic-con model itself—a multi-day convention featuring the participation of fans, vendors, celebrities and industry professionals in various programs and activities about comic-related popular art forms—has become an immensely popular phenomenon and spawned many imitators across the United States and around the world. Today, there are roughly 40 comic-cons in major cities across the United States: San Jose, Portland and Seattle on the West Coast; Boston, New York, Baltimore and Atlanta on the East Coast; and many others in between, including Chicago, Nashville, Dallas and Salt Lake City. Worldwide, there are roughly 50 more comic-cons across six continents, from Europe to Africa, South America to North America, as well as Asia, the Middle East, Australia and New Zealand (Wikipedia n.d.).

Not surprisingly, Europe has a growing number of comic-cons modeled after SDCC. However, not all comic conventions emphasize the pop-cultural aspects (i.e., movies, television, games) common to the San Diego model; some are dedicated exclusively to the professional art of comics. For example, the Komikazen International Reality Comics Festival in Ravenna, Italy, celebrates non-fiction and 'reality-based' comics as a politically and socially conscious art form (Komikazen International Reality Comics Festival 2015). The Angoulême International Comics Festival in France was founded by the French Ministry of Culture in 1974 and is considered to be one of the most prestigious awards ceremonies in the comic book industry, including awards for local student artists and creators with disabilities (Angoulême International Comics Festival 2017; Schofield 2008; Shiach 2016). And, the Caption Comics Festival in England, which was discontinued in 2015, specialized only in 'small press' and 'independent' comic creators (Caption Comics Festival 2015).

Nonetheless, there are U.S.-style comic-cons across the European continent. The United Kingdom, for example, is home to a large number of them, such as the London Super Comic Con, Edinburgh Comic Con and Wales Comic Con. Many appear to be centrally organized by event-management companies. For example, Showmasters hosts "Film & Comic Con" events in London, Sheffield, Glasgow, Bournemouth, Cardiff and Exeter (Showmasters 2016). Likewise, MCM Central hosts comic-cons in Midlands, Liverpool, Birmingham, Northern Ireland, London, Manchester, Ireland and Scotland, as well as Belgium and Hanover (MCM Central 2017a). Interestingly, MCM began as a memorabilia collectors' show in 2001, but its organizers made a deliberate effort to alter it a few years later. "In 2005, we took the first steps that would transform it from a collectors' and autograph event into a US-style comic con, with the addition of dedicated comics, anime and videogame areas plus film and TV content." (MCM Central 2017b) A similar approach has taken root in Australia and New Zealand. The Supanova Comic Con & Gaming Expo organizes events in Melbourne, Sydney,

Perth, Brisbane, Adelaide and Gold Coast, while the Armageddon Expo describes itself as "THE New Zealand sci-fi, gaming, anime and comic family entertainment event" and hosts events in Auckland, Wellington, Christchurch, Dunedin and Tauranga (Armageddon Expo 2017). The Oz Comic Con, on the other hand, is part of a global conglomerate of conventions and expositions under the management of ReedPOP, which oversees comic-cons in cities around the world, including the United States (New York, Chicago and Seattle), Europe (Paris and Vienna) and Australia (Melbourne, Sydney, Perth, Brisbane and Adelaide), as well as other parts of the world (mentioned below) (ReedPOP 2017).

Italy hosts several prominent events in Rome, Mantua and Ravenna, as well as the largest comic festival in Europe—Lucca Comics & Games— with nearly 500,000 visitors annually (Lucca Comics & Games 2017). In Finland, the Helsinki Comics Festival claims to be the largest comics event in Northern Europe, dating back to 1979 (Helsinki Comics Festival 2017), while the International Festival of Comics and Games in Lodz, Poland, claims to be the biggest comics event in Central-Eastern Europe, drawing nearly 20,000 people in 2016 (International Festival of Comics and Games in Lodz 2017). In Bucharest, Romania, attendance at the East European Comic Con more than doubled from its first annual event in 2013 (9400 attendees) to its second in 2014 (22,000) (Davies 2014). Interestingly, while they proudly express their connection to SDCC, organizers also proclaim the event's potential as an important tourist attraction for the country of Romania, overall:

East European Comic Con (EECC) is an event based on pop culture... [aiming] to bring together all those who love comic books, movies, TV series, Sci-Fi and fantasy, Japanese culture, anime, manga, board games, trading card games and last but not least, technology. The idea for this convention came from the famous Comic Con San Diego International. East European Comic Con is one of the most important events of its kind in Europe and the most important one in Eastern Europe...EECC intends to become one of the most important pop culture based events in the world. As it addresses geeks from all over the world, EECC will play a key role in increasing the number of tourists that visit Romania. (East European Comic Con 2017)

As discussed below, this kind of acknowledgment may lead some to claim that the globalization of Comic-Con is yet another form of Americanization or cultural imperialism, but some attendees at the first "Comic Con Russia", in Moscow in 2014, explicitly disagreed, noting the universality of this culture. "'I've wanted to come for years,' says 31-year-old Elena Formina. 'There have always been geeks and fans here, it's just now they call it Comic-Con. American, Russian—all fans are the same. They love their heroes. It's about sharing that love.'" (quoted in The Guardian, Davies 2014). Said 23-year-old Dmitri Makyorov, "'A lot of the films may be American, but it's an international culture and it is becoming more and more global.'" (quoted in The Guardian, Davies 2014).

Recently, comic-cons have proliferated rapidly throughout Asia and the Middle East. IGN Entertainment, an Internet media company that caters to fans of comic con-related activities, has managed multiple conventions on the Arabian Peninsula, including events in Abu Dhabi, Bahrain, Oman, Qatar and the United Arab Emirates (IGN Convention 2017). Comic Con India (under the management of ReedPOP) had its inaugural event in Delhi in 2011 and has now expanded to four other cities—Mumbai, Bengaluru, Hyderabad and Pune. Once again, their self-description is noteworthy for declaring the importance of this particular form of pop culture fandom.

> From inception, we have steadily expanded the scope of our events by involving the various industries that can help expand popular culture. We plan to continue reaching many more communities of dedicated fans as well as bringing our unique events to many more cities in India. We provide a platform for brands to not only be part of our mission to expand popular culture, but to also engage with passionate fans across the country. We are dedicated to creating unique events and giving our fans, exhibitors and partners a platform to celebrate their undying love and passion for comics and pop culture. (Comic Con India 2017)

Likewise, AsiaPop Comicon in Manila, Philippines, also describes their event as organized around "the various genres of geek and pop culture". However, they have also used the comic-con model as a foundation to expand into a multi-genre event with even broader appeal by incorporating "lifestyle elements of beauty, sports and technology to create an all-inclusive experience for fans, families and visitors of all ages and interests" (AsiaPOP Comicon 2017). Meanwhile, Comic Fiesta in Kuala Lumpur, Malaysia, claims to be "one of Southeast Asia's largest and longest-running animation, comics and games (ACG) events" (Comic Fiesta 2016). In addition, ReedPop now manages events in Seoul, Beijing, Shanghai, Jakarta, and Singapore (ReedPOP 2017). However, the largest comic convention in Asia is Comiket in Tokyo, Japan. Launched in 1975, it is now held twice a year to accommodate over 500,000 attendees, which also makes it the largest comic convention in the world. From the beginning, Comiket has celebrated its own domestic history of manga, anime and cosplay, and therefore is not directly connected to SDCC per se. The event revolves around the sale (largely non-profit) of doujinshi, which are self-published comics focusing on manga, anime, video games and other related genres (Comic Market Committee 2014).

Finally, Africa and South America also boast several comic-cons. The International Festival of Comics in Algiers, Algeria, was established by the Ministry of Culture in 2008 and includes activities with local schools and hospitals, much like the artsy Angoulême Festival in France (Adair 2015; Algerie Presse Service 2016). However, like other comic-cons, their program also includes exhibitions, conference panel discussions, autographs, film screenings and an awards ceremony for the best African comic artists (Marasligil 2011). Brazil has two comic festivals—Comic Con Experience (CCXP) in Sao Paulo, and Festival Internacional de Quadrinhos in Belo Horizonte. Amazingly, even though the Belo Horizonte event focuses solely on comics, rather than games, television or Hollywood movies, it boasts a higher attendance than the San Diego Comic-Con, drawing 148,000 attendees at the 2011 event (Johnston 2011). And to the north, Comic Con Ecuador hosted its inaugural event in Guayaquil in 2016, with plans for a three-day event in 2017 (Comic Con Ecuador 2017; Guayaquil es mi Destino 2015).

Explaining Comic-Con

Why has Comic-Con become such a popular, global phenomenon? While there are many different ways to express a passionate interest in the realm of popular culture and entertainment (e.g., as a music, sports or celebrity fan), the growing passion in recent years for this particular form (i.e., comic-related fandom) is worthy of additional investigation. To address this question, I will briefly explore several mainstream approaches to the globalization of popular culture as potential explanations: cultural imperialism, neo-Marxism and functionalism/contagion. Next, after a brief critique of these approaches I will offer an alternative explanation that incorporates insights from the sociology of religion and related approaches that emphasize the mythological aspects of comic culture.

Mainstream Approaches

One of the most popular critiques of globalization is the cultural imperialism thesis (Mattelart 1979; Schiller 1976; Smith 1980; for a critique, see Tomlinson 1991). Proponents of this thesis argue that after World War II the West could no longer impose its way of life over the rest of the world via military imperialism and colonization; these forms of domination were effectively outlawed under the United Nations system that enshrined the virtue of national self-determination in global doctrines such as the Universal Declaration of Human Rights (1948) and the Declaration on the Granting of Independence to Colonial Countries and Peoples (1960). Instead, Western nations and corporations, particularly those from the United States, have used their monopoly over the media and the diffusion of popular culture to impose their values, preferences and other ways of life around the world. The result is a 'Westernization' or 'Americanization' of the globe. Today, despite the popularity of regional variations such as Bollywood movies from India, telenovas from Latin America and Korean pop music ('K-pop'), less developed countries struggle to push back against the onslaught of English-speaking media and information and the cultural values they carry (Thussu 2007). Thus, from this perspective, one could argue that the globalization of Comic-Con, especially with its celebration of superheroes, is part of this process; the United States exalts its power and superiority via nationalistic heroes like Captain America and Superman (Dittmer 2013), promotes core virtues of capitalist wealth and technological advancement via Batman and Iron Man (White 2010), and depicts ideals of feminine beauty via Wonder

Woman (Aizenman 2016). What is more, the increasing popularity of video games at Comic-Con could be seen as a way to promote American preferences for games that are hyper-competitive, individualistic and violent.

Related to the cultural imperialism thesis are neo-Marxist approaches to globalization that emphasize the economic domination of Western countries, multinational corporations and other capitalist entrepreneurs who continually seek out market advantages and profit opportunities around the world, especially in developing countries (McMichael 1996; Sklair 2001; Wallerstein 1979). In the process, a culture of consumerism has spread worldwide, where individuals are transformed into rabid consumers constantly bombarded by capitalist marketing and promotion strategies (Jameson 1991; Klein 2002; Sklair 2001, Chap. 8). From this perspective, the globalization of Comic-Con could represent a new market opportunity driven by management companies like ReedPop and IGN that have found new markets for the promotion of American comic culture in Asia, Australia and the Arabian Peninsula. Indeed, the event itself could be seen as a commodity of sorts that is marketed in big cities around the world, generating profit from admission fees for the organizers, but also for vendors and industry professionals who profit from the sale of merchandise, memorabilia and autograph signings. In addition, Hollywood has for decades used SDCC as a platform to promote, and thereby profit from, its latest comic-related movies and television shows (Comic-Con International 2009, pp. 96–100).

Finally, functionalist theories tend to view modern societies as complex organisms that naturally evolve and develop differentiated institutions in response to changing environmental conditions (i.e., different institutions serve different *functions* to maintain social stability) (see Coser 1956; Luhmann 1982; Parsons 1971). Thus, from a functionalist point of view, the creation of new comic *conventions* around the world could be seen as a natural response to the rapid diffusion and popularity of comic *culture*, especially via new technologies like the Internet that enable ready access to comic-related movies, television, books and video games. Indeed, if Western societies have created comic conventions in response to popular enthusiasm for comic culture, it is natural that the same thing would happen in other modernizing societies that have generated similar enthusiasm. Data by the International Telecommunications Union (2016), for example, support the timing of this relationship. According to their latest global and regional statistics, the percentage of individuals using the Internet worldwide has increased dramatically, from 8% in 2001 to 47% in 2016. And while the average for developing countries in 2016 (40%) was slightly lower than the global average, the percentage of individuals using the Internet in Arab states (42%) and in Asia and the Pacific (42%) was slightly higher, precisely where the most comic-cons are now appearing. Using a similar logic, some scholars in media studies explain how trends in popular culture spread through a process of mass contagion, where new fans are created as they are exposed to or 'infected' by other fans and the cultural products they carry (see Duffett 2013, Chap. 5 for a summary). Thus, from this perspective the globalizing process is similarly automatic and natural.

A Brief Critique

While these approaches offer some well-known and widely accepted observations about globalization that are potentially applicable here, they have similar flaws that raise serious issues. Regarding the cultural imperialism thesis, Tomlinson (1991) has insightfully exposed several fundamental problems. To begin, this thesis assumes there is, in fact, an imperialist message present in a cultural product, such as a song, movie or television program. Second, it assumes this imperialist message is received and understood by the target audience. Third, it assumes different members of the target audience understand this imperialist message in an identical way, otherwise it would not be an effective weapon. Thus, cultural imperialism arguments assume a direct intent to construct, embed and deliver an imperialist message, which is more or less successful at significantly influencing (perhaps brainwashing) other people in different parts of the world. Likewise, neo-Marxist and functionalist/contagion approaches assume whatever is heavily marketed or widely trending will be automatically or naturally adopted by others. Indeed, as Tomlinson and others have long argued (see Ang 1985, for example), audiences are not 'blank slates', mindlessly consuming cultural products. Audiences have different cultural preferences and apply different perspectives to the interpretation of popular culture. Thus, their responses can be varied and complex, not only from country to country but from person to person. As the Russian convention-goers explain above, they are well aware that comic-related *products* (books, movies, television shows) are American, but the passion for comic-related *culture* is more universal—they (and others around the world) love comic culture for its own sake, not because Americans do or because they have been brainwashed to like it.

Thus, a central issue that these approaches have difficulty explaining is why comic culture is popular to begin with, beyond the fact that it originates from America or receives some form of capitalist marketing. Indeed, to further complicate the logic of cultural imperialism, one could ask why Americans *themselves* have become so passionate about comic culture, assuming that American audiences are not the target of American cultural imperialism. In addition, the logic of neo-Marxist and functionalist/contagion arguments has a glaring empirical problem—if every cultural product that is mass marketed is automatically consumed, or if every cultural trend that disseminates has the potential to naturally 'infect' others, we would all be consumers and fans of *everything*! Ultimately, in order for a particular product or genre of pop culture to have a passionate following, it needs to resonate and connect with an audience. This raises fundamental questions that mainstream approaches cannot adequately answer: why does comic culture, in particular, resonate and connect with so many people around the world; why do some fans react so fervently to it?

Insights from the Sociology of Religion

There have been numerous descriptions of comic culture, and similar genres, as a form of modern mythology (Kantor and Maslon 2013; Knowles 2007; Levitz 2010; Maslon and Kantor 2013; Morrison 2012; Reynolds 1994; Teampau 2015). Mary Henderson (1997), for example, explains the mythological aspects of the *Star Wars* movies and how they intentionally employ archetypes common to ancient myths of many kinds—good vs. evil, the hero's journey, temptation and redemption, the importance of heroism, compassion, wisdom, etc. (see also, Wagner 2000). This is not to imply that ancient myths are all the same; they tell different stories that reflect different cultures and time periods. Nonetheless, in general thematic ways, they tend to dramatize common experiences that we all share as human beings (Campbell 1949); most of us, regardless of culture, valorize heroic acts, experience love, rely on mentors to guide us, and face trials and tribulations as we grow up and mature. As Cowen (2002) argues, the dominance and popularity of Hollywood movies around the world does *not* reflect a pure case of American cultural imperialism; this would not a viable financial strategy:

> For better or worse, Hollywood strives to present the universal to global audiences. As Hollywood markets its films to more non-English speakers, those films become more general. Action films are favored over movies with subtle dialogue. Comedy revolves around slapstick rather than verbal puns. The larger the audience, of course, the more universal the product or celebrity must be. …Greater universality means that the movies are relevant to general features of the human condition. …Critics allege that American culture is driving the world, but in reality the two are determined simultaneously, and by the same set of forces. (Cowen 2002, p. 93)

And to be sure, the highest grossing movies worldwide over the past decade tend to be those with clear archetypal elements and therefore broad appeal: action/adventure films, animated children's films and (of course) superhero films (Box Office Mojo 2017; The Numbers 2017).

Thus, one explanation for why comic culture has become so popular around the world is its tendency to be defined by characters and stories that are mythological and universal, yet also modern and entertaining. Indeed, as Henderson (1997) explains, the original *Star Wars* movies not only embodied mythical archetypes; they also reflected social issues and events that were part of popular consciousness at the time (e.g., the Space Age, the threat of nuclear weapons, our relationship to technology and machines), further bolstering their resonance. Famed comic book author, Grant Morrison, comes to a similar conclusion in his analysis of superheroes:

> Batman, Spider-Man, X-Men, Green Lantern, Iron Man. Why have super-heroes become so popular? Why now? On one level, it's simple: Someone somewhere, figured out that, like chimpanzees, superheroes make every-thing more entertaining. ...Superheroes can spice up any dish. But there's even more going on beneath the surface of our appetite for the antics of outlandishly dressed characters who will never let us down. ...In a secular, scientific rational culture lacking any convincing spiritual leadership, superhero stories speak loudly and boldly to our greatest fears, deepest longings, and highest aspirations. ...They're about as far from social realism as you can get, but the best superhero stories deal directly with mythic ele-ments of human experience that we can all relate to, in ways that are imagi-native, profound, funny, and provocative. (Morrison 2012, pp. xvi–xvii)

For devoted fans in particular, comic culture may be more than just a form of entertainment; it may be deeply meaningful. Here, Emile Durkheim's sociology of religion offers potential insight. One of the most enduring and controversial legacies of Durkheim's *The Elementary Forms of Religious Life* (1912) is how he conceptualized religion as revolving around beliefs and practices about 'the sacred' rather than 'gods' or 'the supernatural' specifically. The sacred, he explained, is set apart by society as something powerful, transcendent and holy, and is clearly distin-guished from the mundane world of everyday affairs. The primary means of distinguishing and experiencing the sacred is through collective rituals, which are central to Durkheim's theory. This conception of religion obviously *includes* beliefs and practices about gods or the supernatural, which is the typical focus of sociologists of religion. But it is not exclusive to them—other beliefs and practices can be sacred. While his theory challenges us to expand our understanding of what is traditionally con-sidered 'religious', it represents an underexplored legacy that has enjoyed only limited application to non-religious or secular activities (see Bailey 1997; Bellah 1967; Boli et al. 2003; Ellul 1975; Luckmann 1967), despite pleas in the sociology of religion literature to further explore the varieties of sacred experiences today (Demerath 1999).

I hypothesize that for fans who are noticeably passionate and devoted, comic culture may involve beliefs and practices that are sacred. To be fair, some scholars have described fandoms as actual religions (Bickerdike 2016; Jindra 1994; Melero 2010; Porter 2009; see also, Lyden 2003). This has generated some controversy, as critics claim that this comparison is empirically inaccurate and portrays fans as religious zealots (Duffett 2013; McCloud 2003). Indeed, fandoms are not religions in the traditional sense, à la world religions that have developed a wide-ranging theological belief system and a congregation with longstanding social and cultural bonds over many centuries. Nonetheless, in a more modest and general sense, comic fandom and religious devotion may share some fundamental similarities as sacred, ritualistic experiences. While not a 'god' in the traditional sense, the superhero represents idealized human virtues and aspirations that fans may find meaningful, inspiring and worth celebrating. As a result, while not a 'church' in the traditional sense, comic-cons may serve as a powerful ritual by which to experience and celebrate sacred aspects of comic culture and to bond with like-minded fans. What is more, key features of the comic-con model could be compared to ceremonial rites whose performance is crucial in making the ritual proper and complete: a proper comic-con should have cosplay or a masquerade where fans can enact the look and mannerisms of their favorite characters; it should have celebrity autographs and panel discussions where fans can physically see, hear and talk to the creators and purveyors of comic culture; it should have merchandise for sale so fans can purchase and collect particular objects or totems of their devotion; and, at larger events like SDCC, a comic-con will have lengthy periods of 'queuing' where fans stake-out their place in line (waiting for autographs, panels, etc.) and commune with fellow fans in various ways (Bolling and Smith 2014; Spurlock 2012). Ultimately, to suggest that fan experiences are powerful, transcendent or holy is *not* to imply that they are fanatical or irrational. My approach stems from sociological curiosity first and foremost and does not seek to pass judgment upon fans, either positively or negatively.

Conclusion

Popular culture occupies a prominent place in modern life. With increasing access to technology around the world, many people can routinely engage with popular television shows, movies, music, video games, books, and the internet in their leisure time. No doubt, this has become an easily accessible means of diversion, relaxation, and entertainment for many. But for others, such as devoted 'fans', popular culture may represent something more meaningful, perhaps even sacred. In this chapter, I have explored the growing popularity of comic book conventions worldwide, specifically those based on the famous San Diego Comic-Con in California that began in 1970. I have also sought to explain *why* this particular form of popular culture—comic book (or comic) culture—has successfully globalized and developed such a passionate following. Common theories about the globalization of popular culture such as cultural imperialism, neo-Marxism and functionalism offer overly simplistic mechanisms that cannot adequately explain the particular appeal of comic culture over any other cultural genre that is mass marketed, currently fashionable or comes from America.

Borrowing insights from the sociology of religion and other comic book scholars, I contend that comic culture has globalized because it embodies aspects of mythology that are universally relatable. Comic book heroes and adventures tell entertaining stories of heroism, sacrifice, compassion, coming of age and so on that appeal to all cultures because every human being experiences these things, albeit in less dramatic and entertaining ways. I also suggest that comic fandom may involve beliefs that are sacred to devoted fans, and that comic-cons represent a powerful ritual for celebrating and experiencing sacred beliefs via common practices such as cosplay, panel discussions, autograph signings and merchandise collecting. Overall, there is little systematic information about different fan beliefs and practices. To further explore this, new research is needed to assess not only the presence (or absence) of sacred experiences within fan communities but also to examine how these experiences vary among individual fans; just as religious commitment and devotion vary from person to person, there are certainly variations of commitment and devotion among fans that make their experiences more or less sacred. Given the increasing proliferation of comic-cons around the world, this is an ideal environment to survey fan beliefs and practices and to learn about the potentially sacred role of comic culture in the everyday lives of fans.

Notes

1. Overall, there are other special interest conventions in the realm of popular culture and entertainment that may involve a model similar to SDCC and have equally large followings. For example, there are conventions dedicated to sports, board games and video games, Japanese pop culture, Star Wars, Star Trek and other genres. While these are worthy of social scientific study in their own right, I restrict my analysis in this chapter to those events that (a) identify as 'comic' conventions and (b) closely resemble the model of San Diego Comic-Con.
2. See the original SDCC logo from 1970 at https://secure.comic-con.org/about, which reflects these particular interests.

References

Adair, T. (2015, October 6). To Do: The International Festival of Comics of Algeria. *The Beat*. Available from: http://www.comicsbeat.com/to-do-the-international-festival-of-comics-of-algieria/. [14 July 2017].

Aizenman, N. (2016, October 20). Is Wonder Woman Suited to Be a U.N. Ambassador? *National Public Radio* (NPR). Available from: http://www.npr.org/sections/goatsandsoda/2016/10/20/498569053/is-wonder-woman-suited-to-be-a-u-n-ambassador. [8 June 2017].

Algerie Presse Service. (2016, September 27). Algeria: Forty Countries Participate in 9th International Comics Festival of Algiers. *AllAfrica*. Available from: http://allafrica.com/stories/201609280336.html. [14 July 2017].

Ang, I. (1985). *Watching Dallas: Soap Opera and the Melodramatic Imagination.* London: Menthuen.

Angoulême International Comics Festival. (2017). *2017 Press Kit*. Available from: http://www.bdangoulemepro.com/upload/pro/colonne_blocs/documents/30_61_2017dossierpressefibdangouleme44_673.pdf. [14 July 2017].

Armageddon Expo. (2017). *About*. Facebook Post. Available from: https://www.facebook.com/pg/Armageddonexpo/about/?ref=page_internal. [2 June 2017].

AsiaPOP Comicon. (2017). *Show Info*. Available from: https://asiapopcomicon.com/manila/showInfo. [2 June 2017].

Bailey, E. (1997). *Implicit Religion in Contemporary Society*. Kampen: Kok Pharos.

Bellah, R. (1967). Civil Religion in America. *Daedalus, 96*, 1–21.

Bickerdike, J. O. (2016). *The Secular Religion of Fandom*. Los Angeles: Sage.

Boli, J., Elliott, M. A., & Bieri, F. (2003). Globalization. In G. Ritzer (Ed.), *Handbook of Social Problems: A Comparative International Perspective* (pp. 389–415). Thousand Oaks: Sage Publications.

Bolling, B., & Smith, M. J. (Eds.). (2014). *It Happens at Comic-con: Ethnographic Essays on a Pop Culture Phenomenon*. Jefferson: McFarland & Company Inc.

Box Office Mojo. (2017). *Yearly Box Office (Worldwide)*. Available from: http://www.boxofficemojo.com/yearly/?view2=worldwide&view=releasedate&p=.htm. [2 June 2017].

Bramlett, F., Cook, R. T., & Meskin, A. (Eds.). (2017). *The Routledge Companion to Comics*. New York: Routledge.

Campbell, J. (1949). *The Hero with a Thousand Faces*. New York: Pantheon Books.

Caption Comics Festival. (2015, February 20) *Archive Account*, Facebook post. Available from: https://www.facebook.com/Captioncomicsfest/. [2 June 2017].

Comic Con Ecuador. (2017). *Home Page*. Available from: http://www.comic-conecuador.com/index.html. [2 June 2017].

Comic Con India. (2017). *Comic Con India Story*. Available from: http://www.comiccondelhi.com/cci-story/. Accessed 14 July 2017.

Comic-Con International. (2009). *Comic-con: 40 Years of Artists, Writers, Fans & Friends*. San Francisco: Chronicle Books LLC.

Comic-Con International. (n.d.). *About Comic-Con International*. Available from: http://www.comic-con.org/about. [2 June 2017].

Comic Fiesta. (2016). *What Is Comic Fiesta?* Available from: http://comicfiesta.org/2016/what-is-comic-fiesta/. [2 June 2017].

Comic Market Committee. (2014). *What Is Comic Market?* Available from: http://www.comiket.co.jp/info-a/WhatIsEng201401.pdf. [2 June 2017].

Coser, L. A. (1956). *The Functions of Social Conflict*. New York: The Free Press.

Cowen, T. (2002). *Creative Destruction: How Globalization Is Changing the World's Cultures*. Princeton: Princeton University Press.

Davies, K. (2014). Comic-Con Lands in Moscow as a Sign of Geek Culture's Global Domination. *The Guardian*, October 5.

Demerath, N. J., III. (1999). The Variations of Sacred Experience: Finding the Sacred in a Secular Grove. *Journal for the Scientific Study of Religion, 39*(1), 1–11.

Dittmer, J. (2013). *Captain America and the Nationalist Superhero: Metaphors, Narratives, and Geopolitics*. Philadelphia: Temple University Press.

Duffett, M. (2013). *Understanding Fandom.* New York: Bloomsbury Academic.

Duncan, R., Smith, M. J., & Levitz, P. (2015). *The Power of Comics: History, Form, and Culture* (2nd ed.). London: Bloomsbury Academic.

Durkheim, E. ([1912] 1995). *The Elementary Forms of Religious Life.* New York: The Free Press.

East European Comic Con. (2017). *About.* Available from: http://comic-con.ro/info/about/. [2 June 2017].

Ellul, J. (1975). *The New Demons.* New York: Seabury Press.

Guayaquil es mi Destino. (2015). *Comic con Ecuador.* Available from: http://www.guayaquilesmidestino.com/en/content/comic-con-ecuador.

Helsinki Comics Festival. (2017). *Info in English.* Available from: http://www.sarjakuvafestivaalit.fi/in-english. [2 June 2017].

Henderson, M. (1997). *Star Wars: The Magic of Myth.* New York: Bantam Books.

IGN Convention. (2017). *Events.* Facebook Post. Available from: https://www.facebook.com/pg/ignconvention/events/?ref=page_internal. [14 July 2017].

International Festival of Comics and Games in Lodz. (2017). *About Festival.* Available from: http://komiksfestiwal.com/en/o-festiwalu/. [2 June 2017].

International Telecommunications Union. (2016). *Global and Regional ICT Data.* Available from: http://www.itu.int/en/ITU-D/Statistics/Documents/statistics/2016/ITU_Key_2005-2016_ICT_data.xls. [8 June 2017].

Jameson, F. (1991). *Postmodernism, or, the Cultural Logic of Late Capitalism.* Durham: Duke University Press.

Jindra, M. (1994). Star Trek Fandom as a Religious Phenomenon. *Sociology of Religion, 55*(1), 27–51.

Johnston, R. (2011, December 13). The Biggest Comic Convention in America… Is in South America. *Bleeding Cool.* Available from: https://www.bleedingcool.com/2011/12/12/biggest-comic-convention-america-south-america/. [2 June 2017].

Kantor, M., & Maslon, L. (2013). *Superheroes: A Never-Ending Battle.* PBS/Ghost Light: Films.

Klein, N. (2002). *No Logo.* New York: Picador USA.

Knowles, C. (2007). *Our Gods Wear Spandex: The Secret History of Comic Book Heroes.* San Francisco: Red Wheel/Weisner Books.

Komikazen International Reality Comics Festival. (2015). *Komikazen 2015 English.* Available from: https://www.komikazenfestival.org/komikazen-2015/komikazen-2015-english/. [14 June 2017].

Lefevre, P. (2017). Newspaper Strips. In F. Bramlett, R. T. Cook, & A. Meskin (Eds.), *The Routledge Companion to Comics* (pp. 16–24). New York: Routledge.

Levitz, P. (2010). *75 Years of DC Comics: The Art of Modern Mythmaking.* Hollywood: Taschen America.

Lucca Comics & Games. (2017). *About*. Facebook Post. Available from: https://www.facebook.com/pg/luccacomicsandgames/about/?ref=page_internal. [2 June 2017].

Luckmann, T. (1967). *The Invisible Religion*. New York: Macmillan.

Luhmann, N. (1982). *The Differentiation of Society*. New York: Columbia University Press.

Lyden, J. C. (2003). *Film as Religion: Myths, Morals, and Rituals*. New York: New York University Press.

Marasligil, C. (2011, October 17). A Dispatch from FIDBA, the International Comics Festival of Algeria. *Words Without Borders*. Available from: http://www.wordswithoutborders.org/dispatches/article/a-dispatch-from-fidba-the-international-comics-festival-of-algeria. [8 June 2017].

Maslon, L., & Kantor, M. (2013). *Superheroes: Capes, Cowls, and the Creation of Comic Book Culture*. New York: Crown Archetype.

Mattelart, A. (1979). *Multinational Corporations and the Control of Culture: The Ideological Apparatuses of Imperialism*. Sussex: Harvester.

McCloud, S. (2003). Popular Culture Fandoms, the Boundaries of Religious Studies and the Project of the Self. *Culture and Religion, 4*(2), 187–206.

MCM Central. (2017a). *MCM Shows*. Available from: http://www.mcmcentral.net/shows/. [14 July 2017].

MCM Central. (2017b). *The MCM Story*. Available from: http://www.mcmcentral.net/about/. [14 July 2017].

Melero, C. (2010, August 14–17). *The Religion of Sports: How Collective Rituals and Beliefs Reinforce Community Bonds*. Paper presented to the Annual Meetings of the American Sociological Association, Atlanta.

McMichael, P. (1996). *Development and Social Change: A Global Perspective*. Thousand Oaks: Pine Forge Press.

Morrison, G. (2012). *Supergods*. New York: Spiegel and Grau.

New Oxford American Dictionary. (2017). Oxford: Oxford University Press.

Parsons, T. (1971). *The System of Modern Societies*. Englewood Cliffs: Prentice-Hall.

Porter, J. (2009). Implicit Religion in Popular Culture: The Religious Dimensions of Fan Communities. *Implicit Religion, 12*(3), 271–281.

ReedPOP. (2017). *Our Shows*. Available from: http://www.reedpop.com/Events/. [2 June 2017].

Reynolds, R. (1994). *Super Heroes: A Modern Mythology*. Jackson: University Press of Mississippi.

Schiller, H. (1976). *Communication and Cultural Domination*. White Plains: International Arts and Sciences Press.

Schofield, H. (2008, February 16). France Takes Its Comics Very Seriously. *BBC News*. Available from: http://news.bbc.co.uk/2/hi/programmes/from_our_own_correspondent/7246634.stm. [8 June 2017].

Shiach, K. (2016). Angouleme International Festival of Comics Announces Official Selections for 2017. *Comics Alliance*. Available from: http://comicsalliance.com/angouleme-official-selection-2017/. [2 June 2017].

Showmasters. (2016). *Showmasters Home Page*. Available from: http://www.showmastersevents.com/. [2 June 2017].

Sklair, L. (2001). *The Transnational Capitalist Class*. Oxford: Blackwell Publishers.

Smith, A. (1980). *The Geopolitics of Information: How Western Culture Dominates the World*. New York: Oxford University Press.

Spurlock, M. (2012). *Comic-Con, ep. IV: a fan's hope*. Necca Films.

Teampau, G. (2015). Comic Books as Modern Mythology. *Caietele Echinox, 28*, 140–155.

The Numbers. (2017). *Worldwide Genres Box Office Records*. Available from: http://www.the-numbers.com/box-office-records/worldwide/all-movies/genres/. [2 June 2017].

Thussu, D. K. (2007). Mapping Global Media Flow and Contra-Flow. In D. K. Thussu (Ed.), *Media on the Move* (pp. 11–32). Abingdon: Routledge.

Tomlinson, J. (1991). *Cultural Imperialism*. Baltimore: Johns Hopkins University Press.

Wagner, P. M. (2000). *The Mythology of Star Wars, with George Lucas and Bill Moyers*. Films for the Humanities & Sciences.

Wallerstein, I. (1979). *The Capitalist World Economy*. Cambridge: Cambridge University Press.

White, M. D. (Ed.). (2010). *Iron Man and Philosophy: Facing the Stark Reality*. Hoboken: John Wiley & Sons, Inc..

Wikipedia. (n.d.). *List of Comic Book Conventions*. Available from: https://en.wikipedia.org/wiki/List_of_comic_book_conventions. [2 June 2017].

12

Examination of Leisure and Practical Environmental Education in Japan

Munehiko Asamizu

Introduction

This chapter briefly discusses the relationship between leisure activities and outdoor environmental education in Japan. Even though Japan offers many leisure activities, this chapter specifically focuses on nature-based and rural tourism experiences, which have increasingly become economically, socially and environmentally important. An exposure to life in rural areas is an eye-opening experience for urban residents; many rural villages and towns are already known as domestic tourism destinations in Japan. Further, some primary and secondary urban schools are sending students to rural areas to learn about the different ways of life closely related to the natural environment.

However, many rural municipalities are now suffering from depopulation and aging. Primary industry has been the main source of income for these municipalities, but, due to the decline of older industries, new ones are now required. Similar to many European countries, rural tourism—often called 'green tourism' in Japan—is becoming an important economic source for

M. Asamizu (✉)
Faculty of Economics, Yamaguchi University, Yamaguchi-shi, Japan

rural municipalities. Some rural destinations are also seeking to attract international visitors. As the Japanese population continues to shrink, a commensurate decline in domestic tourism is expected. However, as international tourism to Japan has been increasing each year, many rural municipalities are looking at ways to attract foreign tourists.

As society is changeable, law, policy and governmental organizations also change, and following these, educational institutions and academic societies change as well. The establishment of institutions and associations in Japan follows trends. Understanding leisure policies and associations can in turn lead to an understanding of trends in leisure activities.

The methodology in this study is simple: To understand leisure phenomena chronologically, specialist research was examined, and to fully understand macro tourism trends, government statistics were extracted. Further, as the author is engaged in arranging tourism volunteer activities, some basic data have also been included to analyze local cases at the micro level.

History of Remote Area Outdoor Leisure Activities

To understand outdoor leisure activities in Japan, we referred to previous documentation and research. Even though modern transportation systems were developed during the Meiji (1868–1912) and Taisho (1912–1926) periods, the advent of the Second World War saw a decline in the tourism industry (with the exception of religious tourism). When Japan started to recover, however, the tourism industry redeveloped and also recovered, and it has been growing since the 1950s.

Yamada (2008) summarized the chronological changes in tourism in remote Japan. Ski resorts started to be developed in 1950s and some farmers without agricultural winter employment began using their own homes as inns (*Minshuku*) for tourists. In Hakuba, Nagano Prefecture, for example, there were only 8 of these *Minshuku* guesthouses in 1950, but by 1960 there were 102 guesthouses (Yamada 2008, p. 16).

Since the 1960s, with increasing economic development along with growth in heavy manufacturing, Japan began to rapidly urbanize. To reward workers and give them some time to relax, Japanese companies started organizing group worker tours to rural locations. Tourism facilities for the large group tour were built at *onsen* (hot springs), beach resorts, ski fields and other tourist destinations. To make up for the shortage of recreation facilities, the Japanese government also built some of these facilities.

Kaji's (2009) research also found that around the same time, nature-loving urban people started visiting national parks, further increasing the demand for tourism facilities. Because of the demand for lodging in the more remote areas, the former Ministry of Health and Welfare (now Ministry of Health, Labor and Welfare) planned *Kokumin Kyuka Mura* (National Holiday Village) in 1960 and nominated a further 10 facilities in 1961 (Kaji 2009, p. 37). Recreational facilities such as accommodation, campsites, ski fields and *onsen* were included in *Kokumin Kyuka Mura*. There were 20 recreational facilities at *Kokumin Kyuka Mura* in 1971 and 32 in 1981 (Kaji 2009, p. 77). Similar to the French VVF (*Villages Vacances Families*), *Kokumin Kyuka Mura* provided lodging for local citizens at reasonable prices to promote and encourage social tourism.

After the Tokyo Olympics in 1964, there were significant improvements in the road networks, an increase in car ownership, and an expansion of outdoor activities to remote national forests. Oura (2004) chronologically analyzed forest developments in Japan, finding that the *Kokusetsu Yaeijyou Seido* (National Campsite System) was established in 1966 and that campsites were developed in national forests (Oura 2004, p. 43). To expand leisure activities in the national forests, the former Ministry of Agriculture and Forestry (now the Ministry of Agriculture, Forestry and Fishery: MAFF) initiated *Shizen Kyuyou Rin* (Nature-based Recreation Forests) in 1967 (opened in 1969) and *Recreation no Mori* (Recreation Forests) in 1972 (Oura 2004, p. 44).

During the 1960s, agricultural activities also gradually become a hobby for some urban residents. Some farmers located near urban areas offered a type of agricultural tourism that included fruit picking or livestock experiences on farms (Yamada 2008, pp. 17–18). Following this trend, the former Ministry of Agriculture and Forestry also initiated *Shizen Kyuyou Son* (Nature-based Recreation Villages) in 1971. In the *Shizen Kyuyou Son*, the above-mentioned agricultural activities were introduced as tourist attractions. By 1979 there were around 200 *Shizen Kyuyou Son*, and by 1997 there were 511 (Nakayama 2006, pp. 15, 51).

After the short depression caused by the oil crisis in 1973, there was a shift in Japan from heavy manufacturing to newer industries. The Resort Law of 1987 encouraged the development of large resorts in remote areas such as ski fields, beach resorts, golf courses, theme parks and other large outdoor facilities that also encompassed tourism infrastructure developments in national forests and agricultural areas. Many of these large resort developments, however, were environmentally unsound, and after the bubble economy burst in 1991 many of these mega-facilities in remote areas went bankrupt and closed down.

Post Bubble Tourism

Small-scaled tourism operations, however, survived this economic turmoil. As a result, small, peaceful *onsen* in rural forested areas such as Yufuin in Oita Prefecture and Kurokawa in Kumamoto Prefecture became high-end tourist destinations. Some rural municipalities such as Ajimu (now a part of Usa city, Oita Prefecture), Tono in Iwate Prefecture, and Iida in Nagano Prefecture also attracted green tourism. As Japanese tourists moved from group-oriented activities to independent travel, small tourist destinations became popular after the bubble burst.

The bursting of the bubble economy was a turning point for Japanese society in many areas. Since the initiation of the Green Tourism Law in 1994 (enacted in 1995), rural tourism without the need for huge facilities became popular in more remote areas. Agro-tourism before and during the bubble period was focused on agricultural activities. For example, the Law of Civic Farm Garden Development (*Shimin Nouen Seibi Sokushin Hou*) initiated in 1990 was targeted at weekend farmers from urban areas, with most agricultural activity locations being concentrated around the urban areas (Shinpo 2015, p. 40).

Rental farm gardens are still increasing. According to MAFF, there were about 1000 rental farm gardens in 1993 and more than 4000 in 2013 (Fig. 12.1). However, the geographical location of rental farm gardens remains quite concentrated. In 2015 more than half the rental farm gardens were located in the Kanto region, which includes the Tokyo metropolitan area (Fig. 12.2).

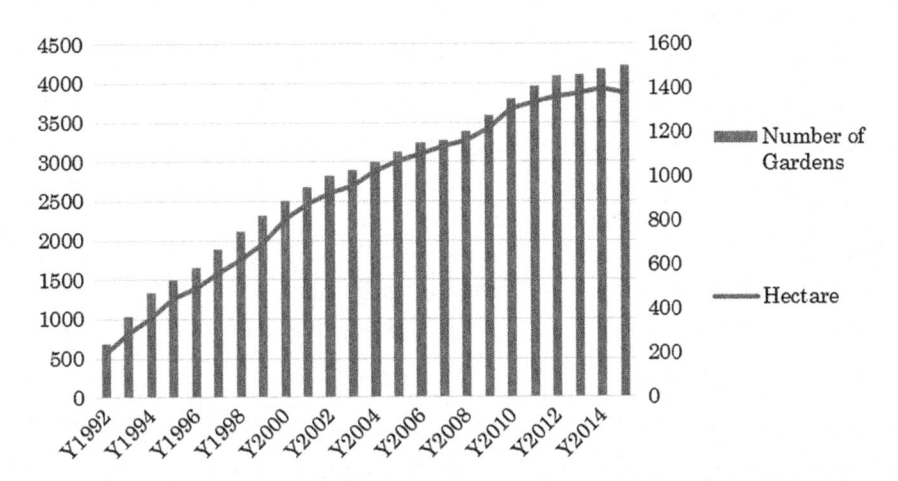

Fig. 12.1 Rental farm gardens 1992–2015 (Source: Ministry of Agriculture, Forestry and Fisheries 2016)

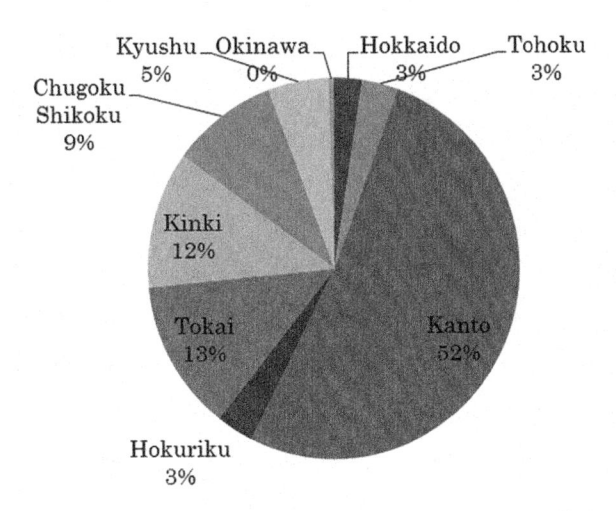

Fig. 12.2 Location of rental farm gardens (2015) (n = 4223; Source: Ministry of Agriculture, Forestry and Fisheries 2016)

However, as the current Japanese government green tourism policy is focused on developing in-depth human relationships between urban residents and remote or rural area locals, the development of appropriate accommodation is important. The deregulation of farmer's inns and traditional-style farm stays (*Minpaku*) have also become attractions for urban tourists to experience the authentic rural way of life with local host families. Before the bubble period, farmers' inns on the previous scheme (*Minshuku*) were required to have facilities at the standard of small hotels (such as separate toilets for the owner for visitors, separated kitchen sinks for visitors, fire alarms and sprinklers, etc.); therefore, renovation costs were high.

After deregulation, however, traditional houses (*Kominka*) were able to offer *Minpaku* accommodations, thereby attracting many urban visitors. And so, the chance to live with local host families and experience the authentic rural way of life and traditional rural culture has become a major tourist attraction. Except for 2010, the number of tourists staying in green tourism facilities has been gradually increasing every year in Japan (Fig. 12.3).

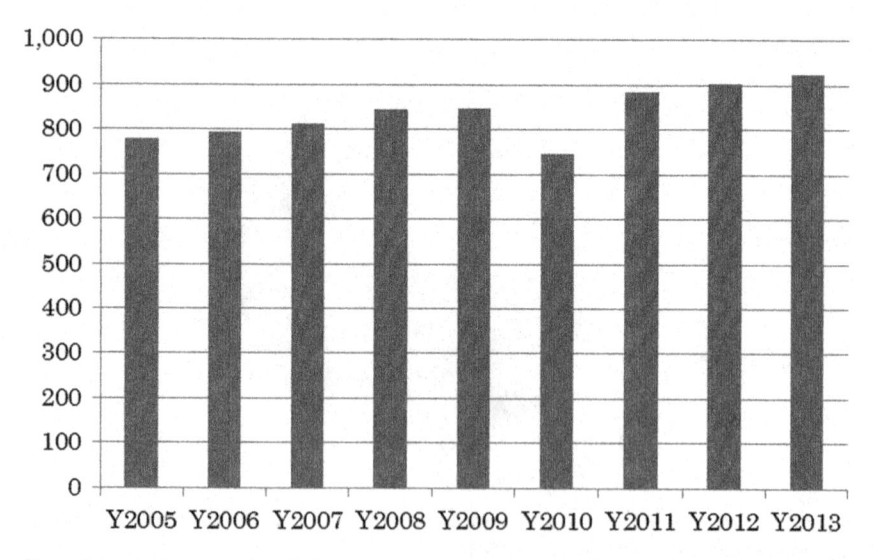

Fig. 12.3 Green tourism facilities lodgers in Japan 2005–2013 (10,000 people) (Source: MAFF 2015, p. 28)

Environmental Education Outside the Classroom

To understand how outdoor environmental education has developed chronologically, past research was examined. Imura (2006) found that the origin of outdoor education as a school activity in Japan was difficult to identify. The reason is that religious activities in remote and rural areas have been a practice for a long time, with youth in some communities being required to visit a holy mountain as a rite of passage to adulthood (Imura 2006, pp. 90–95). However, for school trips longer than one night (*shugaku ryokou*), some records remain. For example, *Tokyo Shihan Gakkou* (Tokyo School of Education), now University of Tsukuba, organized an 11-day hiking/walking trip around Chiba Prefecture in 1886 (JTB, Web) and school trips became popular in Japan earlier in the twentieth century, with some schools continuing these excursions during the Second World War (Ota 2013, p. 5). Interestingly, despite the war regulations, school trips to religious places were still conducted.

After the war, school trip venues were again deregulated. Due to the rapid rise in the popularity of school trips, the Japan School Trip Association was established in 1952 (JTB, Web). Special trains for school trips were also arranged by the former Japan National Railway in 1958. As school trips were usually organized during the week, accommodations in tourist destinations offered reasonable prices. Seki (1980) found that 65.7% of high schools in Japan organized *shugaku ryokou* in 1953, which increased to 92.6% in 1973 (Seki 1980, p. 18).

For nature-based school trips, national centers for outdoor education were initiated (Table 12.1). The first National Youth Friendship Center

Table 12.1 National Institution for Youth Education

Head Office	Planning of institution, program, research projects and grant projects for the private sector
National Olympics Memorial Youth Center	Training for people involved in youth education
National Youth Friendship Center	Planning and implementation of educational programs centered on friendship experiences
National Youth Outdoor Learning Center	Planning and implementation of educational programs centered on outdoor experiences

Source: National Institution for Youth Education (n.d.)

(*Seishounen Kouryu no Ie*) was established in 1959, and the first National Youth Outdoor Learning Center (*Seishounen Shizen no Ie*) was opened in 1975. To educate outdoor instructors and educators of youth, the National Olympics Memorial Youth Center (*Kokuritsu Olympic Kinen Seishounen Sougou Center*) was established at the former Tokyo Olympic Village in 1965 (National Institution for Youth Education, Web).

Due to continuous urbanization since the 1960s, outdoor education for urban youth has become much more important. In 1996, MEXT (Ministry of Education, Culture, Sports Science and Technology) reported an expansion of outdoor education for youth (*Seishounen no Yagai Kyouiku no Kakujyu ni Tsuite*) (MEXT, Web). Following this, the Japan Outdoor Education Society (JOES: *Nihon Yagai Kyouiku Gakkai*) was established in 1997 by specialists and educators (JOES Web).

The rural way of life also became more important for younger Japanese. In 2008, MEXT, MAFF and MIC (Ministry of Home Affairs and Communications) initiated an exchange program so that elementary students could visit and stay in rural communities (*Kodomo Nousangyoson Kouryu Project*) (Kodomo Nousangyoson Kouryu Project, Web). Usually, school trips in Japan are large; therefore, as only around five students can stay in one farmer's house, students were divided at the destination. Former farmers' inns (*Minshuku*) were deregulated compared with the inns in resort areas; however, farmers' inns registered in the newer scheme (*Minpaku*) offer rural farm stay activities for children such as agricultural cultivation and traditional cooking (Fig. 12.4).

As educational tourism in Japan is now diversified, there have been many studies on nature-based educational tourism. For example, Sawauchi et al. (2009) evaluated the agricultural experiences of high school students during their school trips in Hokkaido, and Wakabayashi (2013) examined the nature-based educational tourism development possibilities for an agricultural village from a case in Iida-city, Nagano Prefecture.

Because Japan's population is now declining in size, the domestic tourism market is also expected to shrink; however, the inbound tourist market has been increasing (Fig. 12.5). Tourism development as rural revitalization in the context of globalization is also important for remote

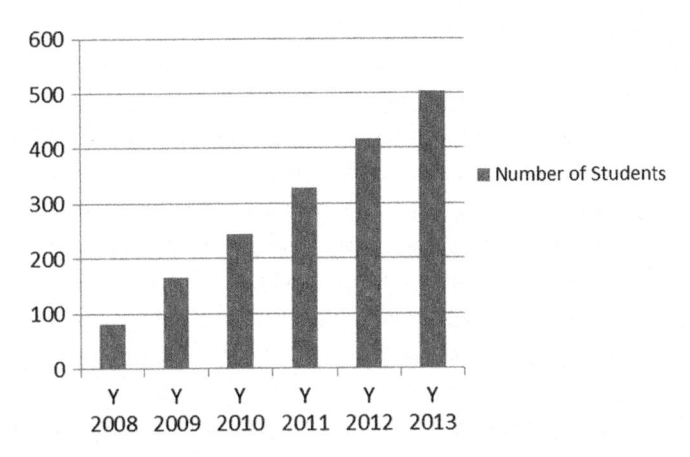

Fig. 12.4 Elementary students attending Japanese government rural visit projects 2008–2013 (1000 people) (Source: Yamaguchi Prefecture 2015, p. 8)

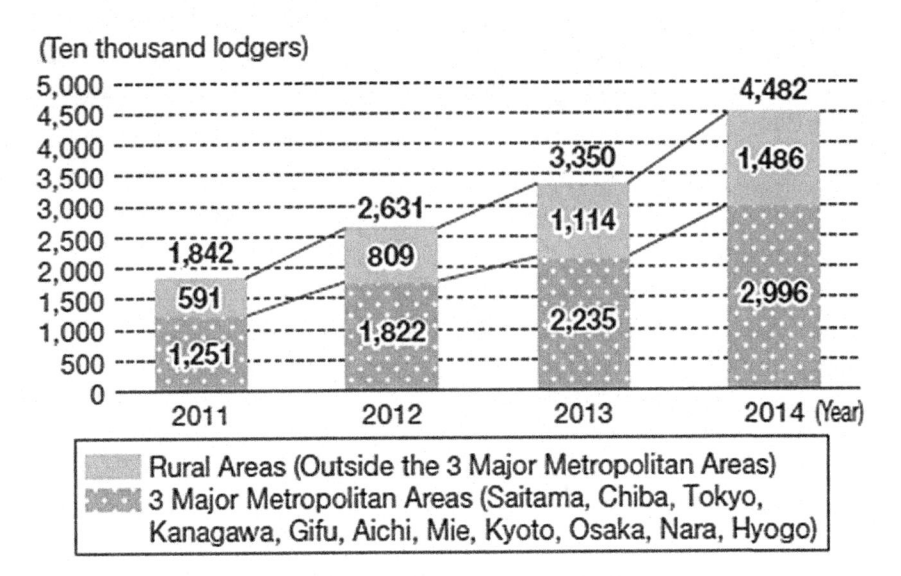

Fig. 12.5 Foreign visitor lodgers in Japan 2011–2014 (Source: MLIT 2015, p. 53)

areas, with Niseko in Hokkaido known as one of the more successful cases (Fig. 12.6).

There have been some case studies on rural global tourism in Japan. Tashiro (2011) examined tourism business development factors on Ojika Island, Nagasaki Prefecture. Ojika was once very successful in attracting international tourists to remote areas by using younger volunteers to cover the depopulation. Tsutsui and Kawabata (2010) examined inbound cases in Tateyama (Toyama Prefecture) and Towada (Aomori Prefecture) and found that the number of international visitors to green tourism facilities was still small; however, Tateyama accepted 77 international visitors in 2007 and Towada had 109 in 2008 (Tsutsui and Kawabata 2010, p. 42).

Many of the remote municipalities are aiming to follow these success stories. However, except for a few case studies, international educational tourism in remote areas has received little research attention despite the increasing importance of inbound tourism in Japan. Even though many remote municipalities in Japan have had some success in attracting international educational tourists, in general, there appears to have been few continuing success stories. As statistical research is limited in this field, case studies that monitor tourist information have become increasingly important.

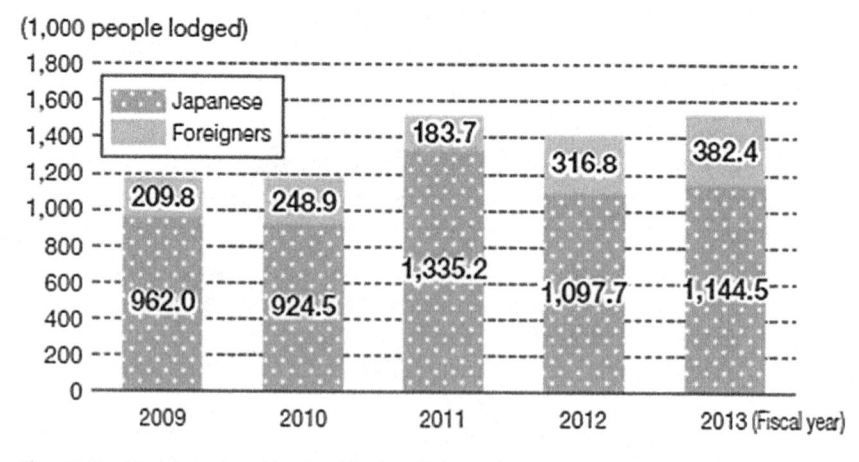

Fig. 12.6 Nights lodged in the Niseko Sightseeing Zone 2009–2013 (Source: MLIT 2015, p. 61)

Leisure Studies in Institutions of Higher Education and Academic Organizations

To develop and sustain new industry, human development and effective education are important. However, leisure education in Japan is concentrated on tourism. Although there are many professors of leisure studies in Japan, apart from vocational schools, only Tokai University (Table 12.2) has a department of sport and leisure management (Sport and Leisure Management *Gakka*) in its school of physical education (Taiiku *Gakubu*) as of 2017 (Tokai University, Web).

In Japan, a *gakubu* (faculty or school) generally has at least 20 professors, whereas a *gakka* (department) has at least 10 professors. A 'course' is usually at least five professors. These names of divisions are useful for quickly categorizing academic institutions. Certain websites allow searches of universities by subject: Study Sapuri, produced by Recruit, is a popular one of these (Study Sapuri, http://shingakunet.com/). According to Study Sapuri, as of June 2017, there are 24 *gakubu* (Table 12.3) and 70 *gakka* focusing on tourism in Japan, excluding courses.

Another way to search for Japanese academic organizations in leisure studies is through academic societies called *gakkai*; Gakkai Nenkan, maintained by JST (Japan Science and Technology Agency) lists relatively large academic societies in Japan (Gakkai Nenkan, https://gakkai. jst.go.jp/gakkai/). According to Gakkai Nenkan, the Japanese Society of Leisure and Recreation Studies (http://jslrs.jp/jslrs2014/), the Association for Leisure and Tourism Studies (http://www.leisure-tourism.com/), and the Japanese Association for Lifelong Education (http://www.j-lifelong. org/) are listed as of June 2017 among academic societies focusing on leisure. On the contrary, 15 academic societies, including the Association

Table 12.2 Department of Sport and Leisure Management

Key features
Sport and leisure as the key cultural feature of the department
Creating new lifestyles
Management tailored to globalization

Source: Tokai University (n.d.)

Table 12.3 Major tourism schools in Japan

Postgraduate
Hokkaido University, the Graduate School of International Media, Communication and Tourism Studies
Rikkyo University, Graduate School of Tourism
Ryukyu University, Graduate School of Tourism Sciences
Sapporo International University, Graduate School of Tourism
Wakayama University, Graduate School of Tourism
Undergraduate
Atomi Gakuen University, Faculty Tourism and Community Studies
Bunri University of Hospitality, Faculty of Service Management
Chiba University of Commerce, Faculty of Service Innovation
Hannan University, Faculty of International Tourism
Heian Jyogakuin University, Faculty of International Tourism
Jyosai International University, Faculty of Tourism
Meikai University, School of Hospitality & Tourism Management
Nagano University, Faculty of Tourism and Environmental Studies
Niigata University of Management, Faculty of Tourism Management
Osaka University of Tourism, Faculty of Tourism Studies
Rikkyo University, College of Tourism
Ryukyu University, Faculty of Tourism Sciences and Industrial Management
Sapporo International University, Faculty of Tourism
Shoin University, Faculty of Tourism, Media and Culture
Shumei University, Faculty of Tourism Business
Tamagawa University, College of Tourism and Hospitality
Tokai University, School of Tourism
Toyo University, Faculty of International Tourism Management
Wakayama University, Faculty of Tourism

Source: Study Sapuri (n.d)

for Leisure and Tourism Studies, are listed among academic tourism associations.

Although tourism studies are dominant in higher education today, Japanese leisure education has historically been well developed on a practical level. Nihon Recreation Kyoukai (National Recreation Association of Japan) was established in 1947, and during the 1940s and '50s, folk dances and other activities influenced by the US gained popularity among the Japanese. To instruct the Japanese in these imported activities, local instructors who had studied foreign recreation were needed (Nihon Recreation Kyoukai, Web-a).

During the high economic development of the 1950s and '60s, Japanese companies offered recreation activities to their workers. To systematically educate many recreation instructors, supported by Nihon Recreation Kyoukai, recreation *gakuen* (recreation academies) started being established in 1963 (Nihon Recreation Kyoukai, Web-a).

As the leisure boom of the 1960s became a social phenomenon, in 1965 Nihon Recreation Kyoukai established a research group and began to publish the *Journal of Recreation Studies* (renamed as *Journal of Leisure and Recreation Studies* in 1992). This research group expanded and became Nihon Recreation Gakkai (Japanese Recreation Academic Society) in 1971 (renamed as Japanese Society of Leisure and Recreation Studies, or Nihon Leisure Recreation Gakkai, in 1991) supported by Nihon Recreation Kyoukai (Japanese Society of Leisure and Recreation Studies, http://jslrs.jp/jslrs2014/). Because of the oil crisis of 1973, however, fewer recreation activities were offered by companies to their workers.

Local municipalities established local recreation policies for the locals in 1970s. *Kominkan* (public halls) and other local public facilities played an important role in local recreation during the 1970s. Through these community-based activities, the Japanese Society for Leisure Study and Development (Nihon Yoka Gakkai) was established in 1973 (Nihon Yoka Gakkai, http://www.yokagakkai.jp/).

Universities and colleges also started offering the recreational instructor licenses authorized by the Nihon Recreation Kyoukai beginning in 1983 (Nihon Recreation Kyoukai, Web-b). As of April 2016, 57,592 recreation instructors had been licensed by this association and approximately 400 educational institutions including vocational schools were in its network (Nihon Recreation Kyoukai, Web-c).

Although the Japanese economy recovered quickly, turning to the bubble economy boom in the 1980s, population aging gradually overtook Japan. Activities for the elderly gradually became important. In 1980, the Japanese Association for Lifelong Education (Nihon Shogai Gakushu Gakkai) was established (Japanese Association for Lifelong Education http://www.j-lifelong.org/). According to Nihon Yoka Gakkai, many members moved to this newer association (Nihon Yoka Gakkai, http://www.yokagakkai.jp/). Nihon Yoka Gakkai was reconstructed as the

Association for Leisure and Tourism Studies (Yoka Tourism Gakkai) in 2012 (Association for Leisure and Tourism Studies, http://www.leisure-tourism.com/).

To combine social welfare and recreation, in the face of aging, reclamation instruction became an essential subject for social welfare workers in 1987 (Nihon Recreation Kyoukai, Web-a). As of April 2016, there were 5071 licensed recreation workers in social welfare (Nihon Recreation Kyoukai, Web-c).

These movements also become academically important. One example is the former Nihon Kenkou Recreation Kyoukai (Japanese Health and Recreation Association), which was renamed Nihon Kenkou Recreation Gakkai (Japanese Health and Recreation Studies Association) in 2014 (Nihon Kenkou Recreation Gakkai, http://www.geocities.jp/recgatukai/). This organization has been publishing *Health and Recreation Research Journal* (formerly Kenkou Recreation Kenkyu Ronbunshu, renamed as *Japanese Journal of Health Recreation* in 2014) since 2004 (National Library, http://iss.ndl.go.jp/books/R100000002-I023389548-00). As remote areas are the front runners in aging and depopulation, the relation between recreation, social welfare and local revitalization are becoming an important issue practically and academically.

Green Tourism Education in Yamaguchi Case Study

Yamaguchi Prefecture (Fig. 12.7) is located in the far west of Honshu Island and has many natural attractions (such as Akiyoshido Cave and Akiyoshidai Limestone Plateau) and historical spots (such as Hagi castle town and the Rurikouji five story pagoda). Despite Yamaguchi being once famous for mass tourism, different types of tourists are needed to ensure tourism sustainability. Hagi has been nominated as a UNESCO world heritage site and Akiyoshidai is attempting to become a World Geopark.

However, as many places suffering from shrinking primary industry do not have any famous tourist attractions, they are trying to find alternative

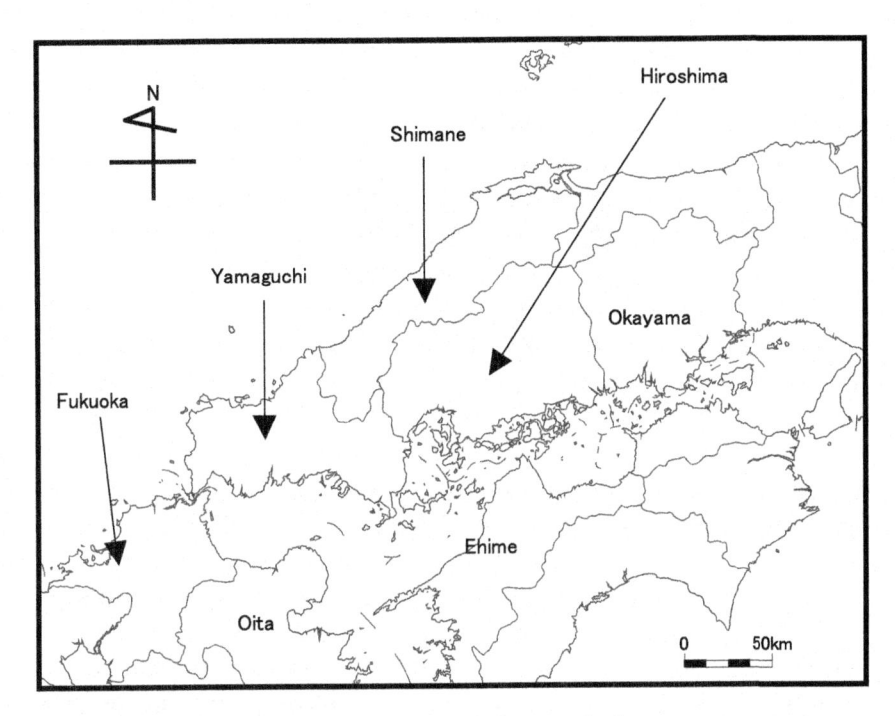

Fig. 12.7 Map of Yamaguchi (Source: Made by Asamizu)

attractions. One solution is to initiate farm stays at farmers' inns to give students agricultural experiences on their nature-based school trips. As previously mentioned, many rental farm gardens are concentrated around large cities, which is a disadvantage for remote prefectures such as Yamaguchi. On the other hand, as school trips in Japan are usually a few days long, it is possible to attract urban students to Yamaguchi. Since the Yamaguchi Prefectural Government established a rural school trip association and began inviting students from Osaka and Tokyo (Fig. 12.8), there has been a significant increase in education tourists.

In Yamaguchi Prefecture, the front runner for rural educational tourism is the Suo Oshima Island. Even though Suo Oshima residents have attracted around 4000 domestic educational tourists to their homes, the area is also suffering from aging and depopulation, which is challenging for any future improvements. Kitakaze et al. (2010), in a case study on

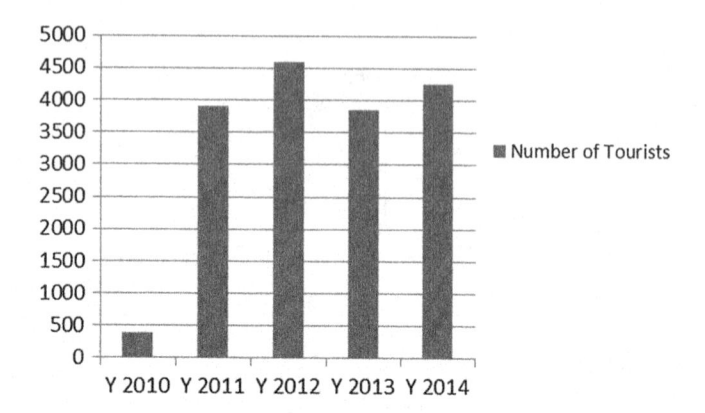

Fig. 12.8 Rural educational tourists in Yamaguchi Prefecture 2010–2014 (People) (Source: Yamaguchi Prefecture 2015, p. 12)

Suo Oshima, reported on an effort involving industry-university-government cooperation to encourage local reactivation. Kota et al. (2011), also in a case study on Suo Oshima, reported on the conduct of an entrepreneurs' course for the tourist industries. This island also arranged homestay programs for international secondary students during the World Scout Jamboree in Yamaguchi in 2015.

Except for the period of the World Scout Jamboree, at which there were more than 30,000 international students, there have been only a few international educational tourists visiting Yamaguchi. However, according to JASSO, there were 1832 international students in Yamaguchi Prefecture in 2015 (JASSO 2016), and Yamaguchi University, the largest university in Yamaguchi Prefecture, had more than 300 international students in the same year (Fig. 12.9).

During the World Scout Jamboree, Yamaguchi Prefectural Government called for volunteer guides and international students from Yamaguchi University, with the volunteer rate for Japanese students being higher than for international students (Fig. 12.10); more Japanese students than expected worked as volunteers during the Jamboree as they enjoyed the opportunity to communicate with international visitors, since very few tourists visit Yamaguchi on a regular basis.

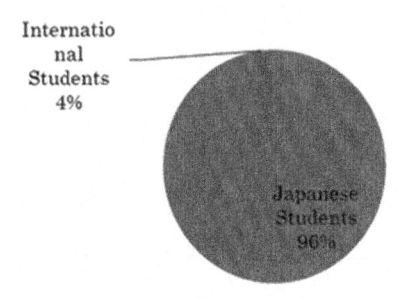

Fig. 12.9 YU students (as of December 2015, n = 10,209) (Source: Yamaguchi University 2015)

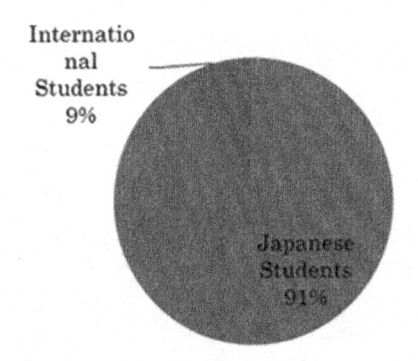

Fig. 12.10 Student volunteer guides from YU, World Scout Jamboree 2015 (n = 54) (Source: author)

International students, however, are seeking more local experiences. Yamaguchi Prefectural Government and some of the municipalities are seeking to develop newer tourist destinations and are also calling for student monitors. Mine City is a neighboring city to Yamaguchi and is adjacent to the main Yamaguchi University campus. The Mine Tourism Association expected Japanese students to volunteer as monitors; however, more than 40% of the attendants were international students despite being only 4% of the student population (Fig. 12.11, Photo 12.12).

Mine City's case is no exception. In Hagi Okan, which is located between Hagi to Hofu via Yamaguchi City, the majority of student

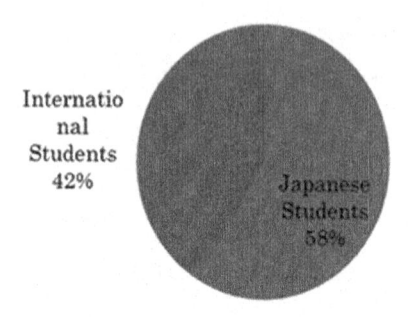

Fig. 12.11 Student monitoring volunteers from YU, Mine City 2013–2015 (n = 60) (Source: author)

Photo 12.12 Mine monitoring tour (Photo by author, Akiyoshidai, November 2014)

monitors were international students (Fig. 12.13, Photo 12.14); however, as these samples are limited, it is difficult to generalize, as international students in Yamaguchi University are interested in attending local Japanese events. Generally speaking, tourists wish to visit places that are different

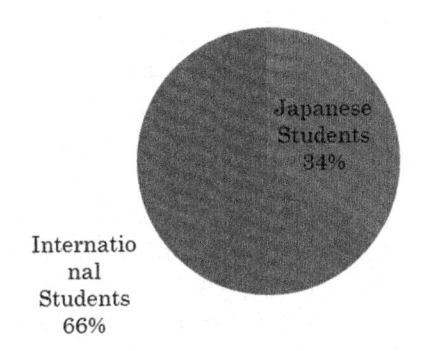

Fig. 12.13 Student monitoring volunteers from YU, Hagi Okan 2015–2016 (n = 32) (Source: author)

Photo 12.14 Hagi Okan monitoring tour (Photo by author, Hanchomon, December 2015)

from their daily lives. Further, international students are not really tourists; however, the interest shown by the students strongly indicates that local resources could attract international tourists.

Conclusion

This paper briefly introduced historical changes in leisure and tourism in Japan. Industrialization, urbanization, human mobility, depopulation and aging are important areas to examine to enable understanding of these changes.

Just after WWII, as outdoor nature activities were popular with the Japanese, beach resorts, ski fields and other facilities were established both privately and by the government. As urbanization grew after the war, rural leisure activities became gradually more important in Japan.

In addition to the Second World War, the oil crisis of the early 1970s and the bursting of the bubble economy in the early 1990s were also major turning points in Japan. Many policies related to leisure and tourism changed during these times. In particular, the post-bubble depression with its attendant depopulation required various changes. As remote areas suffer greatly from depopulation and aging, fundamental changes regarding these are required.

Urban-rural exchanges were popular leisure activities for senior citizens, and they provided important educational activities for younger people. As urbanization in Japan has continued for more than three generations, the rural way of life is unfamiliar to many young people in large cities. For rural residents, rural leisure tourism by individual tourists and by group education tourists from primary and secondary schools has become an important revenue source. As visiting patterns of leisure-oriented tourists and education tourists differ, management and activity has diversified.

More recently, to develop greater cross cultural understanding, rural experiences in Japan have become more important for international visitors. However, to attract more international tourists, alternative tourist attractions are needed. As voluntary work is also important educationally, sometimes international student volunteers contribute to rural community tourism as interpreters and monitors.

The rural areas of Japan face deep and complicated problems. To address them, the national government and municipal authorities have altered their policies. To develop newer human resources, educational institutions have also systematically changed. To study complicated problems, researchers and specialists have organized working groups and academic associations. Collaboration between fields may bring innovation and solutions.

References

Gakkai Nenkan. (n.d.). *Kensaku.* https://gakkai.jst.go.jp/gakkai/. Accessed 1 June 2017.

Imura, H. (2006). The Origin of Outdoor Education in Japan. *Japan Outdoor Education Journal, 10*(1), 85–97.

JASSO. (2016). *Heisei 27 Nendo Gaikokujin Ryugakusei Zaiseki Jyoukyou Chousa Kekka.* http://www.jasso.go.jp/about/statistics/intl_student_e/2015/. Accessed 1 Mar 2017.

JOES. (n.d.) *History.* http://joes.gr.jp/?page_id=1535. Accessed 1 Mar 2017.

JTB. (n.d.). *JTB Group no Kyouiku Jigyou.* http://www.jtbcorp.jp/jp/colors/detail/0063/. Accessed 1 Mar 2017.

Kaji, T. (2009). *Study on the Significance of the Establishment of the National Park Resort Villages and Effectiveness of Usage of the Natural Park in Japan.* Tokyo: Tokyo Kankyo Kouka Gakuen Shuppanbu.

Kitakaze, H., Miyamoto, A., Okanouchi, S., Okamura, K., & Okataku, Y. (2010). An Activity Report on Industry-University-Government Cooperation Aimed for Local Reactivation. *Oshima Shousen Koutou Senmongakkou Kiyou, 43*, 1–10.

Kodomo Nousangyoson Kouryu Project. (n.d.). *Homepage.* http://www.kodomo-furusato.net/. Accessed 1 Mar 2017.

Kota, M., Kitakaze, H., Iwami, Y., Okataku, Y., Kubota, T., & Moriwaki, C. (2011). A Report of the Entrepreneur Course for Tourist Industries. *Oshima Shousen Koutou Senmongakkou Kiyou, 44*, 123–130.

Ministry of Agriculture, Forestry and Fisheries. (2015). *Summary of the Basic Plan for Food, Agriculture and Rural Areas.* Tokyo: MAFF.

Ministry of Agriculture, Forestry and Fisheries. (2016). *Shimin Nouen wo Meguru Jyoukyou.* http://www.maff.go.jp/j/nousin/nougyou/simin_noen/zyokyo.html. Accessed 1 Mar 2017.

Ministry of Education, Culture, Sports Science and Technology. (n.d.). *Seishounen no Yagai Kyouiku no Jyujitsu ni Tsuite.* http://www.mext.go.jp/b_

menu/hakusho/nc/t19960724001/t19960724001.html. Accessed 1 Mar 2017.

Ministry of Land, Infrastructure, Transport and Tourism. (2015). *White Paper on Land, Infrastructure, Transport and Tourism in Japan, 2014.* Tokyo: MLIT.

Nakayama, A. (2006). *Shizen Kyuyou Son no Chiikiteki Tokusei.* Chiba: Moegi Shuppan.

National Institution for Youth Education. (n.d.). *History.* http://www.niye.go.jp/english/history/. Accessed 1 Mar 2017.

Nihon Recreation Kyoukai. (n.d.-a). *Recreation Undo no Rekishi.* http://www.recreation.or.jp/association/folder/. Accessed 30 May 2017.

Nihon Recreation Kyoukai. (n.d.-b). *Ayumi to Enkaku.* http://www.recreation.or.jp/association/transition/. Accessed 1 June 2007.

Nihon Recreation Kyoukai. (n.d.-c). *Kounin Shidousha Suu.* http://www.recreation.or.jp/association/coach/. Accessed 1 June 2007.

Ota, T. (2013). *Showa Zenhanki ni Okeru Shugakuryoko to Ryoko Bunka.* PhD Dissertation, Yokohama City University.

Oura, Y. (2004). Recreational Enterprises in National Forests and Their Influence on Local Society. *Nagoya Daigaku Shinrin Kagaku Kenkyu, 23,* 19–98.

Sawauchi, D., Kuraoka, K., Sajiki, T., Toguchi, T., & Yamamoto, Y. (2009). Evaluation of High School Students' Agricultural Experiences During a School Trip. *Nouringyou Mondai Kenkyu, 174,* 133–136.

Seki, N. (1980). Gakkou Kyouiku ni Okeru Shugaku Ryoko no Ichiduke. *Shin Chiri, 27*(4), 17–26.

Shinpo, N. (2015). *Studies on the Change of Urban Gardening in Japan.* PhD Dissertation, University of Tokyo.

Study Sapuri (n.d.) *Keyword Search.* http://shingakunet.com/. Accessed 1 June 2017.

Tashiro, M. (2011). The Factors for Development of the Tourism Business in a Disadvantaged Place. *Keizairon Kenkyu, 139,* 77–98.

Tokai University. (n.d.). *School of Physical Education.* http://www.u-tokai.ac.jp/english/academics/undergraduate/physical_education.html. Accessed 30 May 2017.

Tsutsui, K., & Kawabata, T. (2010). Perspective of Green Tourism for Foreign Tourists in Rural Japan. *E-journal GEO, 5*(1), 35–49.

Wakabayashi, N. (2013). Development Possibility for Inn and Agriculture/Agricultural Village by Educational Travel of Green Tourism Case Study: Iida-city, Nagano. *Chiiki Seisaku Kenkyu, 15*(3), 159–179.

Yamada, K. (2008). Change in Rural Tourism in Japan's Mountainous Agricultural Areas: A Study of the Period before 1992 and 'Green Tourism. *Kyouei Daigaku Ronshu, 6,* 13–25.

Yamaguchi Prefecture. (2015). *Yamaguchi Ken Taikengata Kyouiku Ryokou Action Plan.* Yamaguchi Prefecture.

Yamaguchi University. (2015). *Gakuhou* No.141. http://www.yamaguchi-u.ac.jp/info/_3120/_4187/_4675.html. Accessed 29 Jan 2016.

13

Internalizing Serious Leisure to Enhance Well-Being in Adventure Recreation

KoFan Lee

Introduction

Adventure recreation (AR), which includes such activities as rock climbing, skiing and snowboarding, kayaking, stand-up paddling and triathlon, has received increased attention in recent decades. The growth of the industry enables people to access it as a casual leisure experience or to embrace it as a central life interest or lifestyle. Media exposure and Internet access allow enthusiasts and people who want to explore, learn and master those activities to connect with others worldwide (Wheaton 2010). AR activities contain real and perceived risks and challenging conditions, which require participants to possess certain levels of competence to enjoy and sustain such experiences (Ewert and Hollenhorst 1994). Words like 'extreme', 'risky', 'adventure' and 'deviant' are sometimes used to describe the sensation-seeking nature of AR and its participants' risk-taking behaviors (Barrett and Martin 2014; Woodman et al. 2013). Such labels, however, are not accurately applied across all AR activities, settings

K. Lee (✉)
Department of Health, Exercise Science and Recreation Management, School of Applied Sciences, University of Mississippi, Oxford, MS, USA

© The Author(s) 2018
A. Beniwal et al. (eds.), *Global Leisure and the Struggle for a Better World*, Leisure Studies in a Global Era, https://doi.org/10.1007/978-3-319-70975-8_13

and populations. Past studies have found that adventure recreationists are drawn to those activities not only due to sensation seeking (Gilbertson and Ewert 2015) but also to seek mastery (Kerr and Mackenzie 2014), freedom (Brymer and Schweitzer 2013), connection to nature (Brymer and Gray 2010), social support (Allman et al. 2009; Ewert et al. 2013) and emotional regulation (Woodman et al. 2010), among other reasons. Furthermore, AR activities have a long history of application in outdoor experiential education to help participants reflect on and redevelop their intrapersonal and interpersonal skills (Priest and Gass 2005; Whittington et al. 2015). It is clearly evident that AR provides a venue for its participants to enhance their well-being and development.

In response to the title of this book, *Global Leisure and a Struggle for a Better World*, I first want to recognize AR as a global phenomenon. Subsequently, to better understand AR experiences and justify the appropriateness of AR as an avenue to well-being, I explain how adventure recreationists commit to AR activities by using the notion of serious leisure (SL) (Stebbins 2007). Serious leisure provides a comprehensive framework concerning leisure as a central life interest that recreationists commit to personally and socially. Recreationists acquire fulfilling experiences from leisure commitments, which enrich their lives and enhance their well-being (Heo et al. 2013). Furthermore, self-determination theory (SDT) will be used to explain motivations for sustaining serious pursuits of AR. Hence, this chapter serves to develop a framework to integrate internalization with serious pursuits in AR.

Adventure Recreation

According to the adventure model (Ewert and Hollenhorst 1989), AR is defined as "a variety of self-initiated activities…that contain elements of real or apparent danger, in which the outcome, while uncertain, can be influenced by the participants and circumstances" (p. 125). In addition, Priest and Carpenter (1993) propose the adventure experience paradigm. Adventure recreationists experience the interaction between perceived risk and perceived competence. The equilibrium of risk and competence leads to peak experiences; imbalances, on the other hand, can bore or distress recreationists. Although both definitions recognize the presence of perceived risks and dangers in AR contexts, risk alone does not lead to optimal experiences. The intrinsic nature of AR experiences, which stresses the need to develop personal competences to gain a sense of control or mastery in challenging conditions, is implied by these two models as well as other studies (Csikszentmihalyi and Csikszentmihalyi 1999; Lee 2013; Stebbins 2005).

Although the intrinsic value of AR suggests an ideal state of AR experience, realistically, not everyone can attain this ideal state (Buckley 2012; Kerr and Mackenzie 2014). Recreationists without sufficient knowledge of an activity need experienced counterparts to keep them secure and motivated. Nonetheless, the beauty of AR experience is the mastery or peak experience that makes them insiders. An insider not only possesses sufficient skills and knowledge to engage in AR experiences but is also socially connected: interacting frequently with other enthusiasts, communities and media in an AR context to gain competences, social status and personal identity (Wheaton 2010, 2004).[1] A meaningful AR experience is then developed through one's efforts to acquire these types of capital in order to develop and sustain a career in AR.

Nowadays, the consumption of AR has become a global phenomenon, and its accessibility is unprecedented. Industry-conducted surveys reveal the growth trend in AR participation (Outdoor Foundation 2016; Sport England and Outdoor Industries Association 2015) and the significant economic impact made by the outdoor industry (Outdoor Industry Association 2012). The World Tourism Organization (UNWTO) has recognized adventure tourism as a worldwide phenomenon and advocates the need to develop it in a sustainable way (UNWTO 2014). Modern infrastructure (e.g., indoor climbing facilities), the evolution of AR activities [e.g., ski versus snowboard (Coates et al. 2010)] and developing technology [e.g., social media, weatherproof garments and light-weight equipment (Berger and Greenspan 2008)] make AR more publicly visible and attract people with diverse backgrounds to different AR forms (e.g., sport versus traditional climbing), spatial areas (e.g., urban versus backcountry), ways of travel (e.g., domestic versus international) and so on. More importantly, AR provides an alternative approach to the pursuit of well-being, such as the use of AR to reduce stress (Gilbertson and Ewert 2015) and to express emotions (Woodman et al. 2010).

With its growing popularity, the sustainability of the AR industry relies not only on consumers who seek novelty or excitement but also committed members who represent authentic identities, define the meaning of participation and enrich the subculture of a given activity (Wheaton 2004). For example, Chris Sharma pioneered the development of difficult sport climbing routes, founded an indoor climbing facility and presented rock climbing as a lifestyle (About Chris Sharma n.d.). Through media exposure he has become an inspirational figure to motivate others to join the sport. The achievement of other elite AR athletes, such as Tony Hawk in skateboarding (Official Tony Hawk 2017), has also enhanced participation in those activities.

It should be noted that although elite recreationists, to some extent, define norms, standards, performances and values in an AR context, not everyone needs to follow this path to becoming an elite recreationist. Instead, the evolution of AR creates new opportunities to accommodate the various needs of participants with diverse backgrounds and help them develop diverse identities within an AR context (Lee et al. 2017; Wheaton 2010) (see note 1). For example, in addition to pursuing personal excellence, a rock climber can also choose to participate in climbing-related experiences such as promoting ethnic diversity (Johnson 2017) and promoting land conservation (Access Fund 2017).

Serious Leisure

Serious leisure (SL) describes committed leisure experiences. It is defined as "the systematic pursuit of an amateur, hobbyist or volunteer activity sufficiently substantial and interesting for the participant to find a career there in the acquisition and expression of a combination of its special skills, knowledge, and experience" (Stebbins 2007, p. 5). SL reveals diverse and complex participation activities within a recreation context. In terms of diversity, past studies have examined participants at different career stages, exploring how their motivations, perceptions and behaviors vary (Brown 2007). In terms of complexity, some participants may play different or multiple roles in a recreation context. While their skills may not improve, their knowledge and experience regarding the activity continue to grow (Bendle and Patterson 2009; Heuser 2005).

The characteristics of SL have been commonly used to explain leisure commitment in AR activities such as endurance sports (Lamont and Kennelly 2012; McCarville 2007; Shipway and Jones 2008), water sports (Barbieri and Sotomayor 2013; Bartram 2001; Gould et al. 2008; Kane and Zink 2004), mountain sports (Dilley and Scraton 2010; Lee 2013; Stebbins 2005) and others (Rosenbaum 2013; Shupe and Gagné 2016). Six characteristics of SL (perseverance, significant effort, career, unique ethos, identification and durable benefits) describe fulfilling experiences in which recreationists explore, learn and master an activity, build social networks and develop personal leisure identities (Stebbins 2007).

To elaborate, perseverance is typified by the adventure recreationist's resilience to address challenging situations during pursuits, which in turn glorify their reputation and enrich their credentials in a recreation activity [e.g., the discomforts runners confront in a race (Shipway and Jones 2008)].

Effort indicates how hard recreationists strive to acquire and exercise skills, knowledge and experience—the cornerstone of enjoyment and mastery in SL (Stebbins 2007). Serious recreationists—those who desire to progress in a recreation context—are also more active in developing their competences compared to less-serious counterparts (Shupe and Gagné 2016); I discuss this later in depth to connect SL and internalization.

The characteristic associated with career indicates the recreationist's progress in a recreation context; the development of their careers relies on contingencies such as achievements [e.g., the first completion of a full-course marathon (Shipway and Jones 2008)], involvement [e.g., artists actively involved in the development of grassroots organizations (Bendle and Patterson 2009)] and culture in a recreation context [e.g., the way female climbers form social groups to address gender identities in rock climbing; Dilley and Scraton 2010)]. Recreationists use these contingencies to present themselves as qualified members to other enthusiasts in a recreation context (McCarville 2007).

Simultaneously, while engaging in an activity, recreationists establish their personal identities among other participants. They present equipment, stories, skills and other such endeavors to comply with the norms of that context and inform others of their affiliations (Robinson et al. 2014; Shipway and Jones 2008). While the first several SL characteristics mentioned above focus on personal experiences, the SL perspective also stresses the importance of a social world (i.e., unique ethos) and the cultures, norms and values it provides in shaping people into serious recreationists (Patterson et al. 2016; Robinson et al. 2014).

Durable benefits include seven personal benefits and three social outcomes obtained from the recreationist's serious pursuits. The seven personal outcomes are personal enrichment, self-actualization, self-expression, self-image, self-gratification, recreation and financial return. The three social benefits are social attraction, group accomplishments and group maintenance (Stebbins 2007). These durable benefits not only provide fulfilling leisure experiences but also motivate recreationists' continuing participation (Stebbins 2007).

Past studies have supported the notion that the characteristics of seriousness (i.e., perseverance, effort, career, unique ethos and identification) are associated with durable outcomes (Heo et al. 2012; Lyu and Oh 2014). Specifically, the development of personal and social identities is crucial for recreationists to perceive their experiences as beneficial and meaningful. In addition to positive recreation experiences, serious leisure also contributes to senior volunteers' subjective well-being (Pi et al. 2014), supporting the idea that leisure commitment plays an important role in enhancing well-being.

Motivation, a Piece Connecting Serious Leisure and Adventure Recreation

While the characteristics of SL explain *how* people commit to AR, Stebbins' work also provides a theoretical foundation for understanding *why* people commit to AR. First of all, although risk is a core element in AR not all activities considered AR are equally risky (Woodman et al. 2013; Wheaton 2010); thus, risk should not be considered the only reason people pursue AR (Ewert et al. 2013; Stebbins 2005). The primary intrinsic reward of pursuing AR is to fulfill the need to build and use competences to address challenging situations in AR contexts, or enjoy a sense of flow (Csikszentmihalyi 1991), which Stebbins considers as a 'cardinal motivator' for devotees of mountain sports (Stebbins 2005, p. 42).[2]

Although the intrinsically rewarding nature of SL adequately explains how adventure recreationists strive to address challenging situations by developing and exerting their skills and knowledge in order to gain a sense of control, such mastery may only apply to recreationists who are adept at their hobbies (Buckley 2012). Recreationists with different individual attributes, such as levels of specialization, can be motivated differently (Ewert et al. 2013).

For example, past SL studies have indicated that recreationists at different career stages have different social motives (Heuser 2005; Shupe and Gagné 2016). For recreationists at a beginning stage or for those who are externally motivated, the social motive is to fulfill the expectations of people close to them; their participation is contingent upon others' participation. On the other hand, experienced and internally motivated recreationists actively seek out community events that allow them to advance their careers or help others progress. The SDT framework, borrowed by Shupe and Gagné (2016), indicates that internally motivated recreationists actively work to progress their piloting capacities, develop piloting communities and reach out to bring others into the activity. Their findings also indicate that quality of motivation is crucial to recreationists' commitments.

Therefore, instead of discussing surface-level motives, as listed in the beginning of this paper, the following discussion focuses on the motivational mechanism facilitating ongoing serious commitments in AR, given that participants' long-lasting benefits and well-being are gained through ongoing commitment rather than casual participation. Therefore, it is necessary to understand AR motivation at a deeper level by discussing source-level motives (Mullan et al. 1997),[3] emphasizing how motivation with various levels of self-determination influences engagements into different life domains such as exercise (Ryan and Deci 2000).

Internalization

To further discuss the link between source-level motivation and serious pursuit of AR, I first introduce SDT. Source-level motivations (Mullan et al. 1997) derive from the SDT perspective. SDT explains intrinsic motivation—the natural propensity for human beings to learn, explore and grow. It also identifies multiple extrinsic motivations to explain why some participants present commitment and vitality when not intrinsically motivated, while others give up or experience drudgery in leisure, job or school contexts (Ryan and Deci 2000).

Ryan and Deci (2000) propose a motivation continuum to conceptualize multiple types of motivation, and they indicate a process of internalization that explains how well people integrate external regulation with personal value systems. When a regulation is highly internalized, one will perceive his/her behavior as self-endorsed, not coerced.

On the left-most extreme of the continuum is 'amotivation', which indicates no intention to act. This happens when an individual does not value the action, and the potential consequence of such action is impersonal. Intrinsic motivation, at the opposite extreme, coincides with full interest. Ryan and Deci (2000) define intrinsic motivation thus: "The construct of intrinsic motivation describes this natural inclination toward assimilation, mastery, spontaneous interest and exploration that is so essential to cognitive and social development and that represents a principal source of enjoyment and vitality throughout life" (p. 70). Intrinsic motivation implies ideal AR experiences in which recreationists strive to acquire psychological flow or peak status and actively seek out contingencies to repeat such fulfilling experiences, leading eventually to enhanced well-being (Csikszentmihalyi 1991; Ryan and Deci 2000; Priest 1992).

Extrinsic motivation is classified into subtypes. External regulation is the least self-determined force. Externally regulated behaviors indicate that one's action depends completely upon external contingencies such as reward or punishment. The removal of stimuli halts continued participation. 'Introjected regulation' occurs when individuals take in some values of external regulations without integrating them into their value system. Introjected regulations include the heightening of self-worth or the avoidance of a sense of guilt (Assor et al. 2009); even though the regulation is internal, the behavior is not self-endorsed, but instead it fulfills the demands of society. These two types of regulation are classified as 'controlled motivation' (Wilson et al. 2012).

On the other hand, identification regulation and integrated regulation present high and completed levels of self-determination, respectively, in which one feels that a behavior is congruent with her/his value systems and is personally meaningful. These two types of regulation, combined with intrinsic motivation, constitute autonomous motivation (Teixeira et al. 2012; Wilson et al. 2012). Multiple extrinsic motivations indicate not only levels of internalization, but the human tendency to integrate and further internalize environmental contingencies (Ryan and Deci 2000).

Past SDT studies in the exercise domain have shown that, in general, autonomous motivation facilitates commitments to exercise and well-being, whereas controlled motivation has a negligible or detrimental influence on exercise behaviors and intentions (Teixeira et al. 2012; Wilson et al. 2012). To be more specific, in their systematic review paper Teixeira et al. (2012) argue that identified regulation tends to be a more consistent contributor to exercise commitment than intrinsic motivation, but intrinsic motivation may lead to long-term well-being. Introjected regulation provides mixed results and may facilitate or hinder exercise experiences.

Not until recently has the SDT perspective been used to explain motivations behind serious pursuits of AR in more than a few studies (Lamont and Kennelly 2012; Lee 2013; Shupe and Gagné 2016). First, Lamont and Kennelly (2012) studied amateur triathletes' motives using the SDT framework. In their study two major themes, intrinsic and extrinsic motivations, were identified, and each major theme entails multiple sub-themes. Although intrinsic motives, such as competence and enjoyment, are largely recognized, triathletes are also motivated by either personally-meaningful forces—such as pursuing well-being and self-transformation, or external regulations—such as opportunities to travel and own equipment. Their study also reveals the cyclical nature of sport motivation (Ryan and Deci 2007), with extrinsic motivation playing an important role during the training phase, in support of enjoyment and competence in a race. Other studies report similar findings (McCarville 2007).

Shupe and Gagné (2016) classified female airplane pilots into independent, interdependent and dependent groups based on their motivations. Independent pilots present stronger internal motives to actively learn and master piloting than the two other groups, who emphasize shared experiences with significant others. Socially, independent and interdependent pilots become involved in organizations and events for self-progression or promotion of female piloting, whereas Shupe and Gagné describe dependent pilots' leisure experiences as companionate leisure. The results of their study imply that the level of internalization parallels the level of commitment.

Lee (2013) examines the association between quality of motivation and seriousness and SL outcomes. The primary finding is that identified regulation is a consistent variable associated with seriousness and outcomes, and it presents a stronger association with seriousness than with intrinsic motivation. This finding is consistent with the study conducted by Edmunds et al. (2006), which showed that identified motivation as a better contributor to strenuous exercise than intrinsic motivation. Further, intrinsic motivation is associated with personal rewards, whereas introjected motivation is related to social rewards. As with the two other studies previously discussed, adventure recreationists display multidimensional motives in their serious pursuits, and the SDT framework enhances our understanding of internalization's links to leisure commitment.

Taken together, the results of these studies indicate that adventure recreationists' motivations range from extrinsic to intrinsic motivations. The motivation continuum is appropriate to capture the motivational orientations of adventure recreationists. Internalization also facilitates leisure commitment, and internalized motivations enable recreationists to define the purpose and significance of their behaviors and to persist through challenging conditions (Ryan and Deci 2000). Serious pursuits of AR are not always pleasant; however, it is not uncommon to observe recreationists persisting through challenging conditions and using these experiences to energize future participation (Stebbins 2005).

It should be noted that although these studies reveal internalization in serious pursuits of AR, internalization does not occur in isolation. From the SDT perspective, motivation is a social phenomenon, and social conditions promote or hinder the process of internalization (Vallerand and Ratelle 2002). As a result, the notion of social worlds will be revisited to explain how social contexts are related to recreationists' commitments.

Implications: Social Contexts Facilitating Internalization

The notion of a social world exerts a profound influence on the SL perspective. Unruh (1980) defines a social world as an "amorphous and diffuse constellation of actors, organizations, events, and practices which have coalesced into a perceived sphere of interest and involvement for participants" (p. 277). Social worlds entail different levels of interactions between actors, organizations, events and practices at various spatial levels. Actors determine their level of involvement and voluntarily participate in activities within a social world (Unruh 1979). Norms, standards and values guide people's activity within a social world, rather than force them to comply with those regulations.

Past SL studies reveal that recreationists at different career stages act differently in social worlds. Endurance sport athletes in the early stages of their careers use social worlds to obtain social supports and learn the subculture of endurance sports (McCarville 2007; Robinson et al. 2014). Adventure recreationists also strive to acquire social capital to enhance their status in AR communities at local or global levels (Kane and Zink 2004; Shipway and Jones 2008). Finally, established adventure recreationists may impart their legacy to younger enthusiasts and give back to communities (Brown 2007; Heuser 2005; Shupe and Gagné 2016). These findings are consistent with Unruh's classification of actors as strangers, tourists, regulars, and insiders. These four roles portray how an actor evolves in social worlds with increasing levels of identity, attachment and responsibility. An insider takes initiative to shape and operate social worlds and is concerned with the sustainability of social worlds;

this description of insiders applies to experienced lawn bowlers (Heuser 2005), serious shag dancers (Brown 2007) and independent airplane pilots (Shupe and Gagné 2016). I would argue the behaviors these insiders present are highly internalized; they not only understand and embrace the subculture of a given activity, but shape these subcultures and inspire other members.

When recognizing the serious pursuit of AR as a means to enhance well-being with internalization as the underlying motivational mechanism of this pursuit, subsequent discussion must include the social implications of this internalization. Internalization occurs when one's basic psychological needs are satisfied. These psychological needs include competence, relatedness and autonomy. Briefly, competence indicates the perception that one can use or exercise her/his capacities and effectively function in a social environment. Relatedness refers to a sense of community. Autonomy indicates the extent to which one perceives her/his behavior as self-endorsed (Ryan and Deci 2000). Environments that support autonomy are used as an intervention to apply needs satisfaction in reality.

For example, Silva et al. (2008) offer multiple strategies to enhance internalization, including (a) offering a clear rationale for behavioral change, (b) acknowledging internal conflict when adopting new behaviors, (c) providing participants with a menu of options, (d) promoting competence, (e) avoiding the use of external incentives and (f) giving positive feedback. Those suggestions can be applied to the interactions between AR providers and clients. For example, after assessing a climber's body movement, his/her instructor not only selects a route based on its rating, but focuses on certain skills, such as dyno, a dynamic movement used to grab next handhold placed out of a climber's reach, needed to successfully send the route. By working on this selected route, this climber gradually develop those skills and the instructor can give immediate feedback to help a client adjust their movements and mindsets. In this case, a rewarding experience is not only derived from a successful ascend, but also being able to establish physical and mental techniques to address challenging situations in this route. Informational feedback is also given to strengthen their positive changes, rather than external incentives.

Although risk is often used to attract current and potential adventure recreationists, being able to commit to an activity with other enthusiasts is also quite attractive. To help recreationists develop their commitments, service providers must first recognize the complexity and dynamics of social worlds (Unruh 1980; Wheaton 2010). First, Unruh (1980) classifies levels of social worlds as local, regional, dispersed social worlds and social world systems. Service providers link clients with information from proximate to distal levels in order to help clients establish their own networks incrementally.

For example, a 'trail day' in a rock climbing area is a local event to enhance the sustainability of a recreation-use land. Through interactions between local climbers or their affiliation groups (e.g., a climbers' coalition) and other organizations, this event can become a regular occurrence in a region. Further, the values of this event may be influenced by or compatible with upper-level social worlds focusing on ideas such as land-conservation (e.g., Access Fund in the United States), or Leave No Trace principles. By encouraging clients to participate in this event, providers give clients the opportunity to immerse themselves in the complex subculture of rock climbing and to explore their social roles and responsibilities as a rock climber.

Moreover, the development of Internet access may flatten levels of social worlds. Internet access creates opportunities for recreationists to learn from worldwide sources and express their AR identities and experiences to others who reside in proximal and distal areas. The diverse ways people perform AR, identities, performances and local subcultures are presented through traditional media websites, online forums, blogs and social media. This provides an unprecedented opportunity to present the big picture of social worlds to recreationists and the public and to promote communication between sub-worlds; all of which enhances the visibility of local actors, events, organizations and practices to other social worlds. The richness of online information provides appropriate materials to accommodate recreationists' diverse needs and the identities they expect to develop.

On the other hand, although the evolution of AR allows recreationists to commit to an activity in diverse ways, there are social conditions that may hinder participation. Stebbins (2005) documents the negative experiences of mountain sport participants: costs, disappointing personal performance, tensions due to competitions, or peer pressure and dislike of others' attitudes or behaviors. Those conditions may be temporary; nonetheless, when negative experiences recur or are profound, recreationists can be discouraged significantly. Moreover, adventure recreationists may get involved in conditions beyond their skill or confidence levels to acquire others' approval or to avoid negative evaluations (Lamont and Kennelly 2012; Vallerand et al. 2006). To manage those coerced conditions, service providers may help clients identify realistic objectives and focus on career development rather than performance. It is also necessary to understand whether clients perceive their social experiences as autonomous or coerced.

Finally, there remains a need to understand the unique experiences and identities of members of an AR population across social classes such as gender. For example, past studies show that recreation experience is used as a venue for females to define their identities beyond gender stereotypes and to resist masculine-dominant cultures in AR (Dilley and Scraton 2010; Kiewa 2001; Spowart et al. 2010). Gender and other social classes imply contingencies possessed by or lacking in diverse populations that can affect commitment to AR experiences (Scott and Shafer 2001). Therefore, when recognizing that serious pursuits of AR lead to fulfilling and meaningful experiences and well-being, individual differences should be considered and emphasized. Instead of seeing diverse populations as exceptions in AR, their experiences and identities provide us with a better lens to examine how diverse populations, especially previously underrepresented groups, can commit to AR and enrich its social worlds.

Conclusions

The 'motivation-serious' leisure framework discussed in this chapter justifies the appropriateness of AR as an avenue to enhancement of well-being. Instead of pursuing AR for hedonic purposes, recreationists invest their time, energy and money with the goal of personal and social enhancement. Internalization provides a framework to explain the underlying motivational mechanism of leisure commitment. More importantly, internalization is either facilitated or hindered by social conditions. Identifying these social factors, examined in other studies of serious AR pursuit, opens up the ongoing dialogue on diverse populations within the AR experience.

Notes

1. The concept of lifestyle sports, an idea developed by Belinda Wheaton and other scholars, inspired me to deeply observe the subculture of AR and how actors in an AR activity strive to earn their identities as insiders. Another notion, the commercialization and consumption of these non-traditional sports, implies to me that an adventure recreationist nowadays can easily link herself/himself with not only local but worldwide social worlds. This idea helped me develop the implications presented in this study.
2. In a book titled *Challenging Mountain Nature: Risk, Motive and Lifestyle in Three Hobbyist Sports*, Stebbins (2005) discusses how mountain sport devotees use their competence and resilience to address challenging or even devastating conditions encountered in their outings. Mountaineers interviewed in this book learn from those experiences and continually pursue improvement in their careers.
3. I borrow the terms 'surface level of motivation' and 'source level of motivation' from Mullan et al. (1997). They examine the factor structure of exercise motivation, in line with the SDT framework. They use the term 'source level motivation' to describe motivations with different levels of self-determination relative to surface-level motivations such as weight control and sociality in the exercise domain. The motivation continuum presents multiple motivations from none to full level of self-determination. The continuum was proposed in organismic integration theory, a sub-theory of SDT, which stresses the human tendency to integrate regulatory sources in an environment for adaptation (i.e., internalization) (Ryan and Deci 2000). This sub-theory explains why people are willing to do things even when they are not interested (i.e., they lack intrinsic motivation) in it.

References

Accessfund.org. (2017). *Our Passion.* [online] Available at: https://www.access-fund.org/meet-the-access-fund/our-passion. Accessed 2 June 2017.

Allman, T., Mittelstaedt, R., Martin, B., & Goldenberg, M. (2009). Exploring the Motivations of BASE Jumpers: Extreme Sport Enthusiasts. *Journal of Sport & Tourism, 14*(4), 229–247.

Anderson, L., & Taylor, J. (2010). Standing Out While Fitting In: Serious Leisure Identities and Aligning Actions Among Skydivers and Gun Collectors. *Journal of Contemporary Ethnography, 39*(1), 34–59.

Assor, A., Vansteenkiste, M., & Kaplan, A. (2009). Identified Versus Introjected Approach and Introjected Avoidance Motivations in School and in Sports: The Limited Benefits of Self-Worth Strivings. *Journal of Educational Psychology, 101*(2), 482–497.

Barbieri, C., & Sotomayor, S. (2013). Surf Travel Behavior and Destination Preferences: An Application of the Serious Leisure Inventory and Measure. *Tourism Management, 35,* 111–121.

Barrett, E., & Martin, P. (2014). The Surprising Personality Traits of Extreme Adventurers. [Blog] *Discover.* Available at: http://blogs.discovermagazine.com/crux/2014/12/04/personality-traits-extreme-adventurers/#.WN5U9W_yvIV. Accessed 31 Mar 2017.

Bartram, S. (2001). Serious Leisure Careers Among Whitewater Kayakers: A Feminist Perspective. *World Leisure Journal, 43*(2), 4–11.

Bendle, L., & Patterson, I. (2009). Mixed Serious Leisure and Grassroots Organizational Capacity: A Study of Amateur Artist Groups in a Regional Australian City. *Leisure Sciences, 31*(3), 272–286.

Berger, I., & Greenspan, I. (2008). High (on) Technology: Producing Tourist Identities Through Technologized Adventure. *Journal of Sport & Tourism, 13*(2), 89–114.

Brown, C. (2007). The Carolina Shaggers: Dance as Serious Leisure. *Journal of Leisure Research, 39*(4), 623–647.

Brymer, E., & Gray, T. (2010). Developing an Intimate "Relationship" with Nature Through Extreme Sports Participation. *Leisure/Loisir, 34*(4), 361–374.

Brymer, E., & Schweitzer, R. (2013). The Search for Freedom in Extreme Sports: A Phenomenological Exploration. *Psychology of Sport and Exercise, 14*(6), 865–873.

Buckley, R. (2012). Rush as a Key Motivation in Skilled Adventure Tourism: Resolving the Risk Recreation Paradox. *Tourism Management, 33*(4), 961–970.

Cheng, T., & Tsaur, S. (2012). The Relationship Between Serious Leisure Characteristics and Recreation Involvement: A Case Study of Taiwan's Surfing Activities. *Leisure Studies, 31*(1), 53–68.

Coates, E., Clayton, B., & Humberstone, B. (2010). A Battle for Control: Exchanges of Power in the Subculture of Snowboarding. *Sport in Society, 13*(7–8), 1082–1101.

Csikszentmihalyi, M. (1991). *Flow* (1st ed.). New York: HarperPerennial.

Csikszentmihalyi, M. and Csikszentmihalyi, I. (1999). *Adventure and the Flow Experience*. In: J.C. Miles, & S. Priest (Eds.), Adventure programming (pp. 153–158). State College: Venture.

Dilley, R., & Scraton, S. (2010). Women, Climbing and Serious Leisure. *Leisure Studies, 29*(2), 125–141.

Edmunds, J., Ntoumanis, N., & Duda, J. L. (2006). A Test of Self-Determination Theory in the Exercise Domain. *Journal of Applied Social Psychology, 36*(9), 2240–2265.

Ewert, A., & Hollenhorst, S. (1989). Testing the Adventure Model: Empirical Support for a Model of Risk Recreation Participation. *Journal of Leisure Research, 21*(2), 124–139.

Ewert, A., & Hollenhorst, S. (1994). Individual and Setting Attributes of the Adventure Recreation Experience. *Leisure Sciences, 16*(3), 177–191.

Ewert, A., Gilbertson, K., Luo, Y., & Voight, A. (2013). Beyond Because Its There: Motivations for Pursuing Adventure Recreational Activities. *Journal of Leisure Research, 45*(1), 91–111.

Gilbertson, K., & Ewert, A. (2015). Stability of Motivations and Risk Attractiveness: The Adventure Recreation Experience. *Risk Management, 17*(4), 276–297.

Gould, J., Moore, D. W., McGuire, F., & Stebbins, R. (2008). Development of the Serious Leisure Inventory and Measure. *Journal of Leisure Research, 40*(1), 47–68.

Heo, J., Lee, I., Kim, J., & Stebbins, R. (2012). Understanding the Relationships Among Central Characteristics of Serious Leisure: An Empirical Study of Older Adults in Competitive Sports. *Journal of Leisure Research, 44*(4), 450–462.

Heo, J., Stebbins, R. A., Kim, J., & Lee, I. (2013). Serious Leisure, Life Satisfaction, and Health of Older Adults. *Leisure Sciences, 35*(1), 16–32.

Heuser, L. (2005). We're Not Too Old to Play Sports: The Career of Women Lawn Bowlers. *Leisure Studies, 24*(1), 45–60.

Johnson, I. (2017). Diversity in Climbing: A Difficult Conversation. *Climbing Magazine*. [online] Available at: https://www.climbing.com/people/diversity-in-climbing-a-tough-conversation/. Accessed 2 June 2017.

Kane, M., & Zink, R. (2004). Package Adventure Tours: Markers in Serious Leisure Careers. *Leisure Studies, 23*(4), 329–345.

Kerr, J., & Mackenzie, S. (2014). Confidence Frames and the Mastery of New Challenges in the Motivation of an Expert Skydiver. *The Sport Psychologist, 28*(3), 221–232.

Kiewa, J. (2001). Control over Self and Space in Rockclimbing. *Journal of Leisure Research, 33*(4), 363–382.

Lamont, M., & Kennelly, M. (2012). A Qualitative Exploration of Participant Motives Among Committed Amateur Triathletes. *Leisure Sciences, 34*(3), 236–255.

Lee, K. (2013). *An Examination on the Motivations of Serious Leisure in Rock Climbing: A Structural Equation Modeling Study.* Doctoral dissertation, Indiana University.

Lee, K., Bentley, J., & Hsu, H. (2017). Using Characteristics of Serious Leisure to Classify Rock Climbers: A Latent Profile Analysis. *Journal of Sport & Tourism,* [online] *0*(0), 1–18. Available at: http://www.tandfonline.com/doi/abs/10.1080/14775085.2017.1327369. Accessed 2 June 2017.

Lyu, S., & Oh, C. (2014). Bridging the Conceptual Frameworks of Constraints Negotiation and Serious Leisure to Understand Leisure Benefit Realization. *Leisure Sciences, 37*(2), 176–193.

McCarville, R. (2007). From a Fall in the Mall to a Run in the Sun: One Journey to Ironman Triathlon. *Leisure Sciences, 29*(2), 159–173.

Mullan, E., Markland, D., & Ingledew, D. (1997). A Graded Conceptualisation of Self-Determination in the Regulation of Exercise Behaviour: Development of a Measure Using Confirmatory Factor Analytic Procedures. *Personality and Individual Differences, 23*(5), 745–752.

Official Tony Hawk. (2017). *Home.* [online] Available at: http://www.tony-hawk.com/#front. Accessed 2 June 2017.

Outdoor Foundation. (2016). *2016 Outdoor Recreation Participation Report.* [online] Available at: http://www.outdoorfoundation.org/research.participation.2016.html. Accessed 31 Mar 2017.

Outdoor Industry Association. (2012). *The Outdoor Recreation Economy.* [online] Available at: https://outdoorindustry.org/pdf/OIA_OutdoorRecEco-nomy Report2012.pdf. Accessed 31 Mar 2017.

Patterson, I., Getz, D., & Gubb, K. (2016). The Social World and Event Travel Career of the Serious Yoga Devotee. *Leisure Studies, 35*(3), 296–313.

Pi, L., Lin, Y., Chen, C., Chiu, J., & Chen, Y. (2014). Serious Leisure, Motivation to Volunteer and Subjective Well-Being of Volunteers in Recreational Events. *Social Indicators Research, 119*(3), 1485–1494.

Priest, S. (1992). Factor Exploration and Confirmation for the Dimensions of an Adventure Experience. *Journal of Leisure Research, 24*(2), 127–139.

Priest, S., & Carpenter, G. (1993). Changes in Perceived Risk and Competence During Adventurous Leisure Experiences. *Journal of Applied Recreation Research, 18*(1), 51–71.

Priest, S., & Gass, M. (2005). *Effective Leadership in Adventure Programming* (1st ed.). Champaign: Human Kinetics.

Robinson, R., Patterson, I., & Axelsen, M. (2014). The "Loneliness of the Long-Distance Runner" No More: Marathon and Social Worlds. *Journal of Leisure Research, 46*(4), 375–394.

Rosenbaum, M. (2013). Maintaining the Trail. *Journal of Contemporary Ethnography, 42*(6), 639–667.

Ryan, R., & Deci, E. (2000). Self-Determination Theory and the Facilitation of Intrinsic Motivation, Social Development, and Well-Being. *American Psychologist, 55*(1), 68–78.

Ryan, R., & Deci, E. (2007). Active Human Nature: Self-Determination Theory and the Promotion and Maintenance of Sport, Exercise, and Health. In M. Hagger & N. Chatzisarantis (Eds.), *Intrinsic Motivation and Self-Determination in Exercise and Sport* (1st ed., pp. 1–19). Champaign: Human Kinetics.

Scott, D., & Shafer, C. (2001). Recreational Specialization: A Critical Look at the Construct. *Journal of Leisure Research, 33*(3), 319–343.

Sharma. (n.d.). *About Chris Sharma.* Retrieved from http://www.chrissharma.com/about-chris/. Accessed 2 June 2017.

Shipway, R., & Jones, I. (2008). The Great Suburban Everest: An 'Insiders' Perspective on Experiences at the 2007 Flora London Marathon. *Journal of Sport & Tourism, 13*(1), 61–77.

Shupe, F., & Gagné, P. (2016). Motives for and Personal and Social Benefits of Airplane Piloting as a Serious Leisure Activity for Women. *Journal of Contemporary Ethnography, 45*(1), 85–112.

Silva, M., Markland, D., Minderico, C., Vieira, P., Castro, M., Coutinho, S., Santos, T., Matos, M., Sardinha, L., & Teixeira, P. (2008). A Randomized Controlled Trial to Evaluate Self-Determination Theory for Exercise Adherence and Weight Control: Rationale and Intervention Description. *BMC Public Health, 8*(1). https://doi.org/10.1186/1471-2458-8-234

Sport England and Outdoor Industries Association. (2015). *Getting Active Outdoors: A Study of Demography, Motivation, Participation and Provision in Outdoor Sport and Recreation in England.* [online] Available at: https://www.sportengland.org/media/3275/outdoors-participation-report-v2-lr-spreads.pdf. Accessed 31 Mar 2017.

Spowart, L., Burrows, L., & Shaw, S. (2010). 'I Just Eat, Sleep and Dream of Surfing': When Surfing Meets Motherhood. *Sport in Society, 13*(7–8), 1186–1203.

Stebbins, R. (2005). *Challenging Mountain Nature: Risk, Motive and Lifestyle in Three Hobbyist Sports* (1st ed.). Calgary: Detselig.

Stebbins, R. (2007). *Serious Leisure: A Perspective of Our Time* (1st ed.). New Brunswick: Transaction Publishers.

Teixeira, P., Carraça, E., Markland, D., Silva, M., & Ryan, R. (2012). Exercise, Physical Activity, and Self-Determination Theory: A Systematic Review. *International Journal of Behavioral Nutrition and Physical Activity, 9*(1), 78.

United Nation World Tourism Organization. (2014). *Global Report on Adventure Tourism.* [online] Available at: http://affiliatemembers.unwto.org/publication/global-report-adventure-tourism. Accessed 31 Mar 2017.

Unruh, D. (1979). Characteristics and Types of Participation in Social Worlds. *Symbolic Interaction, 2*(2), 115–130.

Unruh, D. (1980). The Nature of Social Worlds. *The Pacific Sociological Review, 23*(3), 271–296.

Vallerand, R., & Ratelle, C. (2002). Intrinsic and Extrinsic Motivation: A Hierarchical Model. In E. Deci & R. Ryan (Eds.), *Handbook of Self-Determination Research* (1st ed., pp. 37–63). Rochester: The University of Rochester Press.

Vallerand, R., Rousseau, F., Grouzet, F., Dumais, A., Grenier, S., & Blanchard, C. (2006). Passion in Sport: A Look at Determinants and Affective Experiences. *Journal of Sport and Exercise Psychology, 28*(4), 454–478.

Wheaton, B. (2004). Introduction: Mapping the Lifestyle Sport-Scape. In B. Wheaton (Ed.), *Understanding Lifestyle Sports: Consumption, Identity and Difference* (1st ed., pp. 1–28). New York: Routeledge.

Wheaton, B. (2010). Introducing the Consumption and Representation of Lifestyle Sports. *Sport in Society, 13*(7–8), 1057–1081.

Whittington, A., Aspelmeier, J., & Budbill, N. (2015). Promoting Resiliency in Adolescent Girls Through Adventure Programming. *Journal of Adventure Education and Outdoor Learning, 16*(1), 2–15.

Wilson, P., Sabiston, C., Mack, D., & Blanchard, C. (2012). On the Nature and Function of Scoring Protocols Used in Exercise Motivation Research: An Empirical Study of the Behavioral Regulation in Exercise Questionnaire. *Psychology of Sport and Exercise, 13*(5), 614–622.

Woodman, T., Hardy, L., Barlow, M., & Le Scanff, C. (2010). Motives for Participation in Prolonged Engagement High-Risk Sports: An Agentic Emotion Regulation Perspective. *Psychology of Sport and Exercise, 11*(5), 345–352.

Woodman, T., Barlow, M., Bandura, C., Hill, M., Kupciw, D., & MacGregor, A. (2013). Not All Risks Are Equal: The Risk Taking Inventory for High-Risk Sports. *Journal of Sport and Exercise Psychology, 35*(5), 479–492.

14

Leisure and Meaning-Making: The Pursuit of a Meaningful Life Through Leisure

Yoshitaka Iwasaki

Introduction

Humans naturally strive for a meaningful, enriching life (Garland et al. 2015; Hicks and Routledge 2013; Raskin et al. 2010; Ryff 2014; Wong 2012). For example, Eagleton (2007) suggested that the meaning of life is life itself: life is made sense of by its meaning; Cottingham (2003) spoke of a meaningful life as "one in which the individual is engaged in genuinely worthwhile activities" (p. 66) that can promote the sense of "flourishing" (Eagleton 2007). This meaning-making process in life is central to this chapter—here, 'meaning-making' refers to the process by which a person derives meaning(s) from engagement in an activity, to find a purpose and significance in life and make sense of her/his life (Ignelzi 2000; Morgan and Farsides 2009).

As supported by the research literature, leisure is a key domain of life, one in which people engage to gain significant, valued meanings of life, doing so in different ways—psychologically, spiritually, socially and/or

Y. Iwasaki (✉)
University of Alberta, Edmonton, Alberta, Canada

© The Author(s) 2018
A. Beniwal et al. (eds.), *Global Leisure and the Struggle for a Better World*, Leisure Studies in a Global Era, https://doi.org/10.1007/978-3-319-70975-8_14

culturally (Carruthers and Hood 2007; Chun and Lee 2010; Deschenes 2011; Heintzman 2008; Hutchinson and Nimrod 2012; Iwasaki et al. 2013; Newman et al. 2014; Watters et al. 2013). Classic theorists/writers on leisure as early as 1960, as exemplified by Joffre Dumazedier (1974), described leisure as activity, apart from the obligations of work, family and society, to indulge one's own 'free will' for relaxation, diversion, amusing oneself, broadening one's knowledge or improving one's skills, such as the free exercise of one's creative capacity, and one's spontaneous social or volunteer participation in the life of the community. John Kelly (1987), another influential theorist, explained that in leisure every experience is a new creation with the following key elements: (a) leisure is a *decision* (an act as well as a state), and it is not external to the phenomenon but integral to its nature; (b) leisure is a *creation*, a product of decision and action; (c) leisure is a *process*, not fixed but developing and created in its time and place; (d) leisure is *situated*, constructed in an ever-new context; (e) leisure is *production* in the sense that its meaning is always reproduced in its situation rather than appropriated from some external source; and (f) leisure is an *act*, whole and complex with its history, emotion, interpretation, episodic development and telos. Since leisure is often considered as time free from work and other obligations, the question of how work and leisure interrelate has been another popular aspect of discussion; Stanley Parker (1976) noted the same in outlining the interconnections of 'extension' (work and leisure are similar), 'opposition' (they are polarized and demarcated) and 'neutrality' (they are distinct but not polarized).

Contextualized within these insights, meaning-making through leisure is a unique, distinct concept, focusing on how or in what ways leisure contributes to making sense of life for people or how they gain significant meanings of life through leisure engagement. For example, to characterize such a unique, distinct nature of leisure, Deschenes (2011) suggested that in contrast to the daily activities of 'production' (or *homo faber*), leisure (or *homo ludens*) can provide a space or opportunity through its activity for 'healing' from everyday life. Specifically, Deschenes spoke about the role of leisure as a meaning-making activity to promote healing and personal development, identified as the 'liberating' effects of leisure to be free from productivity, including this role for individuals with significant life challenges and personal limitations (e.g., people with disabilities).

A recent special issue of *Leisure Sciences* has featured the topic of "leisure research to enhance social justice" (Stewart 2014). One important implication of this growing focus in the leisure studies field is that leisure can play a key role in addressing social justice issues such as power relations, oppression, marginalization, exclusion/inclusion, human rights and social change, potentially as an essential meaning-making activity, for example, through empowering people who face injustice. This claim is also in line with a special issue of *Leisure/Loisir* on 'popular leisure' almost a decade ago (in 2008)—as the guest editors Sharpe and Lashua (2008) noted that "popular leisure is made, unmade, and remade through ever-changing articulations of everyday practices and formations of power" (p. 256)—specifically, "engagement in popular leisure overflows with meaning and significance that extends far beyond pleasure and enjoyment" (p. 247) into power-based social justice issues through liberating meaningful leisure.

More recently, Rowe (2016) has supported the use of a *reflexive approach* to leisure (Fullagar 2011) as a meaning-making activity in order to critically examine "the positive, negative, and shades of grey that constitute the complex moral landscape of everyday life" (p. 3), by "situating it (leisure) at the heart of everyday lives" (p. 4). As suggested by Freire (2013), the role of leisure in meaning-making has important implications for advancing other social science fields such as positive psychology by embedding leisure into the positive science field, considering a unique, distinct characteristic of leisure pursuits as a freely chosen, autonomous and intrinsically motivated activity (Kleiber et al. 2011; Schmalz and Blomquist 2016).

Informed by the above conceptualizations of leisure, leisure is defined here as a freely chosen, potentially meaningful activity, which can constructively engage people to gain a variety of benefits such as healing and liberation (Deschenes 2011), well-being (Carruthers and Hood 2007; Newman et al. 2014) and positive personal and social changes (Sharpe and Lashua 2008; Stewart 2014), among others. The purpose of this chapter is to identify and describe the role of leisure in the pursuit of a meaningful life, informed by the literature on these topics from interdisciplinary perspectives. Specifically, such description focuses on the identification of the key elements or factors of leisure-induced meaning-making functions.

Key Themes of Leisure-induced Meaning-making Functions in Life

By integrating the leisure research literature with the literature outside of leisure studies, this (main) section of the chapter identifies and describes the five key elements or factors concerning the potential contributions of leisure to meaning-making in life. These include the roles of leisure in promoting: (a) a joyful life, (b) a connected life, (c) a discovered life, (d) a composed life and (e) a hopeful and empowered life.

(a) Joyful Life

First, one key role of leisure in meaning-making seems to involve promoting/maintaining a joyful life, as illustrated by such key concepts as mindfulness and savoring. Extending Fredrickson's (2013) broaden-and-build theory, Garland et al.'s (2015) mindfulness-to-meaning theory describes the process of mindful, positive, emotion regulation to facilitate reappraisal of adversity and savoring of positive experience. This process is proposed to culminate in a deepened capacity for meaning-making and greater engagement with life and to foster flourishing in life (Garland et al. 2015). Mindfulness has been traditionally described as engendering positive or pleasurable qualities such as joy, happiness, serenity, gratitude and even bliss (Namgyal 2006). Similarly, savoring focuses on both pleasurable features of a stimulus and positive emotions from encountering it (Frijda and Sundararajan 2007). In these ways, savoring is complementary to mindfulness—by mindfully attending to the positive state that emerges from the encounter with the object, one can deepen and enrich the savored experience (Bryant et al. 2011). Specifically, Garland et al.'s (2015) mindfulness-to-meaning theory suggests that mindfulness promotes a self-reinforcing system of positive reappraisal and savoring—the expanding gyre of an upward spiral that broadens awareness and builds meaning through individual flourishing and greater engagement with life.

According to Carruthers and Hood (2011), mindfulness is intimately connected with leisure in that mindfulness can serve as a meaningful form of contemplative leisure engagement to enhance enjoyment and benefits obtained through leisure experiences. Hood and Carruthers (2007) also noted that leisure can enhance savoring, coined as 'savoring leisure', which is defined as "paying attention to the positive aspects of, and emotions associated with, leisure involvement and purposefully seeking leisure experiences that give rise to positive emotions" (p. 310–311).

Newman et al.'s (2014) literature review based on 363 research articles linking leisure and subjective well-being (SWB) suggested that meaning-making represents a core mechanism to promote SWB, particularly through enhancing tranquility and peace of mind, active engagement, positive emotions and well-being in itself. In Carruthers and Hood's (2007) leisure and well-being model (LWM), helping people engage in leisure to create a life of meaning and purpose is a key focus, whereby emotion regulation (i.e., increase in positive emotion and reduction of suffering on a daily basis) is identified as a main strategy of therapeutic recreation (TR) services especially for individuals with significant challenges and limitations. As noted earlier, Garland et al.'s (2015) mindfulness-to-meaning theory involves emotion regulation, as well.

A key theme identified in Hutchinson and Nimrod's (2012) qualitative study on successful ageing represented "more than managing—living a life of meaning"; in particular, "a shift in perspective, which enabled participants to focus on and appreciate small pleasures" (p. 57) was a key function. Similarly, Phinney et al.'s (2007) phenomenological study with older people with dementia found that leisure activities enhanced meaning-making through promoting pleasure and enjoyment. Indeed, Iwasaki et al.'s (2015) qualitative study with individuals living with mental illness found the role of leisure in promoting a "joyful life", as illustrated by the following quote from a study participant: "Everybody needs some type of leisure to fall back on, because it's what makes us human. It is the ability to enjoy things—life really isn't worth living if you can't enjoy it." (p. 544)

(b) Connected Life

The role of leisure in helping people promote/maintain a connected life has been shown as another theme of leisure-induced meaning-making (Chun and Lee 2010; Phinney et al. 2007; Trussell and Mair 2010; Wensley and Slade 2012). This theme appears to have several dimensions including social, spiritual and cultural connectedness. Not only is building social relationships essential to this theme, but connectedness also has spiritual and cultural elements including one's connections to nature, religion and culture (Heintzman 2008; Iwasaki et al. 2015; Phinney et al. 2007). For example, Heintzman's (2008) leisure-spiritual coping model encompasses all of these elements of connectedness. For another example, Trussell and Mair's (2010) study with individuals living in poverty including those who are homeless conceptualized leisure as a "judgment free space", one which provided the individual with opportunities to maintain "a sense of an ordinary life and feel connected to the community, but in a way that facilitated their power to be private"—this function exemplifies the role of leisure as a meaning-making activity in "building this power and sense of connection" that transcends both private and public spaces (p. 529).

In Petrou et al.'s (2016) study with Dutch employees, a sense of connection was shown a key meaning-making function of "leisure crafting", defined as "the proactive pursuit of leisure activities targeted at goal setting, human connection, learning, and personal development". Also reported through leisure is a sense of connectedness experienced among regular walkers (Wensley and Slade 2012), older people with dementia (Phinney et al. 2007), people with spinal cord injury who endure post-traumatic growth (Chun and Lee 2010) and immigrants (e.g., Kim and Kim 2013; Mata-Codesal et al. 2015). The contribution of leisure to making one's life more connected (with self, others, and spirituality) is a key theme identified in Iwasaki et al.'s (2015) study on recovery from mental illness. For example, as a 'spiritual person' a study participant spoke about his love of outdoor activities: "I do love to be outdoors. The natural world is a constant source of joy for me. It's a real good counterbalance to indoor activity. Gardening is a kind of existential prayer. It's my way of celebrating life in its most basic form." (p. 545)

(c) Discovered Life

Another key theme of leisure meaning-making seems to be the role of leisure in helping people promote and/or maintain a discovered life. In particular, the issue of identity appears to be a key concept to describe this function (Kim and Kim 2013; Mata-Codesal et al. 2015; Phinney et al. 2007). Not only is this concept concerned with personal identity, it also involves collective identity. Discovering who the person is both individually and collectively seems vital for the pursuit of a meaningful life, and such discovery can be facilitated by meaningful leisure (Banfield and Burgess 2013; Csikszentmihalyi 2002, 2014; Iwasaki et al. 2015).

For example, Pignato (2017) regarded recreational music making (e.g., jam sessions) as personal and social meaning-making through developing an identity, whereas Syrjala's (2016) study on the transformation from casual enthusiast to serious hobbyist within the subculture of dog agility devotees found the importance of identity construction for meaning-making in a serious leisure community. In addition, Keller and Kalmus' (2009) study with Estonian tweens on the question "What makes me cool?" found a meaning-making role of leisure especially through its identity creation function. A role of leisure in promoting personal identity was found as a key theme of leisure meaning-making in Phinney et al.'s (2007) study with older people with dementia as well.

Related to this personal identity, creativity has been emphasized as another key notion to describe the role of leisure in meaning-making (Banfield and Burgess 2013; Hegarty and Plucker 2012; Mata-Codesal et al. 2015). Some researchers have coined the term 'creative leisure' to describe opportunities that leisure can present for self-expression as a meaningful form of leisure. Wensley and Slade's (2012) study on walking also found the relevance of self-expression as a way of meaning-making. In addition, Twigger-Holroyd's (2016) study on women's practices of dress-related leisure, namely, shopping, sorting, making and mending, found that creativity (besides social interaction) is essential to such pursuits as meaningful leisure.

Furthermore, it has been shown that meaningfulness of leisure for immigrants goes beyond issues of coping with and adapting to acculturation stress and involves issues of self-realization and self-expression, among others (e.g., Kim and Kim 2013; Mata-Codesal et al. 2015). Self-discovery through leisure (e.g., art and crafts, sewing and knitting, cooking, playing music, 'spiritual leisure' and writing poems) was a key theme identified in Iwasaki et al.'s (2015) study with persons living with mental illness. One participant said, "Creativity is a driving force and a big outlet for me. That's always self-discovery in its own rite. It comes from inside you somewhere, so you're discovering something new every time." (pp. 546–547)

(d) Composed Life

Another meaning-making theme seems to involve the role of leisure in making one's life more composed, collected and/or in control and in promoting/maintaining harmony or balance in one's life (Hutchinson and Nimrod 2012; Iwasaki et al. 2015; Watters et al. 2013). Compared to the other domains of life (e.g., work/employment), leisure provides less restrictive and more flexible and liberating opportunities to change or adjust the pace and tone of life so that the person can experience a more harmonious, balanced and composed life (Deschenes 2011; Newman et al. 2014; Wensley and Slade 2012). For example, Deschenes (2011) spoke about the 'liberating' effects of leisure (or *homo ludens*) to be free and facilitate healing from daily activities of 'production' (or *homo faber*) and maintain a more composed, meaningful life, whereas Kleiber et al. (2002) seminal paper identified self-protection and self-restoration as the key functions of leisure for transcending negative life events to promote/maintain a more composed, meaningful life. Also reported was the role of ikebana (Japanese flower arrangement) in enhancing harmony in life (Watters et al. 2013), and leisure's contribution to promoting a sense of autonomy and control among older people with dementia (Phinney et al. 2007).

Furthermore, Iwasaki et al.'s (2015) study on recovery from mental illness found a key theme of leisure meaning-making through promoting a 'composed life' as illustrated by the following comment by a study participant: "My leisure time keeps me out of trouble and keeps my mind focused. It makes me happy and it keeps me calm, cool, and collected. It motivates me to keep going. It keeps [me] stabilized and intact with everything." (p. 545) Another participant concurred on the role of leisure in keeping one's mind occupied and focused more on positive aspects of life: "It (leisure) keeps my mind occupied and [doesn't] let it focus on stupid things. ...Arts, crafts, crocheting, and needlepoint, making stuff makes me very happy. ...It makes you focus on good things in [my] life." (p. 545)

(e) Hopeful and Empowered Life

Finally, the role of leisure in helping people promote/maintain a hopeful and empowered life seems to be another meaning-making function through leisure engagement. For example, meaning-making through leisure has been found to be a key process for effective stress-coping and healing that can promote a sense of hope and empowerment (Carruthers and Hood 2007; Fredrickson 2002; Newman et al. 2014). Leisure pursuits appear to possess a unique, powerful property of providing a person under stress or trauma with opportunities for effective coping or healing (Deschenes 2011; Heintzman 2008; Iwasaki et al. 2008; Kleiber et al. 2002). Such stress-coping and healing functions of meaningful leisure seem to facilitate growth and transformation, which can help people promote/maintain a hopeful and empowered life (Deschenes 2011; Heintzman 2008; Watters et al. 2013). Resilience, post-traumatic growth and empowerment through leisure (Chun and Lee 2010; Sharpe and Lashua 2008; Stewart 2014; Trussell and Mair 2010) are several key concepts related to these functions.

In addition, as illustrated by the meaning construction of 'flow' experiences (Csikszentmihalyi 2002), giving attention to *existential* aspects of leisure is worthwhile (Banfield and Burgess 2013), those dealing with vitality, authenticity, empowerment, sense of achievement and self-actualization as key leisure-induced meaning-making functions. Also, Ryff (2014) emphasized the resilience (i.e., the capacity to maintain or regain well-being in the face of adversity) of people as striving, meaning-making and proactive organisms who are actively negotiating the challenges of life, while the leisure research literature highlights an important role of leisure in facilitating this humanistic resilient process (Chun and Lee 2010; Stewart 2014; Trussell and Mair 2010). Specifically, such a role has been exemplified in transformation of the self through ikebana (Watters et al. 2013) and in Heintzman's (2008) leisure-spiritual coping model, Newman et al.'s (2014) comprehensive review paper and Hutchinson and Nimrod's (2012) study on successful ageing.

Indeed, a contribution of leisure to generating hope and empowerment as a way to make one's life meaningful was a key theme identified in Iwasaki et al.'s (2015) study on recovery from mental illness. Speaking of poetry, church activities and walking and nature, one participant said, "Leisure helps you. Leisure stimulates you and helps you get through this recovery process. …Life isn't always easy sometimes, you know, but leisure makes you stronger. I'm full of hope and empowerment. And I can give to generate hope to other people." (p. 548)

Interconnectedness Among the Themes

As described above, research has shown that leisure can promote all of those five key elements/factors of a meaningful engagement with life. Rather than seeing each element only independently, it is important to consider the possibility of deriving multiple meanings from a single engagement experience as well as the potential interconnectedness of the five identified themes. For example, Newman et al.'s (2014) literature review paper addressed the notions of a joyful life, a composed life and a hopeful and empowered life altogether, as did Hutchinson and Nimrod's (2012) study on successful ageing. Watters et al.'s (2013) study on ikebana dealt with the elements of both a composed life and a hopeful/empowered life, while Heintzman's (2008) leisure-spiritual coping model addressed the notions of both a connected life and a hopeful/empowered life. In addition, Banfield and Burgess' (2013) study with artists described flow-induced meaning-making phenomena including the elements of a discovered and hopeful/empowered life. The promotion of a connected and discovered life was also identified in Petrou et al.'s (2016) study with Dutch employees on meaning-making functions of 'leisure crafting'.

Furthermore, Iwasaki et al.'s (2015) study with persons who live with mental illness found that creative activities (e.g., arts, crafts and collages) promoted a discovered and connected life, while poetry, church activities and walking through nature promoted a connected, discovered and hopeful/empowered life.

Conclusion

The purpose of this chapter was to identify and describe the role of leisure in meaning-making functions in life, informed by interdisciplinary literature on these topics. Such description focused on the identification of the key elements/dimensions of leisure-induced meaning-making mechanisms in life. Specifically, the chapter emphasized the contributions of leisure pursuits to promoting and/or maintaining: (a) a joyful life, (b) a connected life, (c) a discovered life, (d) a composed life and (e) a hopeful and empowered life. Not only do these elements seem to represent distinct factors of meaningful engagement with life through leisure, but multiple meanings can also be gained from a single leisure engagement experience, and these meaning themes can be interconnected.

Considering a unique distinct characteristic of leisure as freely chosen, autonomous and intrinsically motivated engagement (Kleiber et al. 2011; Schmalz and Blomquist 2016), research on meaning-making and meaningful engagement with life seems to benefit greatly from examining a variety of leisure phenomena in its meaning-making functions. The ideas presented in this chapter seem to provide a useful framework to advance this important, emerging area of inquiry. While the development of a research instrument to measure these leisure meaning-making functions is worthwhile (e.g., Porter et al. 2013), well-designed qualitative, quantitative or mixed-methods studies on those functions are needed to further advance this research area. Among others, one key specific area of inquiry seems to be an examination of the types of leisure engagement that can produce stronger meaning-making benefits than other types and under what circumstances.

Almost 15 years ago, Nakamura and Csikzentmihalyi (2003) suggested eloquently in "The construction of meaning through vital engagement" that "one important way people find meaning in their lives is by becoming deeply involved in activities that afford them scope. Even apparently trivial activities become meaningful over time if done with care and concentration" (p. 83). They discussed that many cultural domains such as the arts, literature, forms of play and social interactions "allow persons to build meaningful lives by providing almost unlimited opportunities for engagement" (p. 83). Their discussion focused on the phenomenon of enjoyable interaction with the environment—in particular, the body of theory and research on the 'flow' state. Their notion of *vital engagement*, defined as "a sustained self-object relationship that is both enjoyed and meaningful", is seen as a key feature of optimal development, while they explained its connections to meaning-making activities by highlighting meaningful leisure pursuits. I believe Nakamura and Csikzentmihalyi's words still hold true today as we continue to study the role of leisure in meaning-making and engagement with life, which has important practical implications for human and social services (Carruthers and Hood 2011; Park 2010; Wong 2015). Apparently, leisure's potential contributions to meaningful, engaged living should not be underestimated both conceptually and practically.

References

Banfield, J., & Burgess, M. (2013). A Phenomenology of Artistic Doing: Flow as Embodied Knowing in 2D and 3D Professional Arts. *Journal of Phenomenological Psychology, 44*(1), 60–91.

Bryant, F. B., Chadwick, E. D., & Kluwe, K. (2011). Understanding the Processes that Regulate Positive Emotional Experience: Unsolved Problems and Future Directions for Theory and Research on Savoring. *International Journal of Wellbeing, 1*(1), 107–126.

Carruthers, C., & Hood, C. D. (2007). Building a Life of Meaning Through Therapeutic Recreation: The Leisure and Well-being Model, Part I. *Therapeutic Recreation Journal, 41*(4), 276–297.

Carruthers, C. P., & Hood, C. D. (2011). Mindfulness and Well-being: Implications for TR Practice. *Therapeutic Recreation Journal, 45*(3), 171–189.

Chun, S., & Lee, Y. (2010). The Role of Leisure in the Experience of Posttraumatic Growth for People with Spinal Cord Injury. *Journal of Leisure Research, 42*(3), 393–415.

Cottingham, J. (2003). *On the Meaning of Life.* London: Routledge.

Csikszentmihalyi, M. (2002). *Flow: The Classic Work on How to Achieve Happiness.* London: Rider.

Csikszentmihalyi, M. (2014). *Applications of Flow in Human Development and Education: The Collected Works of Mihaly Csikszentmihalyi.* New York: Springer Science & Business Media.

Deschenes, G. (2011). The Spiritual Anthropology of Leisure: The Homo Faber-religiosus-ludens. *Counselling and Spirituality / Counseling et spiritualite, 30*(2), 57–85.

Dumazedier, J. (1974). Leisure and the Social System. In J. F. Murphy (Ed.), *Concepts of Leisure.* Englewood Cliffs: Prentice-Hall.

Eagleton, T. (2007). *The Meaning of Life.* Oxford: Oxford University Press.

Fredrickson, B. L. (2002). Positive Emotions. In C. R. Snyder & S. J. Lopez (Eds.), *Handbook of Positive Psychology* (pp. 120–134). New York: Oxford University Press.

Fredrickson, B. L. (2013). Positive Emotions Broaden and Build. *Advances in Experimental Social Psychology, 47*, 1–53.

Freire, T. (2013). *Positive Leisure Science: From Subjective Experience to Social Contexts.* New York: Springer Science.

Frijda, N. H., & Sundararajan, L. (2007). Emotion Refinement: A Theory Inspired by Chinese Poetics. *Perspectives on Psycho- logical Science, 2*, 227–241.

Fullagar, S. (2011). Where Might the Path Less Travelled Lead Us? *World Leisure Journal, 53*(1), 15–18.

Garland, E. L., Farb, N. A., Goldin, P. R., & Fredrickson, B. L. (2015). Mindfulness Broadens Awareness and Builds Eudaimonic Meaning: A Process Model of Mindful Positive Emotion Regulation. *Psychological Inquiry, 26*(4), 293–314.

Hegarty, C. B., & Plucker, J. A. (2012). Creative Leisure and Self-expression. *The International Journal of Creativity & Problem Solving, 22*(2), 63–78.

Heintzman, P. (2008). Leisure-spiritual Coping: A Model for Therapeutic Recreation and Leisure Services. *Therapeutic Recreation Journal, 42*(1), 56–73.

Hicks, J. A., & Routledge, C. (Eds.). (2013). *The Experience of Meaning in Life: Classical Perspectives, Emerging Themes, and Controversies.* New York: Springer Science & Business Media.

Hood, C. D., & Carruthers, C. P. (2007). Enhancing Leisure Experience and Developing Resources: The Leisure and Well-Being Model, Part II. *Therapeutic Recreation Journal, 41,* 298–325.

Hutchinson, S. L., & Nimrod, G. (2012). Leisure as a Resource for Successful Aging by Older Adults with Chronic Health Conditions. *The International Journal of Aging & Human Development, 74*(1), 41–65.

Ignelzi, M. (2000). Meaning-making in the Learning and Teaching Process. *New Directions for Teaching and Learning, 82,* 5–14.

Iwasaki, Y., Bartlett, J., MacKay, K., Mactavish, J., & Ristock, J. (2008). Mapping Nondominant Voices into Understanding Stress-coping Mechanisms. *Journal of Community Psychology, 36*(6), 702–722.

Iwasaki, Y., Coyle, C., Shank, J., Messina, E., & Porter, H. (2013). Leisure-Generated Meanings and Active Living for Persons with Mental Illness. *Rehabilitation Counseling Bulletin, 57*(1), 46–56.

Iwasaki, Y., Messina, E., Coyle, C., & Shank, J. (2015). Role of Leisure in Meaning-Making for Community-dwelling Adults with Mental Illness: Inspiration for Engaged Life. *Journal of Leisure Research, 47*(5), 538–555.

Keller, M., & Kalmus, V. (2009). What Makes Me Cool? Estonian Tweens' Interpretative Repertoires. *Young Consumers, 10*(4), 329–341.

Kelly, J. R. (1987). *Freedom to Be: A New Sociology of Leisure.* New York: Macmillan.

Kim, J., & Kim, H. (2013). The Experience of Acculturative Stress-related Growth From Immigrants' Perspectives. *International Journal of Qualitative Studies on Health and Well-being, 8,* 21355.

Kleiber, D. A., Hutchinson, S. L., & Williams, R. (2002). Leisure as a Resource in Transcending Negative Life Events: Self-protection, Self-restoration, and Personal Transformation. *Leisure Sciences, 24,* 219–235.

Kleiber, D. A., Walker, G. J., & Mannell, R. C. (2011). *A Social Psychology of Leisure.* State College: Venture Publishing.

Mata-Codesal, D., Peperkamp, E., & Tiesler, N. C. (2015). Migration, Migrants and Leisure: Meaningful Leisure? *Leisure Studies, 34*(1), 1–4.

Morgan, J., & Farsides, T. (2009). Psychometric Evaluation of the Meaningful Life Measure. *Journal of Happiness Studies., 10*(3), 351–366.

Nakamura, J., & Csikzentmihalyi, M. (2003). The Construction of Meaning Through Vital Engagement. In C. L. M. Keyes & J. Haidt (Eds.), *Flourishing:*

Positive Psychology and the Life Well-lived (pp. 83–104). Washington, DC: American Psychological Association.

Namgyal, D. T. (2006). *Mahamudra—the Moonlight—Quintessence of Mind and Meditation*. Sommerville: Wisdom.

Newman, D. B., Tay, L., & Diener, E. (2014). Leisure and Subjective Well-being: A Model of Psychological Mechanisms as Mediating Factors. *Journal of Happiness Studies, 15*(3), 555–578.

Park, C. L. (2010). Making Sense of the Meaning Literature: An Integrative Review of Meaning Making and Its Effects on Adjustment to Stressful Life Events. *Psychological Bulletin, 136*(2), 257–301.

Parker, S. R. (1976). *The Sociology of Leisure*. London: Allen & Unwin.

Petrou, P., Bakker, A. B., & den Heuvel, M. (2016). Weekly Job Crafting and Leisure Crafting: Implications for Meaning-making and Work Engagement. *Journal of Occupational and Organizational Psychology*. https://doi.org/10.1111/joop.12160.

Phinney, A., Chaudhury, H., & O'Connor, D. L. (2007). Doing as Much as I Can do: The Meaning of Activity for People with Dementia. *Aging & Mental Health, 11*(4), 384–393.

Pignato, J. M. (2017). Red Light Jams. In R. Mantie & G. D. Smith (Eds.), *The Oxford Handbook of Music Making and Leisure* (pp. 405–421). New York: Oxford University Press.

Porter, H., Iwasaki, Y., & Shank, J. (2013). Conceptualizing Meaning-Making Through Leisure Experiences. *Society and Leisure/Loisir et Société, 33*(2), 167–194.

Raskin, J. D., Bridges, S. K., & Neimeyer, R. A. (Eds.). (2010). *Studies in Meaning 4: Constructivist Perspectives on Theory, Practice, and Social Justice*. New York: Pace University Press.

Rowe, D. (2016). Complexity and the Leisure Complex. *Annals of Leisure Research, 19*(1), 1–6.

Ryff, C. D. (2014). Psychological Well-Being Revisited: Advances in the Science and Practice of Eudaimonia. *Psychotherapy and Psychosomatics, 83*, 10–28.

Schmalz, D. L., & Blomquist, K. K. (2016). Time to Eat: Implications for Leisure-based Eating for Health and Development. In D. A. Kleiber & F. A. McGuire (Eds.), *Leisure and Human Development* (pp. 189–216). Urbana: Sagamore Publishing.

Sharpe, E. K., & Lashua, B. D. (2008). Introduction to the Special Issue: Tuning in to Popular Leisure. *Leisure/Loisir, 32*(2), 245–258.

Stewart, W. (2014). Introduction to the Special Issue: Leisure Research to Enhance Social Justice. *Leisure Sciences, 36,* 325–339.

Syrjala, H. (2016). Turning Point of Transformation: Consumer Communities, Identity Projects and Becoming a Serious Dog Hobbyist. *Journal of Business Research, 69*(1), 177–190.

Trussell, D. E., & Mair, H. (2010). Seeking Judgment Free Spaces: Poverty, Leisure, and Social Inclusion. *Journal of Leisure Research, 42*(4), 513–533.

Twigger-Holroyd, A. (2016). Perceptions and Practices of Dress-related Leisure: Shopping, Sorting, Making and Mending. *Annals of Leisure Research, 19*(3), 275–293.

Watters, A. M., Pearce, C., Backman, C. L., & Suto, M. J. (2013). Occupational Engagement and Meaning: The Experience of Ikebana Practice. *Journal of Occupational Science, 20*(3), 262–277.

Wensley, R., & Slade, A. (2012). Walking as a Meaningful Leisure Occupation: The Implications for Occupational Therapy. *British Journal of Occupational Therapy, 75*(2), 85–92.

Wong, P. T. P. (Ed.). (2012). *The Human Quest for Meaning: Theories, Research, and Applications* (2nd ed.). New York: Routledge/Taylor & Francis Group.

Wong, P. T. P. (2015). Meaning Therapy: Assessments and Interventions. *Existential Analysis, 26*(1), 154–167.

15

Conclusion

Anju Beniwal, Rashmi Jain, and Karl Spracklen

This book deals with the contested nature of leisure in relation to well-being, and then considers current evidence concerning the ways in which leisure had been experienced in contemporary societies across the world. The series combines the views, ideas and studies of leisure for local as well as international level. This kind of collection of leisure studies plays an important role in helping researchers understand society. Leisure as a holistic phenomenon covers individual and social dimensions. Both Indian and foreign scholars contributed papers to this edited volume. Three aspects, which emerged prominently in these discussions, are the

A. Beniwal (✉)
Department of Sociology, Government Meera Girls College, Udaipur, Rajasthan, India

R. Jain
Department of Sociology, University of Rajasthan, Jaipur, Rajasthan, India

K. Spracklen
School of Film, Music and Performing Arts, Leeds Beckett University, Leeds, United Kingdom

© The Author(s) 2018
A. Beniwal et al. (eds.), *Global Leisure and the Struggle for a Better World*, Leisure Studies in a Global Era, https://doi.org/10.1007/978-3-319-70975-8_15

local, virtual and global aspect of leisure. The present volume is an edited collection of best papers delivered at the International Sociological Association's Third Forum of Sociology in Vienna under RC13 (Sociology of Leisure). This collection has a strong focus on global, local and virtual leisure studies and new global leisure theory. All the editors are members of RC13's executive board, and the lead editor, Spracklen, is RC13's Secretary and Vice President for publications. Leisure studies is now taught far beyond its original faculty heart, and this edited collection covered studies from recreation to research on the local, global and virtual level. We hope the collection and contents herein will draw new leisure theories. Nowadays, researchers are applying complex theory to their work and to their teaching in leisure studies, and the related subject fields have appeared in their writings. The contents of this collection demonstrate the critical nature of the field and the growing maturity of theories of leisure in local, virtual and global spaces worldwide. The thirteen chapters of this book are structured into three sections focusing mainly on local, virtual and global leisure. This collection of new concepts promotes a new sociology of leisure and leisure studies, which we fervently hope will be beneficial for scholars, social scientists and policy makers.

Leisure helps improve the health and well-being of individuals and the development of inclusive communities. Types of leisure activities depend upon local context and socio-cultural values in local leisure. Virtual leisure activities are based on virtual mobility and its time and space related transformations, which in turn produce an effect of doubling of places or, potentially, of multiplication of places. In contemporary society, virtual leisure can be considered among the favorite leisure options. Each new virtual technology in the social realm brings challenges and new perspectives and possibilities for replicating reality. This book aims at exploring the features of virtual leisure and their impact on well-being of human being. There are many variables affecting leisure and recreation. Contributors examined that the relative wealth of an individual and the wealth of the society concerned is the most important factor influencing recreation and leisure. Many factors like health, safety, security, longevity, opportunity and awareness influence significantly the amount of quality of leisure and recreation enjoyed globally. Theories that are necessarily still in development, and to which most scholars can contribute, are described in various societies, in a global era.

The chapters of the book are segmented into three sections: local leisure, meaning and resistance; virtual leisure and pop culture; and global leisure and responses. The narrative allows the reader to reflect on each offering. The first section, introduced by Alice Pacher of Meiji University, Japan, examines the current situation of the sexless phenomenon among Japanese couples. The study found that 35 Japanese couples between the ages of 20 to 30 years tended to avoid sexual expressions due to previous negative experiences, pain during sexual experiences, and lack of physical contact with the partner. The common ground of interviewee thinking was an overabundance of pornography and sexual availability and a lack of education relating to sexual health and satisfaction.

Seven writers from Brazil contributed to the second paper, on Singing Group: Ludic as Part of Rehabilitation. The authors are: Miraíra Noal Manfroi; Adriana Aparecida da Fonseca Viscardi; Daliana Stephanie Lecuona; Giandra Anceski Bataglion; Verônica Werle; Juliana de Paula Figueiredo; and Alcyane Marinho. It is refreshing to note how playfulness enhances rehabilitation. Using Florianopolis, in Santa Catarina, South Brazil, as the health institution for field research, the authors investigated relationships between the ludic component, rehabilitation process, treatment and heath promotion. These services were provided by volunteers and professional workers. The study found that music provided by musical instruments and sing-a-longs contributed to the recovery and healing process of patients. The findings indicated that rehabilitation looks at the holistic model more closely involving social and humanistic techniques.

Two authors from Turkey have written on the Celebration of Holy Ramadan: The Case of Turkey. The authors are: Zuhai Yonca Odabas, of CankiriKaratekin University, Turkey and Gunnur Ertong Attar, Mersin University, Department of Sociology, Turkey. The authors state that Ramadan is a holy and preferred month of forgiveness from God (Allah). It is commonly known as a period of fasting during daylight hours. What is not known is that it is: a period to purify the soul; refocus attention on God; and practice self-discipline and sacrifice. At its close , Ramadan becomes a celebration – a justification for fasting, penance, compassion for others and sacrifice. The authors focus on the transforming of Ramadan since the beginning of the twenty-first century. The conflict between secular and religious culture has been played out in the public and private sphere. The ascendency of personal minds has, according to the authors become the 'collective mind'. Drawing from one's past, leisure and recreation activities enhance Ramadan's activities.

Anju Beniwal from India, wrote on Leisure Time and Youth Well-Being. She sees youth as an asset of the present; that young people make an important contribution to accelerated development; and that India's youth bulge holds an edge over other developed nations. She posits that leisure and recreation of young people benefits the nation in so far as they mitigate anti-social behavior. Beniwal examines under what conditions youth leisure is conducive to well-being. The energy, enthusiasm, dynamism, innovative ideas and creative thinking they possess make the youth population an important asset for any country's accelerated development. Leisure is related to health and well-being and if it contributes towards this aspect then it is constructive leisure for youth as well as nation.

The second section dealt with virtual leisure and pop culture. The five chapters in this section dwell on: Japanese culture of idol tourism; virtual reality devices; video games in the family context; the Nigerian musical industry projection of gender, sexuality and body; and the meaning and purpose of leisure activities on Manga/Anime fans (Fujoshi) in Japan. Yuki Tajima, Doshisha University, Japan, reported on the idol culture in Japan. The focus of this culture has shifted from urban (Tokyo) to regional – specific geographical areas. The author used *Amachan* (a TV drama) to focus on the relationship between media content in Japan and the residents of the community known as the Ama Club. The filming site was Kuji-shi, in the Iwate Perfecture of the Tokyo region. The author found that by examining characteristics of regional idols the potential of contents tourism contributed to regional revitalization.

Jonathan Harth of Witten/Herdecke University, Germany, writes on 'Being there and being someone else' which throws light on the massively distributed virtual reality devices. Additionally, he explored the impact on body and identity management. The companies that presented the first generation of Virtual Reality (VR) were: Oculus Rift, HTC Vive and Playstation VR. Harth focused on two questions: What is it that makes VR such a unique experience and what impact it may have on the users' experience of body and identity. He maintains that if one sees the world through someone else's eyes, it would change one's perspective of self, world and others. He concludes that firstly from a sociological perspective one's body must be conceived as a (cultural) observed body – not static but poly-contextual; and secondly that through the medium of computer-games one takes the action of someone else. These possibilities of VR put even a higher degree of the 'space of presence'.

From the Jagiellonian University in Poland, Damian Galuszka wrote on video games in the family context and the influence digital media made between children and parents. The growing popularity of gaming means an increasing investment of time to this hobby with an effect on other leisure activities. The growth is reflected in market revenues. The growing population of gamers includes children, for whom video games are a preferred leisure option and a sphere of socialization that takes place in family surroundings. Through research utilizing quantitative and qualitative methods on 24 families' short comings were noted: cultural and technological deficiencies by parents; insufficient levels of parental control; lessened parent-child communication; and lack of support from the school. The author hoped for a deepened analysis of the impact of video games on the family environment.

Aretha Oluwakemi Asakitikpi, has written on projecting gender, sexuality and body through the music industry. She reports on the historical transformation of the music industry expanding from government to private organizations as providers. The floodgates of diversity and choice have since opened up in Nigeria, particularly in the area of music. Through musical videos, artists have entertained audiences within and outside Nigeria projecting and redefining sexuality, gender relations and the body. The author used three musicals to project her objectives: *Collabo* by Psquare featuring Don Jazzy; *JAMB Question* by Simi featuring Falz; and *Marry Me* featuring YemiAlade and Poe. These videos produced by Nigerians had Nigerians featuring prominently; gender relations were a major theme; and they had high public viewing on social media platforms. Qualitative methods were used to analyze lyrics and songs, visual projection of body movements and physical spacing and clothing to identify gender concepts. The analyses gave support to gender relations in terms of inequalities and power.

Saori Ishida and Hiromi Tanaka of Meiji University, Japan, wrote on the meaning and purpose of leisure activities of Manga/Anima fans called "Fujoshi". The contradictions and ambivalences in Japanese women's fan communities were discussed. *Fujoshi* referred to female comics (*manga*) and related products such as animation (*anime*) fans who enjoy works that feature male-homosexual relationships. The authors' paper examined the meaning and purpose of this unique leisure activity. Through interviews with seven *fujoshi* women the authors identified what makes the women seem satisfied, fulfilled or happy in their activities. On the negative side the process of heightened differentiation between *fujoshi* and others was discussed.

The third section of this collection deals with global leisure and responses. Four papers comprise this section. They are globalization of Comic-Con and sacralization of popular, leisure and environmental education in Japan, using serious leisure and internalized outdoor sport participation to enhance wellbeing and leisure and mean-making. Authors of these papers are from the United States, Canada and Japan.Michael Elliot of Towson University in the United States wrote on globalization of Comic-Con and sacralization of popular culture. The exponential rise in attendances of Comic-Con conventions has made it the premiere event for fans celebrating the popular arts. The focus has moved from comic books to movies, television shows, video games, novels and others. It attracts fans, vendors, celebrities and industry professionals. Among the features of the four-day convention are activities such as costume contests, Celebrity panels and autographs, art exhibits, vendor booths, industry awards and workshops. Internationally Com-Con has occurred in America, Canada, France, India, Brazil and the United Arab Emirates. Comic-Con is an expression of contemporary leisure activity that too may explain cultural imperialism, neo-Marxism, psychological perspective and mainstream media. The author proposes a Durkheimian hypothesis that Com-Con is a sacred ritual for devout fans and has globalized because of key aspects that represent archetypes that transcend national boundaries.

Munehiko Asamizu of Yamaguchi University, Japan, wrote on leisure and environmental education in Japan. The author shows how rural leisure activities are changing historical trends in Japan. In a descriptive paper, Munehiko Asamizu describes changes in rural tourism after the Green Tourism Law of 1994. The enactment of the law encouraged the spread of green tourism development. The rural way of life is promoted locally by inviting high school urban students to experience countryside. The green tourism development also extends to international events and attracts excursionists from US, Korea and Taiwan.

KoFan Lee from the University of Mississippi in the United States combined serious leisure and internalized outdoor participation to enhance wellbeing. The author explains how the use volition and autonomy assist in the internalization of human behaviours. Through the medium of serious leisure the paper discusses how the process of internalization can be facilitated or hindered by social contexts.

Yoshitaka Iwasaki from the University of Alberta, Canada, wrote on leisure and meaning-making. He promoted the notion of pursuing a meaningful life through leisure. He stated that humans seek the pursuit of a meaningful, enriching life. Meaning-making referred to a process by which a person derives meaning(s) from an activity where leisure provides opportunities for meaning-making. An integrated review of literature contextualized the process of meaning-making as remedying the bad and enhancing the good. The former concept is the primary role of therapeutic recreation. The latter is essential for successful ageing. Meaning-making through leisure to enhance human life is designed towards enhanced subjective wellbeing.

It is hoped that the summaries of the arguments and explanatory frameworks- segmented into: local leisure, meaning and resistance; virtual leisure and pop culture; and global leisure and responses – provides a useful and meaning-full perusal of chapters in the book. The authors are congratulated for further opening up of leisure and its diversity to a global readership. Furthermore, we believe that this discussion allows us to introduce a common theory of global leisure that runs across the book's various chapters. This new theory is something we hope will be of immense usefulness in sociology of leisure, leisure studies and related disciplines.

Firstly, the importance of leisure in the life of humans has not changed in the age of globalization. Leisure activities may change, as we can see around the world, and in all societies and cultures. Leisure may be truly global, part of popular culture, or it may be a hybrid between the global and the local, or something that takes place virtually. But the meaning and purpose of leisure does not change. The need for leisure does not change. It is fundamental to our spiritual flourishing, and our psychological and sociological well-being. That meaning and purpose is, however, under threat by the unique circumstances of our age. Globalization has opened up leisure spaces and leisure lives, it has challenged gender norms and other traditional values, but at the same time globalization has contributed to greater inequalities of opportunity and outcome. The neo-liberalism at the heart of globalization serves to concentrate power, to maintain power and to reproduce hegemonic power relations. This explains why some people in the research in this book retreat to local leisure, or virtual leisure – because these are spaces for resisting globalization and the power of the world's new elites. Global leisure in all its forms, then, has the potential to be co-opted by capitalism, by nation-states and ruling elites. As sociologists and theorists of leisure we need to be aware that global leisure has the potential to be both a help in the struggle for a better world, and a hindrance. Our role as researchers is to contribute to leisure studies an awareness of how specific forms and spaces of global leisure might work to give humans agency and belonging, whether we call those leisure spaces Foucauldian heterotopias (Blackshaw 2017) or Habermasian lifeworlds defined through communicative leisure (Spracklen 2009, 2011, 2015). Only careful, empirical research will show which leisure can serve its purpose, and which leisure is usurped.

References

Blackshaw, T. (2017). *Re-imagining Leisure Studies*. Abingdon: Routledge.

Spracklen, K. (2009). *The Meaning and Purpose of Leisure: Habermas and Leisure at the End of Modernity*. Basingstoke: Palgrave Macmillan.

Spracklen, K. (2011). *Constructing Leisure: Historical and Philosophical Debates*. Basingstoke: Palgrave Macmillan.

Spracklen, K. (2015). *Digital Leisure, the Internet and Popular Culture: Communities and Identities in a Digital Age*. London: Palgrave Macmillan.

Index

CPSIA information can be obtained
at www.ICGtesting.com
Printed in the USA
LVOW13*2002220418

574435LV00015B/740/P